THE EMER

A Developmental,
Object Relations A ... to
the Treatment of the Closet
Narcissistic Disorder of the Self

ALSO BY JAMES F. MASTERSON, M.D.

COMPARING PSYCHOANALYTIC PSYCHOTHERAPIES
• Developmental, Self, and Object Relations • Self Psychology
• Short-Term Dynamic
(with Marian Tolpin, M.D., and Peter E. Sifneos, M.D.)

PSYCHOTHERAPY OF THE DISORDERS OF THE SELF
(with Ralph Klein, M.D.)

THE REAL SELF
A Developmental, Self, and Object Relations Approach

TREATMENT OF THE BORDERLINE ADOLESCENT
A Developmental Approach

THE PSYCHIATRIC DILEMMA OF ADOLESCENCE

COUNTERTRANSFERENCE AND
PSYCHOTHERAPEUTIC TECHNIQUE
Teaching Seminars on Psychotherapy of the Borderline Adult

THE NARCISSISTIC AND BORDERLINE DISORDERS
An Integrated Developmental Approach

FROM BORDERLINE ADOLESCENT TO FUNCTIONING ADULT
The Test of Time

PSYCHOTHERAPY OF THE BORDERLINE ADULT
A Developmental Approach

THE EMERGING SELF

A Developmental, Self, and Object Relations Approach to the Treatment of the Closet Narcissistic Disorder of the Self

James F. Masterson, M.D.

Routledge
Taylor & Francis Group
www.routledge.com

First published 1993 by
BRUNNER/MAZEL, INC.

Published 2014 by Routledge
2 Park Square, Milton Park, Abingdon, Oxfordshire OX14 4RN
711 Third Avenue, New York, NY 10017

Routledge is an imprint of the Taylor & Francis Group, an informa business

First issued in paperback 2014

Library of Congress Cataloging-in-Publication Data
Masterson, James F.
The emerging self : a developmental, self, and object relations approach to the treatment of the closet narcissistic disorder of the self / James F. Masterson.
p. cm.
Includes bibliographical references and index.
ISBN 978-0-87630-721-2 (hbk)
ISBN 978-1-138-00500-6 (pbk)
1. Narcissism. I. Title.
[DNLM: 1. Narcissism. 2. Borderline Personality Disorder--etiology. 3. Borderline Personality Disorder—therapy.
4. Countertransference (Psychology) 5. Personality Development.
6. Ego. WM 460.5.E3 M423e 1993]
RC553.N36M369 1993
616.85'85—dc20
DNLM/DLC
for Library of Congress 93-1604
CIP

Acknowledgments

First and foremost I want to thank my patients for their generosity in giving permission for their cases to be used to help other therapists learn this approach. Their identities, of course, have been disguised.

I wish to thank Ralph Klein, M.D., Richard Fischer, Ph.D., Candace Orcutt, Ph.D., and Judith Pearson, Ph.D., for reviewing and commenting on the manuscript. I also would like to thank my wife, Patricia, as well as Nancie Scanlan and Glad P. Nadaner, for their cheerful and helpful attitude while preparing the manuscript.

Contents

Introduction

There is much confusion among clinicians about the diagnosis and psychotherapy of the closet narcissistic disorder of the self. It is the most common problem of therapists who seek consultation with me about a treatment impasse. This confusion is fostered by the fact that DSM-III-R provides no diagnostic category for the closet narcissistic disorder. In addition, although the self psychologists recognize it, that recognition depends on accepting their overarching theories about the self, which many therapists do not accept. Beyond that, my previous writings on the subject were published in 1981 and 1985[1,2] and my own perspective has changed and grown so much in the interim that I felt the need to elaborate on and update the concept of the disorder—an additional piece in the continuing puzzle of the personality disorders.

This book, written for therapists, presents a developmental self and object relations approach to the psychotherapy of the closet narcissistic disorder of the self. It addresses such questions as: What does the clinical picture look like? What is the reason for the diagnostic confusion? How does one resolve the confusion? What other disorders does this disorder mimic? How do you differentiate it from the borderline and/or schizoid disorders of the self? What are some possible etiologic factors? What precipitates a clinical syndrome? What is the intrapsychic structure of this disorder, and how does it compare with other disorders? How do you identify it? What is the central psychodynamic? What are the crucial defenses? What is a mirroring interpretation of narcissistic vulnerability, and why is it the intervention of choice? What are the differences between shorter-term and intensive psychotherapy with regard to goals, indications, therapeutic techniques, and limitations? What is projective identification, and why is it important in countertransference reactions to these patients?

The book, the third of a series on the disorders of the self,[1–3] contiues to reflect the shift in my perspective on the personality disorders from a developmental object relations approach that included a notion of the self indirectly (i.e., individuation and self-representation) to one that considers the developmental arrest of the self as primary.

The personality disorders are disorders of the self whose primary psychodynamic theme is what I have called the disorders-of-the-self triad: self-activation leads to anxiety and depression, which leads to defense. This idea began with the study of the borderline personality disorder and was originally called the borderline triad. Further study led to applying it to the personality disorders in general.

Although the triadic psychodynamic theme is common to all the personality disorders, patients differ in the way in which they experience the abandonment depression and in the way in which they defend against it. It is these defenses, viewed through the intrapsychic perspective of object relations theory, that enable us to make the diagnosis. For example, what differentiates the closet narcissistic disorder from the other personality disorders is its intrapsychic structure, the experiencing of the abandonment depression as the self "falling apart" rather than as "losing the object," and the primary defense of idealizing the omnipotent object to regulate the esteem of the grandiose self and defend against the abandonment depression. Throughout this volume, the term "disorder of the self" will be used for personality disorder.

Chapter 1 describes, and gives a number of clinical examples of, the clinical picture of the closet narcissistic disorder. Chapter 2 presents the theory and discusses the etiology of the intrapsychic structure and its clinical manifestations. It emphasizes the crucial dynamic of the disorders-of-the-self triad and the crucial defense of idealizing the omnipotent object to regulate the grandiose self. It is these central, enduring themes that clarify the confusion and place the therapist on the right track.

Chapter 3 on differential diagnosis differentiates the closet narcissistic disorder of the self from the borderline and schizoid disorders of the self, the narcissistic defense against a borderline disorder, and the narcissistic defense against oedipal conflict.

Chapter 4, introducing the psychotherapy, describes the need for therapeutic neutrality implemented by the therapeutic stance and the therapeutic frame. It then describes the therapeutic task: to help the patient convert transference acting out into therapeutic alliance and transference by mirroring interpretations of narcissistic vulnerability. The capacities of the real self are described and the clinical evidence of these capacities as the real self activates and emerges are printed in boldface throughout the clinical chapters to emphasize that emergence.

The next four chapters present detailed process-note descriptions of the psychotherapy of four patients with a closet narcissistic disorder, each of whom was seen for about two years—two in shorter-term psychotherapy and two in intensive analytic psychotherapy. All four cases demostrate the clinical vicissitudes of the disorders-of-the-self triad, as well as how to use mirroring interpretations of narcissistic vulnerability to deal with these vicissitudes.

The two chief obstacles to effective psychotherapy are lack of knowledge and countertransference. Chapter 9 describes why countertransference is such an issue with these patients and defines and illustrates the profound importance of the defense mechanism of projective identification in the evocation of countertransference reactions. Chapters 10 and 11 give detailed process-note descriptions of the supervision and resolution of the countertransferences of three therapists.

The chapters on treatment demostrate the slow, difficult struggle of the real self to overcome the defenses, work through the pathologic affects, emerge, and become consolidated.

THE EMERGING SELF

A Developmental, Self, and Object Relations Approach to the Treatment of the Closet Narcissistic Disorder of the Self

PART ONE
The Clinical Picture

1

The Clinical Picture—
A Chameleon

A therapist baffled by a therapeutic impasse with a "borderline" patient asks for a consultation and gives a good description of the patient's clinical picture: depression, difficulty with self-assertion, clinging in relationships and with the therapist, difficulties with anger and impulse control, an inadequate sense of self, and denial of self-destructive behavior.

The diagnosis of borderline disorder of the self seemed correct, and the therapist used the appropriate therapeutic intervention of confrontation. However, the patient, rather than integrating the confrontations to develop a therapeutic alliance, instead responded either by attacking the therapist and becoming more and more resistant, or by seeming to integrate the confrontations, but without a change in affect or the therapeutic alliance.

The therapist felt more and more frustrated and defeated, and the pressure to blame the borderline patient's stubbornness or intransigence for this turn of events became irresistible as the therapist began to think, "These difficult-to-treat borderline patients . . ." How many papers on the borderline begin with this phrase! This therapist unfortunately had fallen prey to the most common diagnostic error with the personality disorders. He had mistaken a closet narcissistic disorder of the self for a borderline disorder of the self.

The first important reason why this happens is that the revised third edition of the *Diagnostic and Statistical Manual of Mental Disorders* (DSM-III-R) makes no provision for the closet narcissistic personality disorder. As shown in the following, the manual provides criteria for only one form of narcissistic disorder, the exhibitionist.

Narcissistic Personality Disorder

1. Grandiose sense of self-importance or uniqueness.
2. Preoccupation with fantasies of unlimited success, power, brilliance, beauty, or ideal love.
3. Exhibitionism; the person requires constant attention and admiration.
4. Cool indifference or marked feelings of rage, inferiority, shame, humiliation, or emptiness in response to criticism.
5. At least two of the following disturbances in interpersonal relationships.
   a. A sense of entitlement or expectation of special favors without assuming reciprocal responsibilities.
   b. Interpersonal exploitiveness.
   c. Relationships that alternate between the extremes of overidealization and devaluation.
   d. Lack of empathy.

Therefore, the clinician's alertness to the presence of the disorder is dulled.

The second important reason is that the closet narcissistic disorder of the self clinically most commonly can mimic the borderline personality disorder, but also, less commonly, the schizoid personality disorder. This book shows how developmental self and object relations theory pierces the clinical confusion and enables the therapist to identify the consistent, underlying intrapsychic structure and select the effective therapeutic approach.

The closet narcissistic disorder of the self has a consistent underlying intrapsychic structure and an equally consistent defensive theme: idealization or devaluation of the omnipotent object to regulate the grandiose sense of self. The principal emotional investment is in the object, not the self. Despite this, the clinical picture, like a chameleon, can take on the colors of other disorders. There are a number of symptomatic themes that reflect the patient's complaints rather than the aspects of the problem that the patient denies—for example, grandiosity, sense of entitlement, or lack of empathy.

CLINICAL THEMES

The impaired self can be consciously experienced as bad, inadequate, ugly, incompetent, shameful, or weak, or as falling apart. A prominent complaint is difficulties with intimacy or a close relationship. A real, healthy close relationship would interrupt the patient's narcissistic defenses and expose the patient to his or her impaired self and abandonment depression, and so the patient must form relationships based on narcissistic defense. The permutations and combinations of these relationships are endless. The complaint can vary, for the narcissist with a detachment defense, from having no or few relationships, to a lack of responsiveness on the part of a partner (failure to mirror perfectly), to being attracted to people who are not in reality available—for example, having an affair with a married person or with someone who lives far away or travels a lot, with the distance providing the necessary defensive protection.

A seemingly inconsistent picture appears with persons with devaluing narcissistic disorders, who seem to be devoted either to partners whom they consistently attack and devalue or to partners who attack or devalue them. They undergo recurrent experiences of instantly "falling in love" based on sexual attraction, and then being disappointed and falling out of love as the relationship matures. Also, attracted by the other person's money, power, beauty, or sexual appearance (narcissistic supplies), they may evince a genuine feeling for the person that quickly leads to disappointment when the quality that attracted them disappears.

Narcissistic rage emerges at the partner's failure to meet entitlement needs without awareness of the entitlement.

Problems with sexual functioning arise that derive not from a specific sexual conflict, but from the need to defend against the anxiety and depression produced by the emotional pressure for intimacy that occurs in a sexual relationship. One can be sexually competent with a partner with whom one is not involved, but when one is involved, one has to detach affect to function sexually.

The difficulties with real-self–activation also vary widely, from the patient's not knowing what he or she wants to do to the patient's being able to identify it but not being able to initiate it, or being able to initiate it but not being able to follow through. Or the patient is able to activate only through a relationship with an idealized other, but if he or she becomes separated from the idealized other, the ability to activate deteriorates.

The difficulty with self-activation also causes patients to take jobs in which they can function quite successfully, but where they feel no sense of meaning or satisfaction—for example, a lawyer who really wants to be an artist. Or they may initiate a career based on their latent talent and being able to identify what they want (real-self–activation), but find that success so frustrates their closet defenses, thus bringing them onto center stage, that it exposes them to such severe anxiety that they have to avoid following through in order to relieve the anxiety. Often the need to relieve the anxiety can lead to alcoholism or drug addiction. Workaholism as a defense against intimacy and/or the anxiety associated with self-activation is common. The structure of the work partakes of their emotional investment in the idealized object, and while they work long hours, they feel an emotional equilibrium, and the loneliness, isolation, and burnout involved are denied. This difficulty with real-self–activation can extend to difficulties in taking good care of personal needs, such as diet, weight control, exercise, rest, and proper grooming. On the other hand, some patients can spend inordinate time on taking care of themselves.

There can be problems with affect regulation, with either detachment and too little affect or too much affect and outbursts of narcissistic rage. Unlike with the exhibitionist, there is a constant repetitive experience of the disorders-of-the-self triad: self-activation leads to anxiety and depression, which lead to defense. Under separation stress, the depression is full blown and the patient may become suicidal. Otherwise the depression is better defended against and of a lower grade.

There may be a host of neurotic symptoms, from anxiety to phobias, compulsions, and hysterical symptoms. Somatic symptoms are particularly common as the patient experiences the impaired real self as "the body's falling apart." In some patients, acting-out symptoms arise, with sexual promiscuity, alcoholism, or drug addiction. In others, the symptomatic picture can be that of an eating disorder, most commonly bulimia, but also anorexia nervosa. For the adult patient, there may also be a current, ongoing enmeshed relationship with the mother or father, or both, with the patient feeling caught up in the role of psychological caretaker and unable to free himself or herself from that role.

Separation stresses commonly precipitate a clinical syndrome: separation from the idealized or devalued object and/or a loss of narcissistic supplies, such as power, money, beauty, or appearance.

CLINICAL EXAMPLES

The following examples present brief descriptions of patients who will be discussed in greater detail in the chapters on psychotherapy.

Case of Ms. A.

Ms. A., a tall, blond, slender, divorced, 40-year-old homosexual woman who owned a business and had two children, complained of her difficulty in interpersonal relationships. She had had her first homosexual relationship while in college. Later she fell in love with a man, married him, and in so doing, she said, "I lost my sense of self. I became all things to my husband and children." She was married for 10 years, during which time there were no homosexual relationships.

She reported, "After 10 years, I realized that I had no self, nor did

I have any intimacy with my husband. I started to drink, and as I had a low tolerance for alcohol, I became an alcoholic and had blackouts. I drank for three years, until last year, when I joined AA and started an affair with a woman.

"During the three years that I was drinking, I had two relationships with women and one with a man. All of them were difficult and conflictual. I tended to sell out to women who were attracted to me. I have great difficulty acknowledging myself. I feel I have no self. I have trouble asserting myself."

Comment

This patient's defense of idealizing the object helped her to manage for many years, as long as she denied the cost to her real self. However, as she got older, this defense began to fail with her narcissistic husband. She divorced him, but, on her own without a close object to idealize, she became an alcoholic in order to deal with her abandonment depression, and she started psychotherapy. When the psychotherapy did not help, she came to therapy with the complaint that her lifelong idealizing of the object had not worked, and that she was aware of its cost to her real self.

Case of Mr. B.

Mr. B., a 55-year-old bachelor, in the setting of the death of his closest male friend, conflicts in his relationship with a woman friend, and increases in his asthma symptoms, became anxious to the point of panic for fear that he might have a coronary occlusion and die, as several members of his family had died of heart attacks. He checked his blood pressure and pulse four or five times a day. He denied depression, but the affect was probably absorbed by his somatic preoccupations. He also felt a lessening of his interest and energy and sense of excitement in his work.

He complained of difficulties in his relationships with women, both in the present and throughout his life. He had a close relationship with a 35-year-old woman, whom he liked and to whom he was attracted, but, he said, "She wants emotion and commitment, and I mostly want sex, and I get angry at her demands. As much as I like her, when she's not around and I'm alone, I don't miss her and I feel fine."

Comment

As a child, this patient's abandonment depression had been powerfully reinforced by severe physical illness that threatened death. He had defended by detaching affect from the self and the object and idealizing it, and by performing to receive adulation. The loss of the friend, the pressure of intimacy, his age, and the recurrence of his asthma overcame his defenses and reinforced and precipitated the childhood panic that he would die.

Case of Mr. C.

Mr. C., a single 38-year-old architect, had a chief complaint of "latent heterosexuality, homosexuality, social isolation, depression, and anger and self-destructive behavior." He described himself as a workaholic who worked 16 hours a day. He lived by himself and was socially isolated. He had great difficulty tolerating his feelings when alone in his apartment, and when he was not working, he drank at home or went out to gay bars, either just to observe and be with people or to seek one-night sexual stands. He found it difficult to access his feelings, and so felt detached a good deal of the time, and although he wished to have relationships, he had few friends and felt isolated and lonely. "I couldn't bear to have anything good happen to me," he said. "I don't deserve anything. When anything good happens, I turn around to attack myself. I spend my time observing. It's frightening to get close to people."

Comment

This patient's impaired real self was so fragile that his defense of performing for the idealized object to regulate his grandiose self was not sufficient, and thus he also required detachment of affect from the object and workaholism, and possibly alcoholism, to deal with the profound abandonment depression. It was the failure of this entire defensive system to manage his depression and isolation that brought him to psychotherapy.

Case of Mr. D.

Mr. D., a 50-year-old married businessman, came for psychotherapy after a heart attack with a chief complaint of: "I'm hanging onto a bad marriage because I'm afraid of being abandoned. I've been in codependency groups for years and have read widely, including several of your books. I abdicated to my mother, and since then to two wives. I feel chronically depressed most of the time. I feel lost, with no sense of an identity or of self. My business is successful, but I am a workaholic. Many years ago, I was an alcoholic. However, I've been overeating and am still 25 pounds overweight after my heart attack."

Comment

The patient's heart attack impelled him to come for psychotherapy after a number of previous therapeutic failures. The difficulty with the sense of self, the dependence on attacking women, suggests that his defenses go beyond the usual focus on the object to an internalization of the aggressor defense that requires an external aggressor to reinforce it. This defense suggests the possibility that the parental negative attitudes may have included physical and/or sexual abuse.

SUMMARY

The diversity of the clinical picture—difficulties with self-image, with affect, with relationships with others, with overt symptoms, with impulse control, as well as workaholism and alcoholism—seem to defy organization, and, therefore, the development of a carefully thought-through and considered therapeutic approach. The advantage of the developmental self and object relations perspective, described in Chapter 2, is that it sifts through this clinical diversity to reach the underlying, enduring, unchanging intrapsychic structure. It allows the therapist to organize the clinical material according to this structure, which then informs the therapist as to what is on the center stage of treatment and how it must be dealt with, and also how to evaluate the results of the efforts to deal with it. In other words, it provides not only a point of view, but also a tool with which to conduct an ongoing evaluation of that point of view.

2

A Developmental, Self, and Object Relations Theory

The term narcissism has become so associated with disorder that it is important to differentiate between healthy narcissism, which is essential to life, and pathological narcissism.

Healthy narcissism, or the real self,[2] is experienced as a sense of self that feels adequate and competent, a feeling derived mostly from reality, with some input from fantasy. This sense of self includes appropriate concern for others, and its self-esteem is maintained by the use of self-assertion to master challenges and tasks presented by reality.

The intrapsychic structure, which underlies this sense of self, consists of a self-representation that has separated from the object representation, has had its infantile grandiosity and omnipotence defused, and is whole—that is, it contains both positive and negative at the same time, and is able to function autonomously. The pathologic narcissism of the exhibitionistic narcissistic disorder or the inflated false defensive self is experienced as being unique, special, adored, and admired. It is called a false defensive self because (1) it is based on fantasy, and (2) its purpose is to defend against pathologic affect, not to deal with reality. The intrapsychic structure consists of a grandiose-self–representation fused with an omnipotent-object representation with the major emotional investment in the grandiose self, whose grandiosity is maintained by seeking perfection and the perfect mirroring of others. The pathologic narcissism of the closet narcissistic disorder or the deflated false defensive self is experienced as feeling special or unique in the glow of the omnipotent perfect other. The intrapsychic structure consists of the same grandiose self fused with the omnipotent-object representation, except that the major investment is in the omnipotent-object representation that is idealized and projected on others, the grandiose self basking in the glow of the idealized object.

Whether the narcissism is pathologic or healthy turns upon the quality of the sense of self feeling and its relationship to the external object. To illustrate: If you are reading this book to glean information that will make you a better therapist and enable you to help your patients more, and you acknowledge me as the source of this information, then that is healthy narcissism. On the other hand, if you are reading the book in order to gain some knowledge that will make you feel unique and special, and you cannot acknowledge my contribution as the source of the feeling, then that is the narcissism of the exhibitionistic disorder. Finally, if you are reading this book because you have idealized me and are basking in the glow of that idealization as you read, that is the narcissism of the closet narcissistic disorder.

On the other hand, to turn this around, if I wrote the book in order to teach what I have learned so that it can be used by others, and I acknowledge the importance of students to the process, that is healthy narcissism. If I wrote the book in order to exhibit my special, unique, grandiose self for perfect mirroring and do not acknowledge the student, that is exhibitionistic narcissism. Finally, if I view the audience as idealized and the source of my self-esteem, and wrote the book to gain admiration and thereby reinforce my grandiosity, that is closet narcissism.

It is also important to keep in mind that a patient can have narcissistic traits without necessarily having a narcissistic disorder. In other words, the patient may have an excessive interest in appearance, power, money, beauty, or the like that is an isolated narcissistic trait that does not result in the creation of the intrapsychic fused omnipotent-object, grandiose-self–representation of the narcissistic disorder of the self.

A DEVELOPMENTAL SELF AND OBJECT RELATIONS THEORY

Developmental self and object relations theory provides some insight into the level of the developmental arrest, the resultant intrapsychic structure, and, finally, the clinical picture of the narcissistic personality disorder. It informs us as to how to evaluate the clinical data and what to do about the data.

LEVEL OF DEVELOPMENTAL ARREST

It is a tenet of object relations theory[4-15] that ego defense mechanisms and ego functions mature in parallel with the maturation of self- and object representations. A controversy has arisen over how to explain that the narcissistic personality disorder seems to violate this tenet in that a very primitive self–object representation is seen alongside a seemingly high capacity for ego functioning.

To put it in developmental terms, although the self–object representation is fused, the narcissistic personality disorder seems to receive the benefit for ego development that is believed to come about only as a result of separation from that fusion. There as yet has been no satisfactory resolution of this dilemma, either by myself* or by other authors. A perspective on the issue can be gained by noting Mahler's observations.[17]

One of the functions of the rapprochement crisis during the separation–individuation phase of development is to bring into accord with reality through phase-appropriate disappointment and

*In turning to developmental theory, one must keep in mind that the line of validation of clinical theory is from the presenting clinical picture to how it is validated in the transference and through the working through of the genetic elements. The line of validation is not from clinical to developmental theory. The reason lies in the differences between the clinical infant and the research infant. In the former, there is maximum subjective reporting and no observation. In the latter, there is maximum observation and little or no subjective report.

The work of Stern [16] has called into question many of Mahler's ideas as adultmorphic pro-

frustration those arachaic structures, the grandiose self and the omnipotent object. The chief characteristic of the practicing period is the child's great narcissistic investment in his or her own functions and his or her own body, as well as in the objects and objectives of his or her expanding "reality." He or she seems relatively impervious to knocks, falls, and other frustrations.

The rapprochement subphase (approximately 15–22 months) begins with the mastery of upright locomotion. Alongside the growth of the child's cognitive faculties and the increasing difficulties of his or her emotional life, there is also a waning of his or her previous imperviousness to frustration, as well as of his or her relative obliviousness to the mother's presence.

An increased separation anxiety is observed: At the height of mastery, toward the end of the practicing period, there is increasingly clear differentiation between the self-representation and the object representation. The toddler starts to lose the sense of grandiosity and omnipotence, and begins to realize that he or she must cope with the world on his or her own. The toddler returns to woo the mother, demanding that she share every aspect of his or her life, but it no longer works. The self-representation and the object representation are well on the way to differentiation. In this manner, the infantile fantasies of grandiosity and omnipotence are brought into accord with reality.

The fixation of the narcissistic disorder of the self must occur before this event because clinically the patient behaves as if the object representation were an integral part of the self-representation—an omnipotent, dual unity. The possibility of the existence of a rapprochement crisis does not seem to dawn on this patient. The fantasy persists that the world is the patient's oyster and revolves about the patient. In order to protect this illusion, the patient must seal off, by avoidance, denial, and devaluation, those

---

jections on the infant. For example, Stern views the infant self as being separate from birth. They both agree, however, that it requires "good enough" mothering or "attunement" of the object to the child's self for the self to consolidate and become autonomous. Developmental studies continue to advance, and are useful as long as we keep their limitations in mind. I am using Mahler's view here because it provides a clear clinical distinction that helps us to understand the narcissistic disorder.

perceptions of reality that do not fit or resonate with this narcissistic, grandiose self-perception. Consequently, the patient is compelled to suffer the cost to adaptation that is always involved when large segments of reality must be denied.

Why the fixation occurs at this level is a complex and poorly understood matter. Presumably, as with the borderline, the etiologic input can come from both ends of the nature–nurture spectrum. However, the input from both sides is much clearer in the borderline than in the narcissistic disorder of the self.

Some of the mothers of patients with narcissistic disorders are themselves narcissistic and emotionally detached. They ignore their children's need for emotional support of the emerging real self in order to mold them into objects that will justify their own perfectionistic, emotional needs. The child's real self suffers as the child resonates with the mother's idealizing projections. The child must be perfect for the mother, rather than be his or her own real self. The identification with the mother's idealization leads to preservation of the grandiose self, which defends against the perception of both the mother's failure to support the real self and the child's associated feelings of abandonment depression.

The developmental dynamics of the closet narcissistic personality disorder show some variations on the theme. Often both parents have narcissistic disorders of the self, the father exhibitionistic, the mother closet. Neither parent supports the child's real self. The mother idealizes the father, who is the narcissistic center of the family, and the child's only recourse is to identify with the mother's closet narcissism. To identify with the father's exhibitionism would threaten the father's position and expose the child's vulnerability. In other cases, the child emerges from separation–individuation as an exhibitionist, but later in childhood, trauma to the exhibitionistic self impels the child to "go underground"—that is, to shift the dominant investment in the grandiose self to idealizing the omnipotent object, which thereby becomes a closet narcissistic disorder of the self.

Another possibility is suggested by the fact that, in normal development, the child, particularly the male, turns strongly in the early practicing phase, before rapprochement has occurred, to identify with the father. The child, experiencing an abandonment depression at the hands of the mother, could use this normal pathway as a vehicle or channel to "rescue" him or her from the abandonment depression at the hands of the mother. Rather than undergo the normal developmental process of identification with the father as a second, new nonsymbiotic object, the child transfers wholesale the symbiotic relationship with the mother to the father in order to deal with the abandonment depression. The father thus becomes a target for the projection of the symbiotic relationship with the mother. If the father has a narcissistic personality disorder, and this transfer takes place before the rapprochement phase, the child's grandiose self will still be preserved and will be reinforced through identification with the narcissistic father, thus producing a narcissistic disorder of the self.

If the transfer occurs after the rapprochement phase has brought infantile grandiosity and omnipotence into accord with reality, the identification with the narcissistic disorder of the father will occur after the formation of the split object relations unit of the borderline, and a narcissistic defense against a borderline disorder will be superimposed on the underlying borderline intrapsychic structure. In other words, once the grandiose self has been brought into accord with reality during the rapprochement phase, it disappears and gives way to the separate split self- and object representations. Any turn to a narcissistic father after this event has taken place can only result in superimposing a later narcissistic identification on top of an underlying borderline intrapsychic structure.

This possibility raises some intriguing, but so far unresolved, developmental questions. It suggests that a narcissistic father may be essential for the production of a narcissistic defense against a borderline disorder. Since this turn to the father occurs earlier and more harmoniously in boys than in girls, it suggests that narcissistic disorders may be more common in boys than in girls, which seems to agree with clinical experience. Beyond that, the male child's rescue by the narcissistic father does not seem to lead commonly to homosexual problems, while the female child's rescue almost always leads to sexual conflicts during the oedipal period.

This developmental turn to the father has been used by

Kohut[18,19] to suggest that if the mother has not established a cohesive self (his terms), the father may be able to do it. I think he overlooks here that in the narcissistic personality disorder, the self that turns to the father is already developmentally arrested, and, therefore, the father can at best provide further defense.

INTRAPSYCHIC STRUCTURE

Exhibitionistic Narcissistic Personality Disorder of Self (Figure 2.1)

Object Relations Fused Units

The intrapsychic structure that results from the developmental arrest on superficial clinical observation of the exhibitionistic narcissistic personality disorder would appear to consist of only one object relations unit, in contrast to the borderline's two part-units. It appears this way because of the unique continuous activation of the defensive unit, while the other underlying unit only reveals itself in treatment as the continuity of the defenses is interrupted.

The defensive or libidinal grandiose-self–omnipotent-object relations fused unit of the exhibitionistic narcissistic disorder consists of an omnipotent-object representation that contains all power, perfection, direction, supplies, and so on. The grandiose-self–representation is one of being superior, elite, exhibitionistic, with an affect of feeling perfect, special, unique, adored, admired. The projection of this defensive unit is so ubiquitous, global, and airtight that it effectively conceals from the casual observer the underlying pathologic or aggressive fused unit. The exhibitionist projects the grandiose self, exhibits his or her specialness, and expects perfect mirroring of his or her grandiosity and unique perfection by others. The underlying aggressive object relations fused unit consists of a fused object representation that is harsh, punitive, and attacking and a self-representation of being humiliated, attacked, empty, and linked by the affect of the abandonment depression that is experienced more as the self fragmenting or falling apart than as

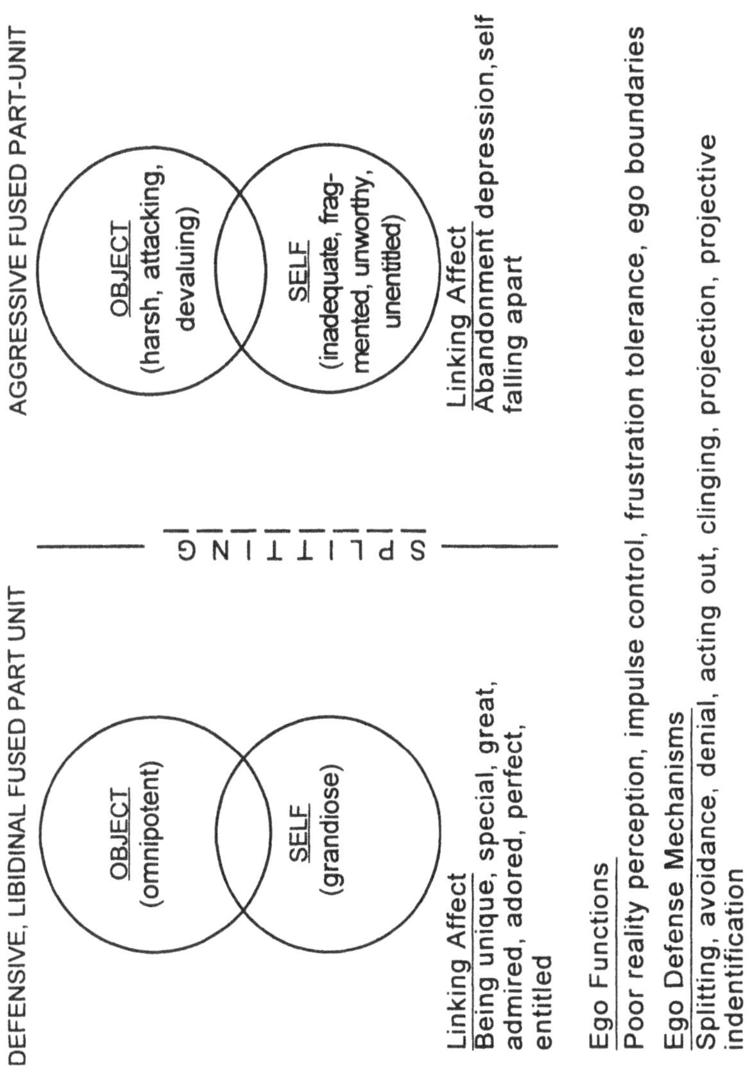

Figure 2.1. Narcissistic Personality Disorder—Intrapsychic Structure of the Object Relations Unit

the loss of the object described by the borderline personality disorder.

Alliance Between the Defensive, Grandiose-Self–Omnipotent-Object Fused Unit and the Pathologic Ego

The defensive or grandiose-self–omnipotent-object relations fused unit forms an alliance with the pathologic ego to defend against the abandonment depression of the aggressive fused unit, but this alliance operates in a manner different from that of the borderline. The abandonment depression of the aggressive fused unit can be precipitated either by efforts at true self-activation (i.e., the pursuit of realistic self-expressive goals as opposed to the narcissistic goals of perfection, adoration, money, power, beauty, and so on) or by the perception of the object's failure to provide perfect mirroring.

The perception of the abandonment depression activates the alliance between the grandiose fused unit and the pathologic ego, and the patient proceeds to avoid, deny, and/or devalue the offending stimulus or perception, thereby restoring the balance of his or her narcissistic equilibrium (i.e., its defensive libidinal fused part-unit) and avoiding the experiencing of depression. The continuous, global projection of this defensive unit allows the patient with a narcissistic personality disorder to minimize the experience of depression and makes it appear that he or she gets emotional supplies from within. In addition, the relatively free access to aggression enables the narcissist either to aggressively coerce the environment into resonating with the narcissistic projects, or, if this fails, to deal with the failure by avoidance, denial, and devaluation.

The Closet Narcissistic Personality Disorder (Figure 2.1)

As illustrated, the intrapsychic structure of the closet narcissistic personality disorder is the same as that of the exhibitionistic. However, the shift in emotional investment from the grandiose-self– to the omnipotent-object representation results in two key clinical differences in how the defensive structure operates: (1) The exhibitionist seems impervious to the object, whereas the closet narcissist is exquisitely dependent on and vulnerable to the object. The patient projects the omnipotent object on others and regulates the grandiosity of the self by "basking in the glow" of the idealized object. (2) The closet narcissist does not have the capacity consistently to maintain the continuity of defense and, therefore, is prone to experience depression and to present the same clinical sequence as the borderline disorder (i.e., self-activation–depression–defense).

When this defensive alliance does not prove adequate, the patient massively projects the underlying attacking object with its associated rage and depression on the external object; feels attacked from without; feels humiliated, shamed, vulnerable, and inadequate; and either attacks back or withdraws, feeling fragmented—having lost the organization of the sense of self.

The Abandonment Depression in the Narcissistic Disorder

The elements of the abandonment depression are the same: suicidal depression, homocidal rage, panic, guilt, hopelessness and helplessness, emptiness and void. However, these affects are experienced differently by one with a narcissistic disorder. The exhibitionist tends not to experience depression because of the continuity of the defense. The depression in the closet narcissist is marked by feelings of humiliation and shame and of the self falling apart. The borderline depression is focused on feelings of inadequacy about the self owing to the loss of the object. Rage in the narcissist is cold and unrelated, filled with outrage, as compared with the borderline's rage, which is warm and extremely related. Envy is prominent in the narcissistic disorder and minor in the borderline. The exhibitionist's feelings of hopelessness and helplessness and emptiness and void are held in check by the defenses, while in the closet disorder, both feeling states are more often consciously experienced. In the closet narcissistic disorder, if the feelings of helplessness and hopelessness are not conscious, they become so in response to the initial therapeutic interventions—"If I don't focus on the object to regulate my self, I don't know what to do and it's hopeless."

The dominating power of these affects is seen in the havoc they wreak on the patient's adaptive life and the extraordinarily tenacious quality of the patient's resistance to facing and dealing with them in psychotherapy.

THE EXHIBITIONISTIC PERSONALITY DISORDER

The DSM-III-R contains only one of the two narcissistic disorders, the exhibitionistic narcissistic personality disorder. The diagnostic symptoms are as follows:

1. Grandiose sense of self, its importance or uniqueness.
2. Preoccupation with fantasies of unlimited success, power, brilliance, beauty, ideal love.
3. Exhibitionism requiring constant attention and admiration.
4. Cool indifference, or marked feelings of rage, inferiority, shame, humiliation, or emptiness in response to criticism.
5. A sense of entitlement, interpersonal exploitation of others, lack of empathy.

The advantage of the DSM-III-R approach is that since it is free of theoretical bias, it can be used to test any number of theories, and since it is based on symptoms, it is based on the most obvious and so most easily replicated phenomena. The disadvantage from the perspective of the disorder of the self theory is that the emphasis on symptoms stresses the most evanescent and fleeting aspects of the disorder and ignores the most stable enduring aspect—the intrapsychic structure and the developmental arrest of the self. Beyond that, there is no provision for a closet narcissistic disorder.

The Developmental Self and Object Relations Approach to Diagnosis

The symptoms listed in DSM-III-R are the patient's calling card and are evaluated first, and then the intrapsychic structure is explored. With the exhibitionistic narcissistic disorder of the self, one looks for the grandiose self, with the omnipotent-object representation projected on the therapist and others, and the patient's relating to the therapist with the expectation of perfect mirroring and responsiveness. The patient is disappointed when the mirroring is not available. At the same time, one observes the defects in ego functioning (poor reality perception, impulse control, ego boundaries, and frustration tolerance) and primitive mechanisms of defense (splitting, acting out, idealizing, projection, projective identification, denial, and avoidance). Underneath this defensive grandiose self is the fused aggressive unit with a harsh attacking object; a self-representation of being empty, inadequate, bad, fragmented, and so on; and a linking affect of abandonment depression.

There are certain clinical implications that flow from this intrapsychic structure. The exhibitionist has a unique capacity to maintain continuous activation of the grandiose-self–defense; therefore, there is an intolerance of depression, and so depressive affect is not common in this individual. In addition, the behavior is motivated by the pursuit of narcissistic supplies—that is, perfection and perfect responsiveness, wealth, power, beauty, and, finally, the capacity, when confronted with a stimulus that frustrates the need for mirroring, either to avoid the stimulus, deny it, or devalue the person presenting the stimulus, all as a means of avoiding the experience of depression.

Clinical Types

Clinical types of the exhibitionistic narcissistic personality disorder can be divided by functioning level into high, middle, and low. High-level patients rarely come for psychotherapy. Often, through their charisma, talent, or skill, they are able to coerce the environment into resonating with their narcissistic needs. They undertake activities that offer narcissistic gratification, such as politics or acting. Only when life deals them a severe trauma such as a profound loss do they consider psychotherapy. The middle-level patients are the ones most commonly seen in psychotherapy. They have great difficulty in object relations, usually along with neurotic symptoms, sexual problems, and difficulties in functioning. Those who function on the lowest level are difficult to separate from those with sociopathic personalities.

Clinical Characteristics of the Grandiose-Self–Omnipotent-Object Defense

The main feature of this defense is continuous activation of the grandiose self, with extreme vulnerability of the underlying, impaired real self. The patient is often able to coerce the environment into resonating with his or her grandiose self, refueling it and creating an illusion of a stable system for the maintenance of self-esteem. The patient feels grand, verified by his or her perception of the world and the world's feedback. The illusory quality of this defense only becomes revealed in psychotherapy as the grandiose self is dismantled and the patient begins to have severe problems with self-activation. Unable to be genuinely involved emotionally, the patient uses his or her narcissistic antennas to simulate involvement. Like a stranger in a foreign land, the patient employs these antennas to assess others' narcissistic needs in order to determine what must be done to inspire others to provide for the patient's needs.

THE CLOSET NARCISSISTIC DISORDER OF THE SELF

The closet narcissistic disorder is not included in DSM-III-R. The self psychologists call it the idealizing disorder of the self. The three key differences between the exhibitionist and the closet narcissist are as follows:

1. The closet narcissist's major emotional investment is in the omnipotent object rather than in the grandiose self. The patient projects this object on others, idealizing them as a way of regulating his or her own sense of grandiosity.
2. The closet narcissist cannot maintain the constant activation of defense and, therefore, exhibits the triad of self-activation–depression–defense seen in the borderline personality disor-

ders, which often leads to a misdiagnosis of borderline disorder.

3. The closet narcissist may seem to respond to confrontation; however, the fact that there is no consequent change in affect or in the therapeutic alliance reveals that the response is not genuine, but a result of defensive compliance.

To make the diagnosis, one evaluates the same intrapsychic structure as in the exhibitionistic disorder; that is, grandiose-self–omnipotent-object defensive fused unit and the underlying aggressive fused unit. However, the difference in style of defense is most important to identify—the patient idealizes the therapist and basks in the therapist's glow.

THE DEVALUING NARCISSISTIC PERSONALITY DISORDER

Most patients with a narcissistic disorder of the self will be found in the foregoing categories; that is, most use the defensive grandiose self or omnipotent object to defend. However, a smaller group of patients defend in the opposite manner—by continually projecting the underlying aggressive fused unit. They project the impaired self on the therapist and act out the role of the harsh attacking object by devaluing the therapist. Or they project the harsh object on the therapist and act out the role of the impaired self. Still other patients alternate between the two styles. It is important to identify the devaluing defense early, before the therapist has become intimidated and the treatment overwhelmed by the patient's projections. If interpretations do not resolve the devaluation, confrontation must be used, as one cannot do psychotherapy (i.e., achieve a transference relationship and therapeutic alliance) under a devaluing projection.

The theory equips us to return in Chapter 3 to the clinical picture to demonstrate how it helps the therapist to make a differential diagnosis.

3

Differential Diagnosis

The exhibitionistic and closet narcissistic disorders can be differentiated from each other by the way in which the patient presents his or her false self—either inflated (grandiose) or deflated (closet). In addition, there can be clinical pictures where the false-self–defense alternates between grandiose and closet.

EXHIBITIONISTIC NARCISSISTIC DISORDER VERSUS BORDERLINE PERSONALITY DISORDER

The two disorders can be distinguished by developmental level, intrapsychic structure, clinical manifestations, and transference acting out, as well as by the psychotherapeutic technique required for treatment.

Developmental Level

The narcissistic personality disorder must be fixated or arrested before the developmental level of the rapprochement crisis is reached, since one of the important tasks of that crisis is not performed—the phase-appropriate deflation of infantile grandiosity and omnipotence. The intrapsychic structure of the narcissistic personality disorder preserves the infantile grandiosity and narcissistic link to the omnipotent object.

The rapprochement crisis, on the other hand, is crucial to the borderline personality, whose pathology can be seen as a reflection of his or her immersion in it and inability to resolve it. Clinically, the patient behaves as if all life were one long, unresolvable rapprochement crisis.

Intrapsychic Structure

The intrapsychic structure of the narcissistic disorder consists of a grandiose-self–omnipotent-object representation fused into one unit that is more or less continuously activated to defend against the underlying aggressive or empty object relations fused unit. This continuous activation minimizes the experiencing of depression.

This narcissistic style of defense differs from that of the borderline, where the self- and object representations are not fused, but separate and split into rewarding and withdrawing part-units. The projections of these two part-units are not continuous, but alternate. The primary defense is regressive behavior that requires the forgoing of the real self and self-assertion. The borderline patient then does not have as free an access to aggression as does the narcissistic patient. Thus self-assertion, coming up against the withdrawing object projection, is not available for self-esteem. The borderline patient defends by clinging to or distancing from the object.

The borderline patient's projections of the rewarding and withdrawing units are not so global, airtight, or intense that reality events can be totally denied, devalued, or avoided. Unlike the exhibitionistic narcissistic patient, the borderline patient is hypersensitive to reality, particularly to rewarding and withdrawing responses to self-activation. The borderline patient perceives the reality as inducing depression, and then clings to or distances from the object for defense, meanwhile denying the destructiveness of these defenses to adaptation.

Clinical Manifestations and Transference Acting Out

The differences in developmental level and intrapsychic structure are seen clinically in the transference acting out. The continuity of the self-representation of the exhibitionistic narcissistic disorder patient in treatment presents a seemingly invulnerable armor of grandiosity, self-centeredness, exhibitionism, arrogance, and ingratiation of or devaluation of others. These characteristics are in marked contrast to the self-representation of the borderline patient, which alternates between brittle, vulnerable, self-depreciative, clinging behavior and erratic and irrational outbursts of rage.

The depression beneath the narcissist's defenses is heavily colored with narcissistic outrage and feelings of humiliation. The rage has a quality of "coldness" or a lack of relatedness. In contrast, the borderline patient's depression is dominated by feelings of inadequacy about and hostility toward the self, and the rage shows intense relatedness. The themes of pursuit of power, perfection, wealth, and beauty so prominent in the narcissist are minimal at best in the borderline patient. Envy is a prominent theme in the narcissist while in the borderline patient it is subordinated to depression and anger at the loss of wished-for supplies. Although all patients come to treatment with mixed motives, the narcissist's primary motivation is to find and fulfill the perfection he or she seeks, as well as to have the therapist provide adulation and perfect mirroring. The key word here is "perfect," as this contrasts so markedly with the borderline patient, who seeks not perfect mirroring of grandiosity, but bare acknowledgment of the existence of a self-representation as well as fulfillment of the fantasy of receiving supplies.

Although the psychotherapy of the narcissistic personality disorder will be presented in detail later, a brief explanation is presented here to emphasize the differences in psychotherapeutic technique between the two disorders.

Therapeutic Technique

The consequences of the idealizing and mirroring projections of the narcissistic patient and the rewarding and withdrawing projections of the borderline patient help to explain why the therapeutic techniques used with these disorders—confrontation with the borderline, interpretation with the narcissistic—are not reciprocally effective.

One would not confront the narcissistic patient with behavior that he or she perceives as being destructive to himself or herself, because with this grandiose self-image, this patient is not able to perceive that fact. Rather, one would have to point out aspects of reality that the patient is denying, devaluing, or avoiding, since the grandiose self does not perceive the harm done to either his or her object relations or real, true self-interests. The confrontation of the harmfulness of the behavior in reality is experienced as an attack that has to be defended against by denial, devaluation, or avoidance, as was the original reality incident. Consequently, confrontation does not work, and therapeutic technique emphasizes instead interpretation of the patient's vulnerability to narcissistic disappointment of his or her grandiosity and need for perfection as seen in the transference acting out. In contrast, the borderline patient who is denying that the defensive behavior is destructive to the self reacts to the confrontation, or the bringing of this fact to his or her attention, not as an attack from without, but as a constructive therapeutic effort that the patient integrates in order not to be any more harmful to himself or herself than necessary.

Beyond that, if the therapeutic technique so useful with the narcissistic disorder is employed too early with the borderline, it forecloses the development of a therapeutic alliance, placing the therapist in the position of reinforcing the rewarding unit and fostering transference acting out of the rewarding part-unit/pathologic-ego alliance.

CLOSET NARCISSISTIC PERSONALITY DISORDER VERSUS BORDERLINE PERSONALITY DISORDER

The most common diagnostic error springs from confusing the closet narcissistic disorder with the borderline disorder. This confusion is compounded by the fact that the DSM-III-R approach to diagnosis provides no category for the closet narcissistic disorder.

Three clinical features promote the confusion:

1. The patient does not present a grandiose inflated false self, but rather a deflated inadequate self.
2. Unlike the exhibitionist, the closet narcissist is unable to maintain continuous activation of his or her idealizing defense and, therefore, overtly presents the clinical triad of the disorders of the self: self-activation, depression, and defense.
3. The idealizing transference acting out of the false self is confused with the clinging defense of the borderline.

The most common clinical experience, as described in Chapter 1, is for the therapist to diagnose the closet patient as a borderline disorder and to confront the patient; then, instead of integrating the confrontation, the patient responds either with attacks and devaluation or with compliance and no change in affect.

The diagnostic differentiation is made by noting that the patient's intrapsychic structure is fused, not separate—the patient may be talking about himself or herself and change the therapist or someone else without any awareness that this is taking place since they are both a part of the same representation. Or the patient looks to the therapist for a "fusion" response, assuming that the therapist has the same thoughts and feelings as the patient and will respond exactly as the patient needs. Although observing that he or she is separate, the patient nevertheless puts this emotional projection on the therapist. In a psychotic transference, the patient does not perceive the therapist as separate. In addition, there is a quantitative difference between idealizing and clinging in the transference acting out. The borderline patient who is clinging will accept a few words of approval, whereas the closet narcissist seeks *perfect* admiration all the time.

In those cases in which it is difficult to make the differentiation, it is necessary to decide on one or the other and to implement that decision through the therapeutic stance taken. For example, if the therapist decides that the patient is borderline, confrontational interventions are used to confirm the diagnosis. A therapeutic stance of confrontation means more than one or two interventions. Barring further evidence to the contrary, this approach should be maintained for a number of interviews until its effects can be determined. If its effects were to prove negative, one could then reevaluate and turn to the use of mirroring interpretations of narcissistic vulnerability to confirm the diagnosis.

There is an important clinical difference between the way in which the borderline patient responds to confrontation and that in which the closet narcissistic patient responds to interpretation. The borderline patient experiences the confrontations, which are mostly directed at maladaptive, self-destructive behavior, as helping the patient to gain control over a chaotic behavioral state.

One can envision the borderline patient's affective experience of life as being similar to the way a cork floats on the ocean. If the tide goes one way, the cork follows; if the wind blows another way, the cork moves in that direction. There is insufficient capacity to identify, discriminate between, and decide which affects are to be expressed under what conditions. Integration of an intervention is seen by changes in capacities that are demonstrated by changes in behavior. In contrast, the closet narcissistic patient experiences the therapeutic interventions not as offering control, but as the patient's "being understood," and then elaborates on the issue raised by the therapist. Integration of the interventions is seen by further explorations of narcissistic vulnerability.

In this differential diagnostic endeavor, it is important to keep in mind that some closet narcissistic patients will appear to respond in behavior to confrontation and will not attack or devalue the therapist, thereby seeming initially to confirm the diagnosis of borderline disorder. However, this response by the patient is a form of defensive compliance to reinforce the idealization. This can be determined by the fact that although the patient's behavior changes, there is no increase in or stirring up of affect, which would be essential if defenses had been interrupted.

Case of Ms. Y.*

The following is an example of a patient diagnosed as borderline who later turned out to have a closet narcissistic disorder of the self.

An attractive, single, 40-year-old graphics artist, Ms. Y., complained that although always unhappy, in the past several years, she had become even unhappier. She began to tear, mentioned that both her mother and brother had died in the past year, and said: "I've been the rock of the family, but I'm not in control anymore. I've always been in control, but lately I'm irritable and demanding. I keep myself busy, obsessively busy. Sometimes, for example, I may do projects all through the night; otherwise I will have trouble sleeping. I often don't go to bed until I'm exhausted. I find myself being angry.

"I've been unhappy with my job for a long time, but I have an inertia about getting out. I've been going along for years doing things I don't want to do. I've been unable to articulate what I want to do. I have no dream. I'm just going along. My boss is like my mother. He puts me down. I have allowed him to break my self-confidence. I try to assert myself with him, but it doesn't work.

"There have always been plenty of men, but whenever a romantic relationship gets close, I do everything I can to destroy it."

Family History

The mother was described as a dynamic, beautiful, and talented career woman, who was very successful in her work but was bitterly, unhappily married. She had an insatiable need for attention and was unable to love. She demanded performance, and she seemed to love the patient's brothers more than she did the patient. The father was very bright, refined, distancing, honorable, and possibly selfish. He had wanted a daughter. He perhaps was an alcoholic. Although bril-

*This case was prepared by Judith Pearson, Ph.D.

liant, he had burned out very early in life. There were two older brothers: one died of a heart attack and the other was a nonfunctional alcoholic. "My brothers never got away from my mother."

Personal History

"I must have gone to 16 schools during my grammar-school and high-school years. My brothers ignored me. I can remember my mother's being at work while I stayed home doing the cleaning and cooking. I functioned very well at school. I was popular and well adjusted, but it was all an act. I was terrified and never knew when I would have to leave one school and go to another. I went away to college, but transferred several times to get away from men. I've been running my whole life. I went with one man for seven years but I couldn't commit to him, I was too afraid."

There was no history of drinking or drugs or sexual abuse. After graduating from college, she taught English and fine arts for five years. She admitted that she had always had sexual problems with men. She has never been promiscuous, but although she claimed to be a one-man woman, she said she has dated two men concurrently. She finally left teaching to get away from a man and came to New York, where she has lived and worked at her present job for 12 years.

Discussion

The separation stress of her mother's and brother's deaths, the clinical presentation of depression and its defense of workaholism, the difficulty with self-acknowledgment and self-activation, the intense conflict with a narcissistic mother, the Cinderella story in childhood of doing the cooking and cleaning, and the panic at relationships with men all pointed toward a borderline disorder of the self in this one session. Let us see whether confrontation will or will not confirm the diagnosis.

The Psychotherapy

Ms. Y.'s initial complaints were feelings of hopelessness and futility about her life ("Nothing gives me pleasure, except doing for others"); depression regarding her lack of a close relationship ("I have always wanted a child and a family; I'm afraid I'll never have one"); and grief over her mother's death and the death of a brother as a result of smoking and alcohol abuse. She was also aware that she did not activate herself and that she had an "inability to say No to others," needing "to put others first." As she pointed out, "The only satisfaction I have in life is trying to please my friends." Recently she had noticed more anger and instability—emotions previously alien to her.

Despite her expressed wish for closeness, Ms. Y.'s history with men showed a pattern of distancing. She described "blowing up" a relationship with a man who was "warm and close" and who wanted to marry her, while at the same time being attracted to men who were "powerful, egotistical, and self-confident." Currently, Ms. Y. is involved with two very successful businessmen, neither of whom is available geographically. One has physical problems that make sex problematic, and they have not slept together. The other, with whom she is having a sexual relationship, lives far away and travels much of the time. It is likely that he is involved with other women. Ms. Y. was clear that although she longs for a warm relationship, her fear that she will be "taken over" by a man in the way that she was controlled by her mother keeps her from having a successful relationship.

Ms. Y.'s relationships with other women include an entanglement with a controlling, narcissistic "best friend." The friend, Ms. B., "wants everything I have. If I buy something, she has to have the identical thing. If I make something for myself, she wants one too." Ms. Y. also described Ms. B.'s envious reactions to Ms. Y.'s successes with men.

Ms. Y. has been successful in her career. She works perfectionistically and too hard, and has difficulty asserting herself with her overly demanding, moody, critical boss. When discussing her professional life, Ms. Y. described disappointment in her parents' refusal to support her intellectual and professional growth. She wanted to go to medical school, but was refused the opportunity, while all the family resources went into providing an education for her two brothers. Ms. Y. acknowledged, however, that she accepted her lot. "I could have pursued it myself, but somehow I never did." Her current job is consonant with maintaining a beautiful, elegant, perfectly finished façade—a false self-image that radiates self-sufficiency and self-esteem. As Ms. Y. stated, "People tell me they find it hard to believe I'm depressed. They see me as having everything. Nobody really knows me, and I'm afraid that if I show people who I really am, they won't like me."

I began treatment with the diagnosis of borderline disorder of the self. Ms. Y. showed characteristic overinvolvement with others at her own expense. Self-activation was difficult and led to depression, which she defended against by immersion in "the lives of others." She had an expressed fear that if she activated herself, she would "pay for it in every other way," that is, that she would lose those whom she cared about. I would confront her about her pattern of putting her needs last; for example, staying up all night to finish a project for someone and going to work tired, or failing to confront her boss when he made an unreasonable demand of her. Her replies were inevitably compliant. She would sigh and acknowledge, "I know I should take care of myself first, but somehow I just can't seem to do it. I guess I want to be irreproachable. It's the only way I know how to be loved. It seems I can only be myself by defining myself by other people."

When I would point out the cost to her of living that way—her overtirednesss, unhappiness, and sense that her life was not her own—and remind her of her own awareness that she was now in midlife and wanted things to go differently, she would respond by looking as though she were being scolded. She would lower her head and say, "I know you are right. Maybe it's just too late for me. Maybe [my brother] is right, and all of us are doomed. Sometimes I think it's just fate or genes. I don't even know if I can do this [the therapy] right."

At these times, I would address the fact that she saw the therapy as something to do "well" for others (in this case, me) rather than as a process in which she was engaged to help herself. Her response again was acknowledgment: "I know I'm here to help myself, and

I want to help myself, but sometimes I just don't know if I have it in me. Maybe I'm just too damaged by now and I'm just wasting time. Sometimes I just feel resigned to my lot."

As the work proceeded, I began to realize that I, too, was feeling unsatisfied with the course of the treatment. I found the sessions essentially sterile. Despite Ms. Y.'s unhappiness, real emotion was rarely expressed in session. Dreams and memories were few and far between. I started to wonder where my patient was hiding herself. I also started to wonder about the diagnosis.

I reviewed the information I had about Ms. Y.: her flawless façade, her use of such terms as "irreproachable" and "perfect," her fear of being "judged and criticized." I also reviewed what I knew about her relationships and her life. Her mother, like her best friend, Ms. B., was controlling, critical, and invasive, but essentially uninvolved. She expected Ms. Y. to be a perfect mirror of herself and her wishes, and treated Ms. Y. as an extension of herself. Thus, although Ms. Y. was beautiful (having once won a beauty contest), her mother was "disappointed because I didn't look like her, I resembled my father's side of the family." Her mother also expected Ms. Y. to take care of her father and brothers and to give over all her resources to their care, much as the mother herself had done.

I began to reflect that the patient may have been the recipient of a narcissistic pattern whereby her mother had projected the idealized unit onto the "genius" boys, gratifying their every wish, while projecting an empty, aggressive self-representation onto my patient. I recalled my patient's indicating that her brother had refused to work out of a sense of entitlement. "He could get a job, but nothing was good enough for him. Mother always told him that he was a genius, so teaching was beneath him. He'd rather starve." I remembered her describing her mother's attitude that if Ms. Y. were to marry, the mother would live in a little house in the backyard. Perhaps the patient's transference acting out, which I had thought was clinging, was actually an idealization of the object to maintain a fusion with it.

Ms. Y.'s pattern with men was also confusing. Given her high level of functioning, should she not, as an upper-level borderline, demonstrate clinging? Yet her pattern with men was consistently one of distancing and detachment and of ultimately becoming what she described as "the ice queen." Was this not more representative of narcissistic withdrawal and detachment than of projection of the withdrawing unit? And what of her involvement with "competent, egotistical, powerful men"? Was this not a repetition of her mother's insistence that she serve the idealized male? And what of Ms. Y.'s relationships with women? Was her need to please more attributable to a fear of abandonment or to a fear of narcissistic attack and retribution? Surely the dynamics of her friendship with the "sticky" but attacking and envious Ms. B. bespoke the latter.

In short, some four or five months into the treatment, I began to wonder whether I was dealing with an upper-level borderline disorder or an upper-level closet narcissistic disorder. To answer my diagnostic question, I changed my form of intervention, shifting from confrontation to mirroring interpretations of narcissistic vulnerability.

The patient's response to these interventions in the following weeks left me with a growing conviction that the new diagnosis was correct. I began consistently to address Ms. Y.'s vulnerability and fear of attack as the inner source of her incapacity to stay with herself (e.g., "It seems to me that inside you feel so vulnerable to being attacked for any self-assertion that you soothe this vulnerability by avoiding standing up for yourself at work"). Her response was: "I was thinking about what you said about vulnerability. I do feel vulnerable. I feel vulnerable to everyone. I think it was because of my mother. I know she loved me, but nothing I could do was enough for her. She always found fault. She hated the way I looked, and she never saw me as smart. I was the ordinary one; only the boys were special because they were the geniuses. I could never please her, so I feel I can't please anyone. I never feel good enough." And finally Ms. Y. began to cry, saying, "I thought I would be free of her when she died, but I'm still trying to get her to love me."

The opening up of deeper content and affect expressed in the following sessions convinced me of the narcissistic diagnosis. Ms. Y. was clearly expressing the conflict of the closet narcissist—a deep wish to be "special" to the parent and to experience the exhilaration that comes with parental mirroring of infantile grandiosity, which is then buried because of fear of the parent's shaming and deflating criticism or attack. To save herself from the continual excoriation of her mother's venom, Ms. Y. buried her own needs to be mirrored and devoted herself to pleasing by continuously mirroring the other.

What confirmed the diagnosis was that I began to observe more emotion and more life during the sessions. I felt more attuned to my patient, and there was certainly more affect present from her side. She also began to look at me when I intervened, rather than to keep her head lowered. I was able to connect her sometimes stilted compliance in the session with her sense of vulnerability, and my interpretations of her transference acting out allowed her to explore her need "to be perfect and have everything under control" in the sessions.

Comment

The key to confirming the diagnosis was the patient's integration of the interpretation, which led to further and deeper exploration of her narcissistic vulnerability.

SCHIZOID DISORDER OF THE SELF VERSUS CLOSET NARCISSISTIC DISORDER OF THE SELF

Some patients with closet narcissistic disorders have such prominent defenses of detachment of affect and social withdrawal and isolation that they appear to have a schizoid personality disorder. At the same time, there is one clinical type of the schizoid disorder with narcissistic defenses that mimics the closet narcissistic disorder. Since the therapeutic interventions with the two disorders differ, it is essential to make a careful differential diagnosis between them.

The concept of the schizoid personality disorder has been enlarged through the developmental self and object relations approach, particularly by the Masterson Institute's clinical director, Ralph Klein, M.D. His conception is briefly summarized and a schizoid patient with closet narcissistic defenses is described, before a detached closet narcissistic disorder of the self that mimics the schizoid disorder of the self is presented.

SCHIZOID PERSONALITY DISORDER*

The schizoid personality disorder of the self is a dimension of psychopathology that has been recognized in one form or another since shortly after the turn of the century. The concept, however, has had differing connotations over time. A more complete picture of the schizoid individual is required—one that addresses not only the clinical picture, but also the nature of the original developmental disturbance, the resultant intrapsychic structure, and the therapeutic manifestation of these features, both in the transference acting out and in responses to specific therapeutic interventions.

Clinical Manifestations

As with other personality disorders, the clinical presentation can serve as a red flag to signal the clinician's attention when making a diagnosis. However, if the DSM-III-R diagnostic criteria for schizoid disorder are rigidly adhered to, many patients with this disorder will be overlooked and consequently misdiagnosed. The schizoid personality disorder, as defined in DSM-III-R, identifies, in fact, only those patients who have severe, generally lower-level character structures that correspond roughly to clinical stereotypes of the schizoid patient—cold, wary, isolated, withdrawn, eccentric, and strange. The avoidant personality of DSM-III-R comes close descriptively to the general picture of the higher-level schizoid individual, which I would propose as part of an overall schizoid continuum or dimension of psychopathology that would take its place beside the borderline and narcissistic dimensions.

Also useful for diagnosis is Guntrip's[20] conception of clinical features with which the schizoid individual might present. These are organized as follows:

*This section was written by Ralph Klein, M.D.

1. The "pure schizoid cluster": withdrawal, introversion, lack of affect.
2. The "narcissistic cluster": narcissism, superiority, self-reliance.
3. The "borderline cluster": depersonalization, regression, loneliness.

The "schizoid cluster" is the most direct expression of the individual's need to maintain a safe, stable interpersonal distance from others. This cluster is a necessary, but not sufficient, feature in making the diagnosis of a schizoid personality disorder. Such manifestations as are present in this cluster may present as overt phenomena, easily identified by the observer, or they may present as a covert phenomenon. The patient could be described as a "secret schizoid" who subjectively and intrapsychically perceives and experiences others and relationships at a great distance that is not obvious (overt) to the observer, but that will only become known when the patient reports such internal, subjective phenomena.

Although the schizoid cluster is necessary to make the diagnosis, the patient may present clinically with symptoms that may at first appear narcissistic or borderline. But the narcissism of the schizoid is different from that of the narcissistic personality disorder. It is a reflection of the patient's need to maintain a safe distance *above* others, a feeling of not having to rely on others, and is not a reflection of an underlying grandiose-self–representation. Also, the borderline features are not reflections of the split object relations units of the borderline personality disorder (especially the bad-self–representation), but rather represent a different way to be apart from, albeit *below,* others, unable or unwilling to participate in their company.

Developmental Considerations

Patients with borderline and narcissistic disorders believe that a "communication" network is in place between themselves and others. However, they are confronted with the task of discovering the specific conditions that will keep open the channels of communication and maintain the pattern of attachment that had been established. Those conditions might include regression, compliance, mirroring, or perfectionistic strivings, to name a few. For the schizoid individual, there is no conviction that a communication network is in place, or even possible, without grave risk and danger. For the schizoid individual, the basic "primitive agony" or "unthinkable anxiety" (Winnicott[21]) is "complete isolation because of there being no means of communication."

How did this state of affairs come about? The best answer at present is that the schizoid individual came to the conclusion that no matter what he or she did, he or she could not satisfy the conditions necessary to negotiate, build, and maintain a means of communication.

What was it in the nature of the interpersonal interaction that led the schizoid person to the sense of near-hopelessness about relatedness? Issues of nature and fate aside, the subjective experience of many schizoid individuals was that their efforts at relatedness were of no avail and would meet with scorn, indifference, or neglect. Their subjective experience was not that of a vital cog in the family system, whether healthy or pathologic, but as a dehumanized, depersonified "function" that would be called upon to serve a purpose and then consigned to the "back shelf" until their services were required further. This experience is expressed with many metaphors, such as feeling like an android, a puppet, or a slave.

Intrapsychic Structure (Figure 3.1)

The intrapsychic structure of the schizoid personality disorder consists of two split, defensive object relations units, which I have described as the "master–slave unit" and the "sadistic-object–self-in-exile unit." The schizoid personality disorder most often pervasively activates the latter unit, and experiences others as potentially

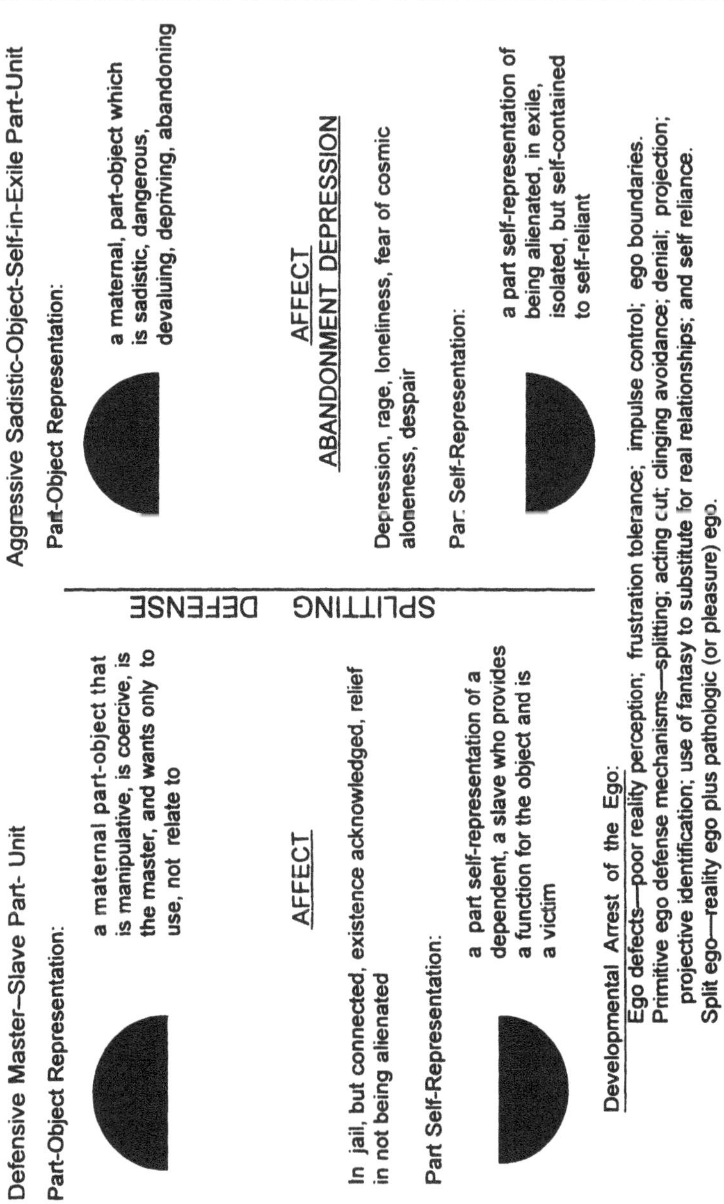

Figure 3.1. Split Object Relations Unit of the Schizoid Disorder of the Self

dangerous, devaluing, or depriving. The benefit of "exile" is safety, while the debit side is the experience of isolation, loneliness, alienation, and "cosmic" aloneness. These individuals we rarely see in treatment.

The schizoid personality disorder who is unwilling to settle for safety at any cost is then likely to activate the master–slave unit, and, furthermore, is most likely to seek treatment voluntarily. The master–slave unit is a "settling" of a different sort, one that is far more related, although again at a cost to the patient. Here the object is perceived as manipulating, coercive, controlling, and appropriating. The individual accepts the conditions of the relationship as a slave would, because he or she feels it is the only condition of relatedness open. This manifests itself as compliance, dependence, submission, and the subjective experience of victimization.

What the patient with a schizoid personality disorder can turn to protectively, adaptively, and defensively are self-reliance, self-containment, self-sufficiency, and/or fantasy. Fantasy and self-sufficiency are "schizoid compromises"—more or less adaptive efforts to regulate the swings between the master–slave and the sadistic-object–self-in-exile units.

Transference Acting Out, Therapeutic Alliance, and Treatment

The nature of the transference acting out of the patient with a schizoid personality disorder reflects or mirrors the nature of the intrapsychic structure. This patient will have to see the therapist in any conflict situation through the screen cast by either the projection of the "master" representation or the "sadistic-object" representation.

The therapist, therefore, is experienced either as manipulative, controlling, and laying claim to whatever the patient possesses of value, or as sadistic, dangerous, and depriving. In the first case, the patient accepts the role of slave as the price for relatedness. In the second case, emotional exile is the condition for maintaining freedom and self-protection.

Unbeknownst to the therapist, usually, another form of transference acting out will involve the schizoid fantasy of intimacy with the therapist. This fantasy, often concealed until a therapeutic alliance is in place or even until the latter stages of treatment, is often the most deeply hidden "compromise" that such a patient will mobilize to defend against the risk of moving closer emotionally in real life outside the therapist's office.

The key word to describe the nature of the therapeutic alliance here is "safety." How does the therapist help the patient convert transference acting out to therapeutic alliance? The therapist must maintain therapeutic neutrality. No major parameter of treatment must be introduced for the patient with a schizoid personality disorder around the frame and therapeutic neutrality. The therapist conveys his or her safety as an object by the primary use of *interpretation of the schizoid dilemma*. The schizoid dilemma is that the patient can be neither too close nor too far in emotional distance from another person without experiencing conflict and anxiety. To be too close exposes the patient to the fear of appropriation and manipulation and is unsafe. Yet to be in exile—too far—is to risk the anxiety of unbearable isolation and alienation. The therapist's interpretation of the patient's behavior, thoughts, or feelings as reflections of the therapist's understanding of the patient's dilemma allows the patient to feel understood and safe.

Especially after the therapeutic alliance is in place—a task that might take months or even years—the therapist must add to the interpretation of the schizoid dilemma the interpretation of the schizoid compromise. Here the therapist must look for all signs of defense and resistance and interpret the patient's willingness to "settle" or "compromise" on a relatively safe and comfortable distance without working through the abandonment depression.

When the patient with a schizoid personality disorder is willing to take risks in getting closer, through sharing experiences, feelings, or thoughts, this precipitates in the patient a series of painful and threatening affects associated with the underlying abandonment depression. In order to avoid these painful affects and memories, the patient has had to resort to defense, first in the form of not getting too close or too far, and then in the form, primarily, of self-reliance, self-sufficiency, and fantasy. Linking the patient's efforts at closeness and sharing to defense (distance, self-reliance, or fantasy) through interpretation of the schizoid compromise interrupts defense and sets the condition for the patient to explore the pathogenesis of the split object relations units.

As with all therapeutic work with personality disorders, one must distinguish the goals of ego repair from those of working through. For the patient with a schizoid personality disorder, ego repair may be quite effective in permitting the patient to establish a far more "related," safe, and comfortable distance—that is, to expand the domain of the public self while shrinking the domain of the private self. The achievement of greater relatedness, stable companionship, and generativity may be successful outcomes. However, the goal of working through permits freedom from vulnerability to the fears of manipulation, appropriation, deprivation, and danger, which further permits the overcoming in a maximal way of the impairments in the real self.

Case of Mr. S.

Mr. S., a 40-year-old psychologist, presented with the chief complaint that despite the fact that he was extremely handsome and appeared to be accomplished and sensitive, he felt himself to be a mass of contradictions and, essentially, a "mess." "Inside I feel like pus," he stated. He spoke of his wish to be with people, and yet, at the same time, said that he didn't want to be with others. He described a chronic sense of isolation and, more strikingly, of alienation: "If I were blue, I would not fit in with a group of blue people." He said he felt that something was "missing" within. He reported that no one in his world had any idea how he felt, except for a woman who had been a friend since childhood and his wife of two years—a recovering heroin addict. He himself was a recovering alcoholic. With these two people, and only with them, could he feel safe. Though it was difficult for him to describe these feelings in the office, he stated that he was willing to risk it because he no longer wanted to live like a "ghost"—never really there, never really feeling, "locked away" from the world and himself.

As a child, the patient had been physically beaten by a sadistic father. He recalled that he had felt somewhat protected by, and protective of, his mother, who, however, seemed unable to protect him and who would join in at times in verbally humiliating him. The father was truly a terror, and the patient recalled specifically fearing for his life. He remembered in dramatic detail how he "survived" by "locking myself away when I was seven." He recalled consciously telling himself "I give up" at that age, and presenting a façade to the world of a competent, yet sensitive and somewhat shy individual. He successfully completed high school, college, and graduate school. Much of the time, he did not feel. "I simply chose not to feel, and when that didn't work, I would drink myself into oblivion." He had been an alcoholic for over 20 years, having stopped two years before beginning treatment. He had dated a few women, "Just going through the motions," until he met his wife. She had been his first sexual experience.

Both parents were now deceased, and the precipitant for his coming to treatment was his wish to make his marriage successful, to be able to feel more intimately and be closer to his wife, and, perhaps, even to have a child. Professionally, he had always worked in clinical settings and had never advanced beyond line positions because of his fear of getting closer to others professionally and personally.

His intrapsychic structure consisted of the following split object relations unit. On the one hand, he avoided close contact with others (except for his wife and childhood friend—although these relationships also were limited) because he feared that he would be manipulated, humiliated, attacked, or abused. He often recognized the irrationality of these fears, but felt them no less intensely. He believed that the only way to be free of feeling endangered and potentially devalued was to be totally self-reliant. However, he sometimes feared that he could withdraw so far from others that "I might never come back." Occasionally, he would describe this as a suicidal idea, but mostly he felt that he would lose access to that "real" part of him that he had locked away as a child.

The part of himself that he had locked away he finally described as follows: He had a persistent fantasy that there was inside of him a small egg with an almost impenetrable shell that his physical body protected. Within that egg existed his real self, which had to be protected at all costs; if it were to be destroyed, he would die. But it could do him little actual good unless he could crack the shell and access the person inside, who was real but vulnerable.

This was a description of the sadistic-object–self-in-exile unit, as well as of the deeply hidden hope of relatedness that he had preserved from assault and psychic death as a child.

On the other hand, he said, he felt that to get closer to people would involve his feeling endangered, unsafe, and vulnerable to being trapped, manipulated, and coerced. For example, he could approach his wife affectionately and sexually, but could not allow her to approach him—literally, to take the initiative and touch him. He immediately, he reported, "tightened up, withdrew all feeling, and just experienced her arms around me like chains. I felt caught in a trap. I would be overwhelmed with fear and rage." This literal experience of his wife as potentially enslaving was repeated figuratively in his emotional interactions with acquaintances and colleagues at work. In all these instances, he felt that in order to maintain some connection and relatedness, he had to comply, at least in part, by "going through the motions" of being related—chatting, socializing, making jokes, and otherwise participating in the normal interactions of everyday life. For him, though, they were far from "normal." It was rather like torture. It was at these times that he felt most removed from himself and without feeling, or felt that his compliance was a result of weakness, "a sickness" of his personality that made him submit and pay such a huge price to feel like a human being. This was an example of the activation of the master–slave unit that accompanied any act of closeness or interpersonal relatedness.

His major defense was his self-sufficiency, his feeling that he could survive anything (and had!). He also had extensive fantasies that occupied much of his time. These fantasies were prominently sadomasochistic in nature.

Course of Therapy

Although highly motivated to make some significant changes in all aspects of his life, Mr. S. found that taking the necessary steps was like walking "through molasses" at best or "through a mine field" at worst. The facts in this history were gathered over a year's time. The information did not flow easily. For the patient, it was "like torture," and my response was an enormous feeling of pathos as I watched him struggle to express his wishes and fears.

As might be expected, each act of self-revelation was accompanied by fears that I would use the material either to attack, humiliate, shame, or abuse him: "You must think I'm a long drink of piss just like my father did"—and which his father had called him frequently. When projecting this aspect of his intrapsychic world, he would often teeter on the brink of leaving treatment, stating that he really didn't need it, that he could manage his problems on his own, as he always had. Alternately, he would feel that to share his feelings and past was an example of his weakness. He would attack himself as pitiful and whining, of wanting me to feel sorry for him. At the same time, he would become enraged at me, believing that I was encouraging his self-revelation as a means to gain control over him, that I would turn him into a project, that he would end up doing what I wanted him to do, and that he was simply a source of my own self-gratification. I would treat him, he thought, as long as I found him interesting or challenging, and then I would discard him or refer him elsewhere.

I would consistently address his back-and-forth movement in treatment by interpreting the schizoid dilemma: "Whenever you take the chance to tell me something about yourself, it feels unsafe, and you then close up as a way to protect yourself and to reassure yourself that you can, as always, manage on your own."

Or, "You describe to me a little of how it felt as a child, so scared, so terrified, and you become afraid that I will see you as weak and vulnerable, but when you get angry at me in order to feel strong again, you feel disconnected and apart from me. It seems to me that you get caught in a dilemma of feeling either too close to me or too far away."

Or, "It strikes me that the violence and quantity of your fantasies this past week might be your way of maintaining control of your life and yourself in treatment—especially when you took such a risk in the last session by sharing your fantasies about the 'real' you that is locked away inside."

Or, "I think that when you ask me at times what I am thinking about what you just said, you are checking out where I stand. I experience it as your wanting to know if it is safe to continue—am I really understanding or just trying to fit you into a preconceived notion? So let me tell you what I was thinking, and then I'll ask you what fantasy you had about my reaction."

And so on for most of the first year of treatment. Clearly, the central task was to clarify the distortions created by the transference acting out through persistent, continuous, albeit varied interpretations of the schizoid dilemma until Mr. S. felt that his dilemma was understood by me and that he was safe from my need to act as either a master or a sadistic object.

Once this was established, Mr. S. moved into a systematic examination of the various defenses he employed in order to manage his life—past and present. His alcoholism, withdrawal (socially and affectively), fantasies, and the reemergence repeatedly of feelings of compliance and isolation were increasingly interpreted as a compromise solution to his dilemma.

"It seems to me that your thoughts about drinking again are a destructive compromise between your struggle to move ahead with investing in others and your almost reflexive tendency to withdraw totally. It strikes me as a lousy compromise."

Or, "You tell me that you found yourself calling yourself a 'long drink of piss,' while coming to your session today. I think that rather than continue to share and take risks with me or to totally withdraw your feelings from the session, you are compromising by reconnecting with your father and settling for being his son again by taking up his old chant and repeating it as your words."

Or, "I sense now that your fantasies this week are less the usual pattern of retreating that you have used them for so often in the past than, seemingly, a substitute for taking more risks with Ann [his wife]. You have come pretty far in being more intimate with her, but it seems to me that you are saying, 'The rest of the way will be filled with fantasy, not reality.' I wonder what is motivating you to settle at this point."

The interpretation of the efforts at compromise led Mr. S. to explore increasingly the origin and evolution of the split object relations units. By now he was coming to treatment three times a week, and the pattern of exploration of his pathologic internal world took on the characteristics of most personality disorders (be they borderline or narcissistic) in identifying in memory and with affect the patterns of misattunement, depersonification, and ultimately abandonment. The unfolding of his relationship with his parents took more than three years of difficult, sustained, complicated unraveling, reexamination, and working through.

THE CLOSET NARCISSISTIC DISORDER

Case of Mr. C.

Mr. C., a single, tall, blond, muscular, well-groomed 38-year-old presented with a chief complaint of "latent heterosexuality, homosexuality, social isolation, depression and anger, and self-destructive behavior." He described himself as a workaholic who worked 16-hour days. He lived alone, was socially isolated, and when not working, drank at home or went out to gay bars either to observe and be with people or for one-night stands.

He said he has great difficulty in getting access to his feelings and felt detached a good deal of the time. Although he wishes to have relationships, he said, he has no friends and feels isolated and lonely. "I couldn't bear to have anything good happen to me. I don't deserve anything. When anything good happens, I turn around and attack myself." He has few friends, except for the acquaintances he meets at the office, and has no integrated social life. "I spend my time observing—it's too frightening to get close to people."

Family History

He described his mother as having had no feelings, as being vengeful and destructive, and as seeming to have wanted to use him as a husband, when she was not ignoring him. She was unpredictable, unreliable, harsh, and punitive. His father was extremely self-centered, and expected the patient to accede to his every wish. He was extremely disappointed with and constantly commented on the patient's lack of masculinity. The patient was the third of four children. He had two older sisters and a younger brother, who was born when the patient was three. In describing his brother, who was now quite successful, he said, "I hated him, I wanted to kill him, he was my father's ideal."

Personal History

The patient described his first three years as idyllic, as his father was away serving in the Army and the patient was the center of attention of his grandmother, mother, and sisters. He was described as being active, garrulous, and sociable. When he was three, his father returned and his brother was born. He hated the brother and had fantasies of killing him. As he grew older, he was constantly criticized by his father for not joining the father in his masculine pursuits, such as hunting and fishing. He recalled being so hurt and angry that he rebelled and refused to do so. "Somewhere around the age of eight, I realized that they were both incompetent and that I would have to be the parent. At this point, I gave up on them, and I decided I was going to be a superachiever and substitute that for a relationship."

He proceeded to carry out this goal, graduating at the top of his high-school class, attending a very good college, and becoming a successful architect. Though he had a number of outside interests, such as photography, reading, travel, and painting, he found it difficult to activate himself to engage in them. He admitted having great difficulty in focusing on himself and activating himself to do "what I want to do."

When left alone in his apartment, he would become overwhelmed by anxiety and would have to drink and/or go out to visit bars. He had had no close friends of either sex while in college or as he became established in his profession.

Comment

The profound detachment of affect and social isolation suggested a schizoid personality disorder. However, the diagnosis of closet narcissistic personality disorder became clarified over the course of several sessions when the patient elaborated on how he had dealt with the conflicts of the parents: "I gave up looking to them for approval, and I decided that I was going to achieve. I was going to put on a show and dazzle them and substitute this kind of response for approval." In other words, rather than relate to the object with a masochistic or distancing defense, he would activate his grandiose self to receive admiration from the object and thereby regain the lost paradise and regulate his grandiose sense of self.

Rather than being indifferent to social interaction, the patient craved it, but was terrified that any involvement with others carried the original threat of being engulfed. For example, during prolonged business discussions, he would have to leave—he had to get more space in order to relieve the anxiety about engulfment. The diagnostic impression was confirmed by his response to an interpretation: It was so painful for him to focus on the self he gave up with his parents that he substituted performance and achievement in an effort to dazzle other people and so gain their admiration as a way of regulating his sense of self. The result, however, was that he was left with feelings of isolation, loneliness, and depression, which he had to soothe through the use of alcohol, sexual acting out, workaholism, and detachment.

EXHIBITIONISTIC NARCISSISTIC DEFENSE AGAINST A BORDERLINE DISORDER

Diagnosis can be further complicated by the fact that some borderline patients develop a narcissistic defense against their borderline problem. This psychodynamic can arise from a childhood experience when a child becomes depressed because he or she feels abandoned by the mother and so turns to a narcissistic father for "rescue" after the rapprochement phase has deflated infantile grandiosity and omnipotence. The narcissistic defense initially may confuse the therapist's diagnosis unless he or she is careful to observe the borderline intrapsychic structure emerging as the narcissistic defense is worked through. On the other hand, if the patient begins treatment in a regressed state, the borderline disorder may be observed first and the narcissistic defense will only emerge later in psychotherapy. This does not indicate a change in diagnosis, but a change in defense. Nor does this have to create therapeutic confusion since the therapist has to begin with whatever defensive state the patient presents and then change as the defenses change.

Case of Ms. B.

When first seen, this young woman was clearly in a regressed borderline state. As the psychotherapy progressed, rather than moving into working through her conflict with her mother (borderline conflict), the patient moved into a full-fledged narcissistic defense against this conflict, which took several years to work through, before she returned to working through the underlying conflict.

The patient illustrated the narcissistic defense against the borderline problem by describing how she had two selves: a mother self and a father self. The mother self was dependent, needy, helpless, and clinging, and the father self was superior, cool, and in control, but had very little affect. Under separation stress, she would regress from the father self to the mother self, which she described as being like "falling through the roof" into helplessness. She had no firm foundation for her self-image. The history indicates the presence of the borderline problem in her symptomatic episodes and the narcissistic defense in her high-level functioning at school between these episodes.

History of Present Illness

Ms. B., 21, who had graduated from college with honors, had recently moved to New York City to live on her own and start her first job. This separation stress brought on attacks of panic: "The terror just swept over me. I was afraid that my legs wouldn't work or that I wouldn't be able to eat or swallow. I thought that perhaps I was going crazy." In addition, she complained of hysterical episodes of impaired consciousness and recurrent depressions. Associated with these episodes of panic were feelings of helplessness and inability to cope. She became obsessed "with what might happen if the fear took over." Clearly the borderline problem and her mother-self had the upper hand at that moment.

She reported previous episodes of depression on the first day of summer camp at age nine, in the 12th grade in high school, and during the first year of college. She reiterated her lack of confidence in herself in this state and her enormous feeling of dependence on her mother. She reported that whenever she became panicky, she would call her mother for reassurance, sometimes several times a day. She currently had a boyfriend whom she idealized and to whom she clung.

Family History

She described her mother as being phobic and excessively preoccupied with the family. At the beginning of psychotherapy, she emphasized that her mother rewarded her infantile behavior; later she reported that her mother had vigorously attacked any of her efforts at self-assertiveness or originality. The mother criticized her body shape, her bodily functions, and, eventually, her emerging sexuality, finding all of them "disgusting." The father, on the other hand, giving a hint of the narcissistic defense, was described as very successful, extremely self-centered, and narcissistic. He showed little affect and patronized and looked down on his wife, but actively sought out and indulged both of his children, particularly the patient. She had one younger sister who was phobic. When the patient was between eight and 10 years of age, severe conflict between the mother and father drove Ms. B. even closer to her father, and she became his favorite and constant companion, participating in many activities with him without the mother. The narcissistic defense was by now becoming institutionalized and was in charge.

Associated with this growing closeness to her father, attacks of separation anxiety in the form of anxiety and nausea before going to kindergarten gradually subsided as the narcissistic defense took over, and she functioned extremely well in grammar and high school, getting straight *A*'s. Despite this high level of functioning, when physically ill, she would become extremely anxious. In the 12th grade, she was depressed for about six months; this ended when she met her first boyfriend.

Although she feared she might become depressed if she attended college away from home, she went anyway, and initially did become extremely depressed, crying and calling home almost every day for most of the first year. However, the narcissistic defense again took over, and she adapted well for the next three years, graduated with honors, and moved to the city to look for a job.

She dated one boy throughout the 12th grade, with whom her relationship was mostly intellectual: "He needed me more than I needed him." While in college, she dated another young man for a few years and had intercourse for the first time, without difficulty. She was currently dating a man exclusively whom she described as gentle, caring, and upright, the family's idea of the perfect mate.

Intrapsychic Structure

The patient had the following a basic underlying borderline intrapsychic structure. It included a rewarding maternal part–object representation that was of an omnipotent, godlike mother who provided safety and the associated affect of relief from panic and anxiety and "feeling good and loved." The part–self-image was that of a helpless and compliant child. The withdrawing maternal part–object representation was that of an extremely angry, attacking, and punitive and vengeful mother who found the patient disgusting in her essence (i.e., her individuation) and who would kill her. The associated affect was composed of fear, rage, and depression. The part–self-image was of being guilty—an insect, a worm, worthless, despicably bad, and inadequate because she was a woman, like her mother.

The triad functioned to maintain the wish for reunion and to abet the fulfillment of the mother's wishes by avoiding separation, self-assertion, and individuation; behaving in a helpless, dependent, unassertive, clinging, needy, and asexual manner; and meanwhile denying the destructiveness of this behavior to her adaptation.

Whenever she was exposed to separation trauma—mother's withdrawal or its symbol or self-activation—she would collapse in a helpless, fearful, hysterical panic that, from the history, was designed to coerce the withdrawing mother to return and "take care of her," which she actually did in real life. The patient referred to this part of her self-image associated with the borderline conflict and the mother as "her mother-self."

The Narcissistic Defense

In an effort to resolve this dilemma with her mother and to get revenge, and aided by the father's seductive behavior, she turned from her mother to her father—again probably after rapprochement had deflated her infantile grandiosity—and made an intense identification with his narcissistic character structure. This produced an overlay of narcissistic defense against the borderline conflict.

In this narcissistic intrapsychic structure, the object representation was omnipotent, controlling, all-powerful. The self-representation was grandiose and special, the affect being that of feelings of superiority, uniqueness, and well-being based on the acting out of this unit through narcissistically manipulating other people to obtain their approval, devaluing them, and using them solely for this narcissistic purpose, and also being able to act without sexual feeling, that is, to use sex as a manipulation for her narcissistic needs. This self–part representation the patient described as "her father-self," which was cool, superior, and affectless.

Phallic Oedipal Stage

The identification with the narcissistic father in the latter part of the separation–individuation phase apparently "rescued" the patient from the intense borderline conflict with the mother at the cost of severe conflict in the oedipal stage. The patient colluded with the father's seduction to get revenge on the mother by taking the father away from her, and she thereby developed a pattern of sexual acting out. The fact that the relationship was so actively acted out, though not in an overt sexual manner, then stirred up her oedipal wishes. She developed intense guilt regarding acting out the revenge on the mother, which then was secondarily reinforced by guilt regarding her oedipal feelings toward the father. The mother's original disparaging of her emerging sexuality combined with the oedipal sources of guilt to produce a feminine self-image of being profoundly bad, revengeful, unworthy, and guilty, and not deserving of a real relationship with a man.

Under separation stress, the shift would take place from the father-self to the mother-self, which she described as "falling through the roof" of her personality, going from being cool, detached, superior, and in control (father-self) to being helpless, needy, and clinging (mother-self).

The patient began treatment in this regressed state as a result of her separation panic so that it was necessary to begin the work with confrontation. As she began to form a therapeutic alliance, she moved in treatment, as she had as a child, from the borderline conflict to the narcissistic identification with the father and her father-self. This happened quite suddenly. One day the patient shifted from being helpless, needy, and clinging, which I had been confronting, to a detached, cool, superior, devaluing transference acting out. It was necessary to shift the therapeutic technique from confrontation to mirroring interpretation of narcissistic vulnerability. Finally, when this narcissistic defense was worked through, the patient moved into the abandonment depression, which then was worked through.

CLOSET NARCISSISTIC DEFENSE AGAINST ABANDONMENT DEPRESSION AND NEUROTIC CONFLICT

A clinical picture of the closet narcissistic personality disorder can also be a regressive defense against both an abandonment depression and a neurotic conflict. When the closet defenses are overcome, the patient moves first into an abandonment depression, and then, when that is worked through, into a neurotic oedipal conflict. The following case, briefly described here, involves a patient whose condition was additionally complicated by dissociative* defenses against loss.

Case of Mr. E.

Loss and Tragedy Haunt the Emerging Self

Mr. E., a single, short, blond, slender, meticulously groomed, 35-year-old banker who was moderately anxious and mildly depressed, presented his problem articulately with very little intervention on my part.

Chief Complaint

"I have a vague anxiety, a lack of sense of authenticity, as if I can't be myself and be successful, and I'm tired of living life on the defensive. I never feel like I'm living directly or free, and I never feel satisfied. I have a lack of entitlement or a lack of courage to follow through and don't feel I deserve anything. I feel I'm cheating and I'm constantly afraid that bad things will happen, and they generally do." (He gave an excellent description of his difficulty with his sense of self—i.e., self-image and self-activation—without providing a clue as to its source.)

Precipitating Stress

In the past 18 months, he had suffered three severe losses: two of his best friends were killed in automobile accidents, and he lost so much money in the market crash that he might not be able to keep his cooperative apartment.

He elaborated on his difficulty with real-self–activation in work and relationships.

*Dissociation: A disturbance in the normally integrated functions of identity, memory, or consciousness. It may be sudden or gradual, transient or chronic (DSM-III-R, 1987).

History of Present Illness

"In college I majored in acting and theater and minored in economics, and I worked at my acting. I did quite well. When I graduated, I continued my study at an acting school in New York City in the company of many who are now famous, and I also had a private acting coach.

"My acting coach eventually lost interest in me, and I panicked about not having enough money, and 10 years ago, at the age of 25, I left the theater world and took a job with a bank in order to make money. I did well until recently. But even so, I didn't like it. I had to force myself. I procrastinated, but I'm fearfully obsessed with not having enough money, which I depend on to validate my sense of self. On the other hand, I feel guilty about not doing what I could in the theater because I think I have a lot of talent. I'm also a perfectionist, but even so I have to force myself to do the work."

Relationship with Women

"I'm addicted to women and money as a way of measuring my sense of self. I have a fantasy of the ideal perfect woman, and I'm afraid that if I marry a real one, I will miss out on the perfect one, that she will probably show up among the guests on my wedding day.

"Until 10 years ago, I dated older women. The relationship would usually last two years and then break up. I've been with my current girlfriend for five years and have lived with her for two years. She initiated the relationship and really has carried it for me. I should marry her, but I'm still keeping my options open for the perfect woman, although I feel I love her and she is awfully good to me.

"My goal or vision is to live life authentically, to be plugged into it, to marry the perfect woman and to become such a good actor that it will validate me."

Personal History

"I was born in the Midwest, the youngest, with an older brother and two older sisters. I was okay until I was three and a half years old, when my father died in an automobile accident. My mother was terribly depressed and cried a lot, so my development was suffused in sorrow. My mother had rages, and if we disobeyed, she beat us with a belt. On the other hand, as the baby of the family, I was spoiled by all three women, but when I started school, my mother went back to work as a teacher, and I resented it.

"However, despite the rages, my mother also seemed to encourage our growth. My functioning in grammar school and high school was average, and my social life was good, with outside interests in acting, music, and sports.

"When I was 18, I became curious about what my father had been like and what my relationship with him had been. I went away to college, majored first in engineering, and in my second year changed to drama, where I did well."

The patient denied any clinical or vegetative signs of depression or any abuse of alcohol or drugs. There was no evidence of an affective disorder.

The Psychotherapy

Mirroring interpretations of idealizing the object to regulate the grandiose self led to overcoming the dissociative defenses against mourning the loss of the father. He had thought that he had had a very distant relationship with his father, and he became intensely and dramatically aware that he had had such a close relationship that he had to block it out—that when his father died, his sense of self died. I interpreted that the loss of his father, and then his mother's need for support, impelled him to give up all self-activation and to focus on his mother (the object). He reported, "Every time I activate myself, I feel disaster will strike and my mother will be upset." With regard to his father, he reported: "There is a hole where Father had been, like he was excised. Father loved me far more than I thought. It's so painful. I don't remember caring about him until just now and that it was fun to be with him." He began to sob.

"The last session led to lots of discoveries, with things falling into place. Fun for fun's sake. Sorrow, all the memories of my father and fun. Terrifying things I avoided. It wasn't true that I was too young to know my father or to miss him. I knew him very well, loved him.

I rediscovered and reclaimed my father. I realized that my little boy's heart was broken when he died. Joyful memories of him, too, are painful.

"I built some myths. I was too young to know him. I had thought I hadn't separated from Mother; I turned to him, saw him as remote, distant, authoritarian. If he had lived, my whole life would have been harder. Family videos reminded me of how he loved us. As he was the one who took them, I adored him. I was about three and a half years old when he died. I detached feelings as soon as I heard, and I kept playing. I had so identified with him that when he died, my sense of self died. I make that slip often. The last four days have been ones of extreme pain and sadness. Mother's need never allowed us to focus on ourselves and our own grief. The central trauma of my childhood really was the love and loss of my father."

This admission allowed Mr. E. to begin to repair his sense of self. "The last few weeks, I've felt grounded for the first time in my life. Feeling a connection, not so dependent on others or work or women. I can feel my sense of self developing. Regaining the connection with my father allows me to father my self."

The working through of the loss of his father led to a focus on the abandonment depression and its defenses, which was related to the earlier developmental arrest in the relationship with the mother before the loss of the father. The defenses against this depression were his avoidance of self-activation at work and his avoidance of intimacy with women. Interpretation of these defenses led to the underlying abandonment depression. The working through of this level of abandonment depression freed his sense of self more, but there still remained a feeling of dread associated with full self-activation.

In searching for the reasons for the continued dread, he explored the possibility of sexual abuse in the early years with his mother, based on emerging feelings of fear, sex, and guilt. However, this turned out to be a dead end. Then he reported a dream that broke through into the oedipal conflict: "I was back at home. I saw a naked woman walk by and she invited a naked man to play music with us. I felt suspicious about myself, and then I ran through the woods. And an older man had a dog, which came after me. I slapped him with my foot. The dog looked hangdog and I tried to soothe him. And then a big, athletic man came and attacked me and I fended him off. I'm ready to poke his eyes out. I felt, how dare he try to intimidate me in my own neighborhood? I woke up angry and frightened."

Free association: "I thought about the big nozzles on a tank in our backyard that reminded me of penises, Father's big penis. I remembered the movie *The Grifters,* where the mother tried to seduce the son and that brought on a feeling of fear. Anjelica Huston in a slip reminded me of my mother, ugly, frightening. My mother was committed for ECT when I was eight and again when I was 16. She almost died of uremia when she had me. They thought she would die. Then she had a hysterectomy, and she had major surgery when I was 12. My mother used to go from sobbing to vengeful anger."

In the next session, the patient began: "It was the fear that led to the idea of sexual abuse. After the last session, I thought, could it be oedipal feelings? I felt the same swirl of fear, sex, and guilt. I realized that the special relationship with my mother stimulated a wish to compete with my father and get rid of him.

"In two dreams, I killed him. Father was pushing me away from my mother to the real world. And at the same time that I was trying to rush him out of the picture he died. The only way I could get to the idea of sex in a three-year-old was to think of sexual abuse, so happy to realize that I wasn't abused, but it was my inner sexual feelings, so relieved that I wasn't guilty of betrayal.

"I had knocked off the big dick. I had to assume its responsibilities. I gained a prize, but it was awful. I turned Mother, Father, God against me. I had to make amends. This self was too horrible to come out.

"As I felt this, everything fell into place. I wasn't abused. I was the abuser."

This breakthrough explained one affect that had been puzzling throughout the phase of mourning and working through of the abandonment depression—guilt. The guilt had seemed both excessive and unexplained. It now became clear that the father's death so gratified the patient's oedipal wishes that he was overwhelmed with guilt that he had killed his father. The work now focused on the oedipal conflict revealed in dreams of sexual desire for married women and dreams of being punished by huge, threatening men.

DIFFERENTIAL DIAGNOSIS: COMORBIDITY

The closet narcissistic personality disorder may also be complicated by the presence of other disorders that have become so prevalent today that they must be ruled out while doing the differential diagnosis. Affective disorder, since it is genetic, can coexist with a narcissistic personality disorder. Posttraumatic stress disorder based on physical and/or sexual abuse may also coexist. Sometimes the posttraumatic stress disorder is obvious, and at other times, it can be quite hidden, not revealing itself until well into the psychotherapy. Finally, drug and alcohol addiction must be ruled out. The propensity of addicted patients for denial suggests that the therapist has to be both active and quite specific in investigating any use of drugs or alcohol. Since they compete with psychotherapy as a way of dealing with feelings, they can effectively sabotage the psychotherapy.

MIXED PERSONALITY DISORDERS

It is a common view that a patient can have a mixed personality disorder—in other words, two personality disorders. It has been my experience that this point of view is based on a lack of understanding of both the psychopathology and its developmental origins. The purpose of the personality disorder defense is to deal with painful affect, and in general it would appear that a developmental arrest at one level is enough to deal with the affect, so that although other symptomatic features appear, they are secondary to the basic personality disorder. For example, a patient can have a narcissistic personality disorder with histrionic features or a borderline personality disorder with obsessive-compulsive features.

This means that the patient has a basic personality disorder with the symptomatic features secondary, and not that he or she has two personality disorders.

This chapter has described how to differentiate the closet narcissistic disorder of the self from its exhibitionistic brother, the borderline disorder of the self, the schizoid disorder, and the narcissistic defense against a borderline or a neurotic condition. The next chapter describes the treatment.

PART TWO
Psychotherapy

4

Therapeutic Neutrality, Frame, Stance, and Task

The initial psychotherapeutic interview is a stimulus to self-activation, and as such it evokes both the patient's painful affects and the defenses against those affects. In addition, the patient has a developmentally derived lack of trust in others, including the therapist. Beyond that, the purpose of the repetition compulsion in the narcissistic disorder of the self is not to master conflict as in the neurotic, but instead to avoid the painful affects associated with real-self–activation.

How does the therapist go about the task of creating the conditions that help the patient overcome mistrust, establish a therapeutic alliance, face up to painful affects, and begin to rebuild and reactivate a real sense of self? It is important to keep in mind that a therapist cannot direct, suggest, seduce, threaten, attack, or torture a patient to self-activate. If it happens, it will be because the patient does it. The therapist can only create the conditions that make it possible.

THERAPEUTIC STANCE AND THERAPEUTIC FRAME

An essential contribution to this task is the therapist's attitude of therapeutic neutrality and objectivity. The therapist's personal emotions are not involved in the treatment, which allows the therapist to be in the best position to make decisions in the patient's best therapeutic interest. When pressed to the wall by a patient's persistent acting out of projections, I will occasionally make the point that the therapeutic relationship is the only place in the world where the patient has another person objective enough to decide what is therapeutically best for the patient.

This therapeutic stance of neutrality does not mean, however, that the therapist is not interested in the patient and is an emotional block of wood. The therapist is most interested in helping the patient with his or her problem. The therapeutic stance contains a number of implied attitudes toward the patient and the work that express the frame for the psychotherapy. The therapist does not directly explain these attitudes to the patient, but they become evident from the way he or she responds to the material.

The therapist presents himself or herself quietly and confidently as a person with expertise in this area, who is open and responsive and interested in helping the patient with his or her problem. A therapist cannot do psychotherapy under any kind of threat, as this compromises objectivity. In addition, the therapist who is insecure and anxious about the patient's rejecting him or her will end up doing things to relieve the anxiety rather than to help the patient.

This implied attitude toward the patient, though unstated, becomes a platform for exploration and a role model for internalization. The therapist assumes that the patient will always behave in a self-activated, mature, adaptive, responsible manner so that when the patient does not do so, the therapist can explore it with the patient. The patient's job is to identify his or her feeling states and report them to the therapist. Since the patient's problem revolves around the lack of autonomy of the self and he or she is caught up in self-destructive defenses, the therapist must, on the one hand, use great caution to avoid further trauma to that self by taking over for the patient functions that he or she must learn to perform for himself or herself in the session. On the other hand, since the patient is metaphorically devoted to avoidance of self-activation, the therapist must be equally devoted to the adaptive virtues of self-activation; that is, the patient who does not activate his or her self will pay a price for it that he or she will not like. In this regard, the therapist should quietly support the patient's real-life achievements and console him or her for real-life defeats. Again, these attitudes are not trumpeted about, but are implicit and dictate how the therapist will handle the material the patient presents.

THE THERAPEUTIC FRAME

To protect the psychotherapy from being overwhelmed by either the therapist's countertransference or by the patient's transference acting out, the therapist should have policies in place to deal with all the practical issues necessary to conduct the treatment that becomes part of the frame, including telephone calls, missed interviews, vacations, payments, and seeing the patient's relatives and friends.

Does the therapist draw up a laundry list of expectations? Absolutely not! Does the therapist make contracts? Absolutely not! It is important to conduct the session in such a manner that every moment is a spontaneous, vivid, emotional experience for the patient. All forms of directiveness that further undermine affect and autonomy of the real self should be avoided.

Each issue that arises is dealt with ad hoc on its own merits. For example, at the conclusion of the consultation interview or interviews, I will tell the patient my view of the problem and what treatment is indicated. Often this involves repeating the patient's presentation back to him or her in slightly different words. I then suggest the frequency of sessions and the cost.

If a patient asks how long treatment will take, I reply that I don't know since it depends so much on how the work goes. However, I emphasize, if it's wise, that I see no reason why it should not go well. Then I suggest that, for financial purposes, the patient should plan for a year, and if at the end of that time the patient still has to ask the question, there is something wrong with the psychotherapy. Patients should know exactly where they are in the process and what remains to be done.

Finances

People have more problems with money than they do with sex. Often they are willing to talk about their sexual problems but balk at revealing their finances. It is important, therefore, that the therapist be open and direct in handling finances. The therapist is often the only person who can determine what fee is appropriate to a patient's finances. I always investigate the finances during the consultation when discussing treatment after I have told the patient my fee. The agreement with the patient is twofold: one part is professional (the agreement to treat the patient) and the other is financial (to reserve a set time for the patient with the agreement that he or she will be responsible for that time).

It seems to be the custom today to ask the patient to pay after every interview. I was brought up with the idea that you give the patient the bill at the end of the month, which is what I still do. I hand the patient the bill and, if asked, will say that it is payable within 10 days; however, the patient must pay before the end of the month. Before I give the next bill, I check to see if the previous one was paid, and if it was not, I bring the matter up.

I will say, "I notice that your bill wasn't paid." I want a concrete answer, not just talk. Unless there is some genuine and clear reason for delay, I want the bill paid by the next session. A therapist who does not keep a close watch on reimbursement can promote the patient's acting out of emotional problems through avoiding responsibility for finances. I learned this years ago the hard way—letting patients procrastinate from month to month about paying their bills. Paying the bill is a very important part of the patient's taking responsibility for himself or herself, and when the patient avoids it, the behavior fits right into defense and absorbs affect that has to be brought into the session.

It is important that the fee be appropriate for the patient, not too high or too low. Is a sliding scale or a set fee preferable? For many early years in practice, I had a sliding scale, which I later learned meant soaking the rich and giving it to the poor. The problem with a sliding scale, particularly in intensive analytic therapy, was that the rich patients felt they were being robbed, which they were, and the poor felt they were being patronized, which they were.

I now set one fee and stick to it. However, that requires me to find other sources for people who cannot afford what I am charging. In my group we have a fee range among our faculty and staff, and we also have a lower-cost referral service for patients who can afford very little.

A reduced fee may not be a problem in once-a-week therapy, but it is not a good idea to do intensive analytic work with a patient who is paying a reduced fee. I think it makes it harder for both therapist and patient. If a therapist is planning to do therapy three times a week, and it is clear to the patient that he or she is getting a reduced fee, and it is also clear to the therapist, it can become a problem of resistance with the patient and often countertransference for the therapist. To use a surgical metaphor, the more exacting the therapeutic goal, the clearer the operating field must be. In other words, the therapist has to be more careful to maintain therapeutic neutrality because he or she is going to have difficult resistances to work through and wants to make sure that conditions are optimum.

Fees with Adolescents and Parents

Everybody has a problem with finances where adolescents and their parents are involved. I decide on some smaller amount that the adolescent might be able to pay and give the adolescent a bill for that, and either give or send a bill for the remainder to the adolescent to give to the parents. Where I do not give the adolescent his or her own bill, I hand the bill for the parents to the adolescent to pass on to them. In this way, the patient is at least involved at some level. One of the big problems is that the people who are paying are not coming into the office. Often a situation will arise where the patient starts to do well and so the parents become resistant and stop paying. The parents then must be called in and the resistance dealt with.

Unpaid Bills

Unpaid bills are always a problem, but its magnitude depends on the type of bill. Most of the unpaid bills in our large group come from consultations consisting of one to three interviews. We consider these an occupational hazard and do not pursue them. Fortunately, this usually represents only a small amount of money. Larger bills that go unpaid as a result of resistance during treatment are a different matter. They must be pursued, and if the patient does not pay, therapy must be stopped. Again, in our experience this occurs rarely. I think that the therapist's attitude has a far-reaching effect. The therapist who, in the mistaken countertransferential notion of being a "good guy," sets fees too low or does not follow up on payments is asking for trouble. If problems recur, it is important to search out one's own countertransference contribution. An open, realistic, firm attitude that the therapist has provided the service and is entitled to payment brings the best results.

I can remember one exception. A male patient came to see me because he had kicked in the television set in a fury at his wife for getting sick, and when he went to his doctor, the doctor suggested that he see a psychiatrist. About halfway through the first session, after he had told me about his present illness, he said that his wife had had a baby 18 months earlier and that he still had not paid the hospital or the obstetrician. He then went on to say that he had not paid all his suppliers and that the sheriff was threatening to throw him out of his apartment because he had not paid the rent. I told him he would have to pay me before the session. I could not treat him for this problem while he was perpetuating it with me.

The therapist should offer his or her trust and learn to be very alert to whether it is followed through, and take the matter up when it is not. In doing so, the therapist has both presented the model deemed important and protected himself or herself against its being abused.

When Patients in Psychotherapy Miss Interviews

If the patient is in a crisis or emergency state, the therapist must call; but, if it reflects resistance, it is unwise to call. In the latter case, the therapist is stepping around the resistance, taking over for the patient, and sending the message that the psychotherapy is more important to him than is the patient. This reinforces the resistance rather than dealing with it. I suggest that the therapist control his or her anxiety and wait. If the patient does not return, then a letter should be sent asking if the patient has decided to stop therapy, and suggesting that, if so, it might be better for the patient to come in to discuss it.

I will reschedule if a patient has to miss an interview because of work in a given week. I tell the patient that I will try to reschedule at another time that week if I have a free hour, but if I am unable to reschedule, he or she will have to pay for the time. The more often one sees the patient, the firmer one has to be about all these policies because the consequences of acting out are so much greater. Thus there is some flexibility with once-a-week therapy and less flexibility in intensive therapy.

The problem with patients' missing sessions because of illness is that one never knows whether they really are sick and one should not be put in the position of having to decide when one does not have the facts. For example, a patient calls and says that he or she has a cold and cannot come in, that may or may not be true. The therapist has no way of knowing.

Patients who must travel for a week or more every month are not candidates for analytic work. The regular monthly one-week absence makes intensive analytic therapy and its goal impossible. There is also more flexibility in this regard with patients seen once a week. If I saw a patient who I thought had pretty good therapeutic prospects and the patient had to be away one week a month, I would be inclined to tell the patient that intensive analytic therapy would not work. On the other hand, if the patient was one I was seeing once a week, where my function was somewhere between that of a counselor and that of a psychotherapist, I would probably go along with the absences. Nevertheless, the patient's being away one week a month drives the truck of resistance right into the middle of the work and destroys continuity, even when the patient is seen only once a week. It is the momentum and drive of the continuity that make the psychotherapy work. Patients who travel once a month are unaware of the cost because it probably provides a distancing defense. Thus, not only does one have a patient who is away one session a month, but also a patient whose being away reinforces a specific defense. That distance defense could be difficult to overcome.

Patients Who Read

In treatment I have never suggested that a patient read a particular book. But since I wrote *The Search for the Real Self,* I have been getting many calls from people who have read it, and I do discuss it with them. If I have a patient who intellectualizes and also asks about reading, I will link the two and try to point out the risks of his or her reading. On the other hand, some patients who are deeper into treatment have read some of the books on their own and this has helped them a lot.

A rule of thumb for therapists is to ask patients why, since they are coming to therapy to try to understand themselves (i.e., they have the live data in the session), they feel a need to read a book. Then the motivation and possible problems that might arise should be explored with them. A therapist cannot stop a patient from reading a book if he or she wants to read it. I have had patients read their own cases in the books without recognizing themselves. The management of reading follows the rule that everything should be done to create the conditions for a live, affective experience in the session.

THE THERAPEUTIC TASK: ESTABLISHING TRUST IN THE THERAPEUTIC RELATIONSHIP

Therapeutic Alliance, Transference, and Transference Acting Out

Crucial to an understanding of the psychoanalytic psychotherapy of the narcissistic disorder of the self is an understanding of the differences between therapeutic alliance, transference, and transference acting out. Failure to understand this difference probably has been responsible for much of our confusion about treatment of this disorder.

Therapeutic alliance is a real-object relationship in which the therapist and patient agree to work together to help the patient improve through better understanding and control. As a real-object relationship, it depends on the capacities of both the patient and therapist to see each other as they are in reality, both good and bad at the same time. In other words, both must have the capacity for whole-object relations.

Transference is not a real-object relationship, but one in which the therapist serves as a target upon whom infantile conflicts and affects are projected. The capacity for a transference, however, also requires the capacity for a therapeutic alliance, that is, to see the therapist as he or she is in reality, both good and bad simultaneously. This forms the reality screen against which the patient's transference projections are identified and measured and worked through. How can a patient tell that he or she is projecting without also being able to see at the same time the screen upon which he or she is projecting?

The narcissistic patient relates by transference acting out, which consists of the alternate projection of these self- and object representations upon the therapist without any awareness of the therapist's independent existence at the time of the projection. To understand the dynamics of the transference acting out, we can go back to an article by Freud.[6] He did not have the term "acting out," so he had to coin his own term, "repeating what is forgotten in behavior." The patient remembers nothing; he or she repeats it in his or her behavior. Narcissistic patients seem to have a poor memory. However, it is not that their memory is really poor, but that there is nothing to remember, as it is all being discharged in their acting out. The proof of this is found when the transference acting out is overcome, and the patient develops an extremely acute memory. The function then of the transference acting out is to defend against both feeling and remembering. For those who are football fans, it is an instant replay of the past in the present.

At the same time, the patient's capacity to establish a therapeutic alliance is fragile and brittle at best because of the developmental arrest. This developmental arrest also has other consequences, such as a difficulty with boundaries, a difficulty in using an observing ego to distinguish between infantile and mature aspects of mental life, and a difficulty in tolerating frustration.

The fact that the patient has a fragile therapeutic alliance and is relating through massive projection and transference acting out without awareness of the independent existence of the therapist indicates the goal of the psychotherapy. This initial and continuing goal is to establish, maintain, and strengthen the therapeutic alliance, which nevertheless, under the influence of the disorder-of-the-self triad, will break down routinely, inevitably, and inexorably under the self-activation stress created by the treatment itself. However, proper management of these breakdowns can lead the patient to mastery of the narcissistic problem.

To define the therapeutic goal more clearly, it is to help the patient convert transference acting out into transference and therapeutic alliance by the therapeutic technique of mirroring interpretations of narcissistic vulnerability.

Mirroring Interpretations of Narcissistic Vulnerability

The patient begins psychotherapy unable to trust or to face the painful affect. Therapists who start by urging patients to trust them not only are wasting their time, but are overlooking the essential nature of the first testing phase of the psychotherapy. Even if the patient did not have an intrapsychic problem of trust, why should he or she trust the therapist at the beginning? The patient does not know the therapist at all, even though the recommendation is good and the therapist's reputation is good. Perhaps this otherwise reputable therapist is currently caught up in an intractable countertransference, or develops one with this patient. When my patients tell me at the beginning that they don't trust me, I reply that that makes sense to me. Trust is something that has to be earned.

The therapist earns trust and helps the patient to establish a therapeutic alliance by the way he or she handles the patient's early testing maneuvers. I think that many patients drop out of therapy early because these maneuvers have not been identified or handled properly. The patient begins therapy by focusing more on defense than on conflict and painful affect. The appropriate handling of the patient's defenses leads him or her to the underlying painful affect and conflict and establishes trust.

Therapeutic neutrality is vital. The therapist must maintain the neutrality of the therapeutic frame and expect the patient to identify his or her feeling states and report them. The therapist must not be personally involved with the patient, and must maintain this neutral position without resonating with either the patient's wish to be admired or feeling of being attacked. The function of transference acting out is to defend against both feeling and memory. The patient externalizes and acts out on the therapist in the present problems from the past without realizing it. The neutral therapeutic frame is vital protection against the treatment's being inundated by the patient's transference acted-out projections and the therapist's countertransference. It forms the essential framework within which these projections will be interpreted.

The therapeutic task is to track the sequences of self-activation–painful affect–defense and to use mirroring interpretations of narcissistic vulnerability to help the patient convert the transference acting out to transference and therapeutic alliance. This establishes trust in the relationship and brings to the center stage of the patient's awareness the painful affects associated with a focus on his or her self and self-activation.

How does the therapist then gain entrance to this seemingly solipsistic defensive system? It is important to keep in mind what I like to call "the narcissistic window" of entrance. In working with a narcissistic patient, the focus must be on the here and now in the interaction between the patient and the therapist. With a borderline patient, one gains entrance by confronting maladaptive behavior that often, but not always, takes place outside the session. This is not the pathway to take in working with the narcissistic disorder. One has to understand that anything outside a narcissistic window can be interpreted as a narcissistic wound by the patient.

The patient with a closet narcissistic disorder begins treatment projecting the fused omnipotent object representation on the therapist, idealizing the therapist to regulate the patient's grandiose sense of self. The therapist then interprets to the patient that it is so painful for the patient to focus on himself or herself that he or she turns to the therapist in order to soothe the pain. Here, the key words are pain, self, and defense. This key interpretation helps the patient to feel "understood." The beginning of the interpretation, "It's so painful to focus on yourself," is a way of joining the patient and empathizing with the patient's pain, which is why we use the adjective *mirroring* with the word *interpretation*. The purpose of the mirroring is to open the defensive door in order to point out affect and defense. One of my patients described the way it works in this way: "I don't know how you do this, but somehow you slip in the back door and the next thing I know I'm thinking about something that makes me uncomfortable that I really don't want to think about."

Repetitive experiences of the patient's idealizing of the therapist as a way of dealing with narcissistic vulnerability gradually produces a consensus between patient and therapist that the patient is exquisitively sensitive to the therapist and easily disappointed in failures of idealization. At this point, the consensus leads to the idea that this operation is defensive against the patient's feelings about himself or herself, which then opens the door to the exploration of the abandonment depression associated with self-activation.

In the treatment of the exhibitionistic narcissistic personality disorder, in contrast to the foregoing approach, one does not interpret how the therapist is idealized as a way of soothing the pain about the self, but interprets the therapist's failures in perfect empathy and mirroring of the grandiose self. This leads the patient to become aware of an exquisite need for perfect mirroring from the therapist, which then opens up the channel of exploration of the need for perfect mirroring.

It is vital to track the patient's response to the intervention, since the patient not only must feel "understood," but then must elaborate on the substance of the interpretation in order to be sure that the interpretation has been integrated. This then should lead to more painful affect and more exploration.

When transference acting out is converted to transference idealization and therapeutic alliance, the transference idealization is not interpreted until the last phase of treatment, unless it blocks progress to that phase.

Tracking the Emerging Real Self in Psychotherapy

Since the therapist's task is to track the sequence of real-self–activation–painful affect–defense, it is important to keep in mind the clinical manifestation of the real self. The capacities of the real self are as follows:

1. Self-image—of being adequate, competent, based on reality, with some input from fantasy. Intrapsychic representation as whole—both good and bad at the same time.
2. Self-assertion—to identify and activate individual thoughts and feelings:
   a. Access to and expression of creativity.
   b. Support self when under attack.
   c. Act in a spontaneous self-supportive, adaptive, realistic manner regarding
      (1) Taking physical care of self—diet, work, exercise, schedule, appearance.
      (2) Expressing self through work, recreation, relationships.
      (3) Soothing self when in conflict.
      (4) Autonomous functioning of sense of self.
      (5) Identifying and expressing one's unique creative ideas and urges.
      (6) Seeing objects as they are in reality, both good and bad at the same time.
      (7) Being able to acknowledge one's own self-activation and to set self limits.
      (8) Maintaining self-esteem by coping with and mastering reality.
      (9) Having the capacity for continuity, commitment, and intimacy, a capacity to feel and express empathy with the object.

Access to the real self may first appear in a dream, a fantasy, or a memory, and it usually is consolidated in action, evoking memories of earlier efforts at self-activation that led to pathologic affects. Access to the real self in response to interpretations may reveal itself in a variety of ways: through actions, fantasy, dreams, or free association. Particular attention should be paid to the latter three modalities as they foreshadow its emergence into actions.

The shift from defense to self-activation occurs slowly and in small steps and takes time to integrate and consolidate. Only when it is consolidated in behavior is the stage set for the onset of enduring intrapsychic change. What are some of the signs of emerging self-activation? For example, a male patient who was in conflict with his wife and whose life was in chaos started to organize and take better charge of his daily schedule and began to set limits on his wife's attacks. He then also set limits on his partner's incursions and restructured his lectures from affectless compulsive but deadening inclusiveness to spontaneity and affect. After nine months, he decided to leave his partner: "The wonderful part is that I feel self-esteem, which opens creative vistas, not guilt."

Another patient, Mr. E., began to focus on his acting career—what he really wants to do—and to rely less on others to make his decisions. He calls it "a real breakthrough." He got acknowledgment of his efforts from his coach: "I was doing the right thing." As he became more involved in acting, he reported feeling for the first time, "I was following my instincts, was free of the burden. What I am to me is an actor."

Mr. D. reported a dream in which he was a baseball player making a comeback and doing well. *Free association:* "I was very interested in baseball as a kid." The dream was full of hope and optimism. He started a diet, and tried to stop his role playing at work. He started to organize his time better. Much later in the psychotherapy: "I feel I can now do what *I* want. My perspective in decisions is different, more realistic. I used to feel helpless. Now I feel hopeful, that there is something there."

Ms. A. stopped attacking herself for minor errors, and at the same time found herself to be more empathic with others. She reported: "I'm ahead in the search for me. I'm trying out painting and bridge and feel more like a mother to my children. I'm feeling so much better about myself." Later on, she discovered her love of music and threw herself into pursuing this avocation.

These are all examples of what to look for clinically to show the emergence of the real self. This process proceeds spontaneously in parallel with the analysis and working through of the painful affect. Only when the innermost intrapsychic aspects of this painful affect are worked through is the self free to find fulfillment.

The question is so often asked: How does one know what activity is "right" or what relationship fits the real self? Of course, one answer is that only experimentation, trial and error, can determine that. However, one must have a spontaneous and flexible sense of self to initiate the experiment in the first place, and then to evaluate the feedback appropriately and realistically. In my clinical experience, the "fit" between an aspect of the real self and work or a relationship announces itself so loudly and clearly in the depth of the affective response and the harmonious nature of the fit that it banishes all doubt on the part of either the patient or the therapist that this is the patient's real self.

The other question so often asked is: How does one find meaning in life? The developmental answer is that it is done through experimentation to identify the unique talents, wishes, and needs of the real self, and then to find what aspects of the external environment fit these needs so that a harmonious feedback can be set up between the real self and the reality of the environment.

Types of Psychotherapy

Shorter-Term Therapy

The term "shorter" is used to distinguish this therapy from short-term therapy, which usually takes a matter of weeks. This psychotherapy can last months or years, with the patient being seen once a week. The goal could be called ego repair with a decrease in symptomatology and an increase in adaptation. It is indicated primarily for lower-level patients who have difficulty functioning and not enough ego strength to work through the abandonment depression. It can also benefit higher-level patients, but they have the alternative of intensive analytic treatment. The patient's need for narcissistic defense lessens, as does his or her denial of reality, so that he or she is able to function realistically and effectively. One of my exhibitionistic patients described it as follows: "I was like a prince closeted behind my castle walls with the bridge over the moat drawn up. The treatment has helped me to come down out of the castle, lower the bridge, cross the moat, emerge from the castle, and put on the clothes of a commoner and mingle with them."

Therapeutic technique consists of mirroring interpretations of narcissistic vulnerability that focus mostly on the here and now in the relationship and not on genetic interpretations. These interventions will lead to affect and memory, which can then be used more to shed light on current narcissistic problems than to work through the genetic elements of the abandonment depression. One limitation is that the therapist should avoid pushing for fantasy, dreams, and the depression, since all of these draw the patient deeper into the depression, and the structure of the therapy does not provide for working through the depression. If the patient needs to talk about these issues, the therapist allows it, but does not take them up for systematic investigation.

The length of treatment varies greatly, from a few months to years. The average length would be from a year to 18 months. However, much longer periods are justified, in my view, as long as the therapist does not collude with regression.

At the end of treatment, the real self has been strengthened and narcissistic vulnerability decreased; however, the developmental arrest has not been changed, so the patient remains vulnerable to separation stress. Should the stress be strong enough, the patient will become symptomatic again and return. In order to regress and become symptomatic, the patient has to give up previously learned insight, but when the patient returns to therapy, it takes far less time to restore the insight and overcome the symptomatic state.

Intensive Psychoanalytic Psychotherapy

The patient most often is seen three times a week with the goal of overcoming the narcissistic defenses and working through the underlying depression, which frees the real self to emerge and resume its developmental pathway through the oedipal stage and beyond. The two cases presented here (Mr. C. and Mr. D.) are unusual in that the patients are seen twice a week. It is the rare patient who can do this level of work twice a week, and even with these patients, the therapeutic momentum is slowed.

There are two dividends of this treatment that strongly recommend that it be tried where possible: (1) It removes the vulnerability to separation stress, and there is separation stress in all of our lives all the time. (2) As the anchor of the abandonment depression is lifted and the real self is freed, a flowering of self-activation occurs. The patient experiences it as being reborn, becoming a new person. But what has happened is that all those talents and capacities of the real self that had been blocked by the developmental arrest now are free to emerge.

It is difficult to set a duration for this treatment, but it can be thought of as taking the same amount of time as a classical analysis—three to five years. However, it could be either longer or shorter.

The best candidates are the high-level patients, but many middle-level narcissists are good candidates. The key is that the patient must have sufficient ego strength to contain the depression when the defenses are overcome so that the abandonment depression can be worked through.

The therapeutic technique is the same as in shorter-term therapy: mirroring interpretation of narcissistic vulnerability. This is what overcomes the defenses and establishes a therapeutic alliance. Once the depression emerges, genetic interpretations can be added. In the final phase of treatment, as the real self starts to flower, an intervention that I call communicative matching must be added. I mean by this that as the patient reports new interests and activities, the therapist should discuss the reality aspects of these interests with the patient. I do not mean discussing the therapist's personal life, but just the patient's new interests. This refuels the real self. In the last or separation phase, the patient must work through the transference fantasy that the therapist is the object that he or she always wished for to acknowledge his or her real self; that is, this phase marks the separation from the therapist.

The analytic therapy consists of three stages: testing, working through, and separation. In the testing stage, a therapeutic alliance is formed in analytic therapy, just as in shorter-term therapy, by mirroring interpretations of narcissistic vulnerability. When the therapeutic alliance and transference are established, the patient's abandonment depression takes center stage through memories, dreams, fantasies, and transference. It is of great importance that the patient's access to historical and genetic material come spontaneously from the patient and not from the therapist. When affect and memories lead the content of sessions, working through has been established. It now becomes possible to make genetic interpretations. The therapy gradually deepens until the patient hits the bottom of the abandonment depression where all six affects are present and expressed as, "If I separate, I will die and my mother will die."

When this stage has been worked through, the real self begins to emerge and must be responded to by the therapist with communicative matching—by discussing the patient's new interests and activities. The patient then enters the final or separation stage, as the object.

Psychotherapy with Acting-Out Narcissistic Disorders of the Self

The more prominent the acting-out defense, the more guarded is the prognosis, as the therapist has to adopt a two-stage approach: (1) The therapist must confront the acting out, which then evokes a narcissistic wound, so that (2) he then must deal with the wound through mirroring interpretations of narcissistic vulnerability. The complexities of this two-stage task make the psychotherapy more difficult and the outcome more uncertain.

CONCLUSION

The therapist can only create the conditions that make it possible for the patient to establish a therapeutic alliance. If the therapeutic alliance is to be achieved, it must be achieved by the patient. The therapist cannot do it for the patient. The therapist creates the necessary conditions by not falling into countertransference reactions, by maintaining the neutrality of the therapeutic frame, and by making mirroring interpretations of narcissistic vulnerability.

In Chapters 5–8, these principles are demonstrated by applying them to the psychotherapy of four patients with a closet narcissistic disorder of the self.

5

The Disembodied Heart and the Latchkey Child

Ms. A., tall, slender, blond, a 40-year-old homosexual woman, was a successful interior decorator and the divorced mother of two children. She complained of difficulties in interpersonal relationships.

HISTORY

History of Present Illness

The patient had had her first homosexual relationship while in college. Later, she fell in love with a man, married, and in so doing lost her sense of self. She became "all things to her husband and children." She was married for 10 years, during which time there were no homosexual relationships.

She reported: "After 10 years, I realized I had no self, nor did I have any intimacy with my husband. I started to drink; I had a low tolerance for alcohol and became an alcoholic. I had blackouts. I drank for three years until last year, when I joined AA and started an affair with a woman. During the three years that I was drinking, I had three relationships with women and one with a man. All of the relationships were difficult and conflictual. I tended to sell out to women who were attracted to me.

"I then met another woman, an older woman who reminds me somewhat of my mother, and I have been having a relationship with her for the past year. I find her very distant. I find myself giving and then pulling back, and we have a lot of conflict.

"I have great difficulty acknowledging myself. I feel that I have no self. I have trouble asserting myself. On the other hand, I have this idea that I can get away with anything. At one point, I took Prozac but put on 35 pounds."

Personal History

"Mother was domineering, paranoid, a will of iron, angry, attacking, stingy, a monster who never let me alone. Mother was also a very successful career woman. Father was a rather inadequate, kind, and distant man, who was never available and who did not help me with my mother."

The patient was the oldest of three children, with sisters five years younger and seven years younger. She had to take care of the sisters, who also had serious problems in relationships.

"I was a latchkey kid, and at one point my mother took me to a psychologist, although I don't remember why."

The patient did well in high school, college, and business school. She had friends and did not become aware of her homosexual impulses until college. She has a son in high school and a daughter in graduate school.

She had had prior treatment with a therapist once a week for several years when she was contemplating divorce, but she felt that this treatment had not been of much help.

CLINICAL IMPRESSION AND INTRAPSYCHIC STRUCTURE

The patient appeared to have a closet narcissistic disorder with a history of alcohol abuse, questionable posttraumatic stress disorder, and possible sexual abuse.

Intrapsychic Structure

The omnipotent-object–grandiose-self fused unit consisted of an idealized, omnipotent object representation that provided admiration for perfect performance and compliance. The grandiose-self–representation was one of being unique and special when performing for and in compliance with the object. The aggressive fused unit consisted of a blatant, draconian, domineering, harsh object representation that monolithically and harshly attacked every aspect of a failure to be perfect and any effort at self-activation. The impaired-self–representation, the target of the attacker, was of being frozen, numb, paralyzed, nothing, dead, nonexistent. "A disembodied heart that couldn't contract." The abandonment depression was seen mostly in the aggressive attacks of the object representation. The depressive element was held in check by the detachment defense.

The disorder-of-the-self triad operated as follows: If she were not perfect in the eyes of the object, or if she attempted real-self–activation, the harsh attacking object was triggered and experienced as a harsh voice in the head. She defended against this by focusing on the object, not on the self. The psychotherapy began by interpreting and investigating both of these defenses against self-activation: the focus on the object and the intensive attacking attitude of the object.

PSYCHOTHERAPY

First Month

Defenses Against Intrapsychic Self-Attacks: The Initial Defense

The patient began by talking about how she attends AA meetings but occasionally has a glass of wine, and also how she cheats in the same way on her lover. "If I can't get her full-time, I feel rejected and go out and look for others and then lie to her, but then, when she calls, I come running.

"Nothing comes from within me; there's a void. Mother told me everything I do is wrong, so she had to tell me what to do. I was yelled at for everything, hurt, not appreciated, not important. My father was passive and nonexistent. I have a voice in my head that attacks me whenever I make a mistake."

She described her difficulties with disciplining and setting limits for her son, who is self-indulgent and avoids responsibility. She gives in to him too much. She described her lover as being loving, in contrast to her mother, who was harsh and attacking, and in contrast to the harsh voice in her head. "It's my lover's evenness that attracts me. I can't manipulate her." The patient then reported: "Whenever I do anything wrong, the voice ends up attacking me the way my mother attacked me."

Seeing the attacking voice as the first defense against exploring the impaired self, I tried to investigate this self-attack, but she changed the subject to focus on her lover. I brought this to her attention: "Why is it that when I ask you to take a look at this attacking voice, you shift to talking about someone else?"

In the next session, she came back to her difficulties with setting limits for her son and with her attacking voice. She said, "I can't win; I should kill myself." When I again asked why she had this attacking voice, instead of exploring the issue, she turned to me and said, "You have an easy job."

I interpreted that she focused on me in order to protect herself against looking at the way she attacked herself. At this, she defended by blocking: "I don't think about myself. I think I have some notion that I can live on the edge without paying the price."

Comment

In the first month, the focus on the object to defend against the painful affect of the impaired self is on center stage—the omnipotent-object–grandiose-self defense.

Second Month

Interpretation of Attacking Voice Leading to History of Mother's Attacks and the Impaired Self

In the next session, she continued to defend by talking about others. She spoke of picking up stray cats (i.e., women) and using them, though she didn't necessarily like them. Her father was a good guy, she said, but absent and scared of her mother. She likes hugging and kissing, which give her a sense of affirmation.

She then reported that her sister was marrying a man she had known for only a short time. She was angry at her sister for not taking responsibility for herself and felt she had to confront the sister, although she is sure she will be rejected. She reported that when her lover leaves, she feels alone, as if she doesn't exist, and that there is nothing there and she has to be told what to do. (This session is dominated by defense.)

At the next session, she reported that she had not attacked herself as much as she had before. (Although she was still in defense, her attitude toward the attacking object had shifted.) I had interpreted in the prior session that it seemed to me that the attacking voice and the inadequate self appeared to be companions in her head. I suggested that attacking herself was perhaps one way of holding on to her mother. She replied: "Mother wanted a boy but lived through me. She put enormous pressure on me for performance, for grades in school."

She described not being able to put up with her son's sloppiness. I pointed out that she kept taking over for him by reminding him to do something about it rather than disciplining him. She replied, "I feel I am wrong to activate myself and set limits." I added, "Because your job is to focus on others, not yourself." (This intervention breaks through the defense.) She replied: "I was never taught to trust my own feelings. I feel cheated, angry at my mother, and sorry for myself." She looked depressed, started to tear. She continued: "Mother's brutal tirades—I couldn't please her. She was so cheap." (She was now facing the painful affects of the impaired self and its relationship to the attacking object in her head and the mother in the environment. Interpretation had overcome defense and the underlying harsh aggressive unit had emerged.

Third Month

Memories of Mother's Intimidating Attacks

She continued the theme in the next session (a sign of either a beginning therapeutic alliance or compliance). "I don't focus on myself because it brings on Mother's attacks; that's it, but where do I go with it?" I responded: "Facing the issue seems to impel you to feel helpless. I wonder why." (The first intervention that focuses on the impaired self is often responded to by helplessness and hopelessness.) She said: "I feel confused and angry at myself, just like my mother. Over the weekend I stayed at home and just took my time and enjoyed myself watching television."

(Some history then emerged as an elaboration of the interpretation.) "As a kid, I was punished for being a kid. Mother ruled with an iron hand. There was nothing right about me. However, my friends thought my mother was great. She used to give me hand-me-down clothes. She dragged me shopping in the summer to get winter coats cheap. Buying shoes was such a big deal. [She sighed.] My mother's family was so negative; they'd scream out nasty things. I have no memories at all of happiness. Mother's angry face, critical, never a kind word, told me who my friends could be. In high school, I rejected the only nice girlfriend I had. It was never all right to do what I wanted. If I wanted to be creative, it was a terrible battle with her. I had to cower to survive, so afraid of her—she screamed, raged at me. We were all morons."

The affect emerged in the next session in parallel with some self-activation. "I went to a movie and cried about never having had a loving mother. I was angry and envious of those in the movie, but **I am starting to do things for myself more. I've started to play bridge. I'm starting to light a few fires just for me, and I was able to be alone and walk around the city with no difficulty.** I feel cried out about Mother." (Getting access to and some release from the harsh aggressive unit enabled her to become more self-activated.)

(Taking up the defense, I interpreted again that one function of the mother in her head was to help her deal with these feelings of being alone; by fusing with the object, she defends against being alone.) She ignored my comment and pointed out that she had overcome her self-centered reaction to her son and was able to empathize with him.

She reported: "**When I screw up, I don't attack myself as I used to. I'm also now more able to empathize with people's pain.** Both my wishes for sex and for affection are frustrated by my lover." I again interpreted the defense. She was projecting the mother's attacking voice on her lover to soothe and to avoid facing this voice in her head. She said, "I want to change my lover (as a way of changing her mother)."

(Interpretation of defense brought her back to the impaired self.) "I never felt loved. I always cried. Mother threatened to put me out of the car and leave me alone on the road if I didn't comply. I don't believe anybody cares for me. With my lover, I set some limits, and I felt good about myself. Then I got depressed and wanted to call her. Not having any sense of self leads to my chameleon behavior, and I had a severe headache and felt depressed. A sick voice like my mother's tells me to be cheap just like her." (Having overcome defense and focused on her impaired self and the abandonment depression, will she continue or go back to defense?)

Fourth Month

Mother's Attacks on Impaired Self

She continued the theme with a dream: "Mother is working, needing money, and I tell her that I would support her." *Free association:* "I don't want to let go of my mother. I feel nobody cares; I'm absolutely alone, crying, but this time I don't call my girlfriend. I felt broken by Mother. I can recall masturbating as a very young child as the only pleasure. Mother was negative about everything about my life. She attacked everybody I was close to. She even used to clean my closets without telling me. Women were worth nothing in the family. My father was kind, but he never supported me."

(The affects of the abandonment depression emerged.) Depression continued with vegetative signs, then gradually diminished. The patient reported that she neither drank nor called her lover, but that she was raging inside and could not express it: "Why don't I take care of myself? Why don't I watch my eating and exercise?"

I pointed out that it seemed to me that this was further avoidance of focusing on herself to soothe the pain. The patient replied: "I was a real swimmer as a kid, but no longer. Without my lover, I feel a loss of love. I never felt approval from her, but she didn't reject me for my acting out."

Depression continued, but there was also more release of self-activation: **"I'm feeling better about myself. I'm going to AA more. I used to be very detached in my work. I'm now feeling empathy for others. I feel I make more flexible efforts at asserting myself, and I can do it without lying or manipulating."**

She then reported a transference dream: "I was cuddling in your arms—it was wonderful." *Free association:* "I love my therapy. I wish I could bring you a gift." Without interpreting her idealization, I said that since we were working together to help her improve, her improvement itself was a gift.

Fifth Month

Acting Out and Transference Acting Out Interpreted

The patient returned to the defensive part of the triad. She reported feeling depressed, thinking mostly about her lover, "my addiction." But instead of calling her lover or drinking, she contained the feelings and called her AA sponsor instead, but then found herself stealing a pair of sunglasses: "I knew what to do about it but had to call the sponsor to tell me. My week had been good." I interpreted the disorder-of-the-self triad that she had activated herself, had done well, and then had become anxious and depressed, and to soothe these feelings she had to steal and then call in another person to take over for her. She seemed to have to preserve the right to this self-destructive behavior. She said, "It keeps me alive," confirming my interpretation, "as if I don't exist if I am alone." I interpreted that the acting out was a defense against the depression and anxiety she feels if she focuses on herself. She answered: "I know who I am as a parent and at work but not when alone. I've grown; I don't feel desperate and panicky and not alive."

The patient reported more self-activation: **"I'm ahead in the search for me, what I want to do today. I'm trying to get a better job, I felt more like a mother with my children, and I resumed my relationship with my lover. I'm also trying painting and bridge."**

In the next session, she said she felt my attention vacillating. It annoyed her, but she made a joke of it. I interpreted that she seemed to feel the need to have my attention intensely at all times, and if it vacillated, she felt disappointed and angry and had to make a joke in order to get me back, to reassure herself; in other words, she was focusing more on the object than on herself. She replied, "If I don't do that, I feel I don't exist and I am dead."

She continued: "I feel I am too interested in money, power, superficial things, being flip and arrogant. I now have a severe headache, and I had a dream in which I was a child and an adult at the same time, having an affair with an older woman. I had a blanket and toys."

Free association: "I was the child. The woman had reddish hair like my mother. Fortunately for me, my lover has very good boundaries and is mature." I interpreted that she seemed to be seeking from her lover what she had been denied by her mother.

Comment

After five months, we observed that the patient had overcome the defensive part of the triad, was contained and focusing on the impaired self and the abandonment depression in the interviews, and then slowly returned to defensive acting out, probably to deal with the emerging depression and the memories of her mother. The relationship with the woman friend is a specific acting-out defense. She reenacts in the present to defend against feeling and remembering in the past. Parallel to this, she also splits self-activation from its associated abandonment depression affects; she self-activates without getting depressed.

Sixth Month

Focus on Narcissistic Object to Deal with Dead Self

She reported: "**I'm feeling so good about myself; I'm handling everything. Do I have to continue? I'm feeling so solid about myself, and I am reevaluating my relationship with my lover. I want something better.** I'm not sure what I like. I'm wondering if she is self-centered."

I pointed out how her change in her perception of herself paralleled the increasing self-confidence she had been feeling. She replied: "AA has helped also. **Only now do I know that drinking is wrong for me, and I know right from wrong, and I'm not going to shoplift again. I am thinking of stopping treatment.**"

She was in truth doing better in terms of self-activation, but the emptiness, deadness, and so on were still being defended against through the relationship with the lover. I suggested that if she were to break up with her lover, she would be more on her own with me, and this might increase her anxiety. Could this, I asked her, be the reason she wanted to stop? I said, however, that the decision was up to her, and she decided to continue.

She reported: "I haven't seen my lover in two weeks, but I had two urges to reconnect with her and controlled them. I am handling being alone better. I'm not lonely. I had a weird fantasy of contacting this old girlfriend whom I know to be very self-centered."

I interpreted that either she was connected with a narcissistic, self-centered woman, or that she faced anxiety and depression about being on her own. She replied: "I feel like a newborn horse learning to walk. I'm feeling a bond with all mankind. Although I am gay, I have always traveled with an elite heterosexual group. I am trying to move into the gay world." I said, "You seem hesitant to express yourself in your sexual life." She replied with a history of masturbation from the age of three on and then again intensely at ages nine to 10. She has orgasm with clitoral stimulation when with men.

In the next session, her serious difficulties with intimacy emerged in bold relief. She had a liaison with a new woman to whom she was attracted and had a very good time, but then felt extremely anxious and uncomfortable: "It was too close, and I wanted to get away. I wanted to shrink up and shrivel away, and I have a terrible headache right now. I'm angry that I started it."

I pointed out that it seemed to me that she was upset by the intimacy and that she used pulling away and detachment of feelings to deal with this anxiety. There was a long silence, and then she said: "Is it my mother? I feel very sad now." (Intimacy is a form of self-activation and brings with it all the anxiety and depression associated with self-activation.)

In the next session, she reported that the interview had helped a good deal with the intimacy. She saw the woman again and had a good time, with less anxiety, but then woke up at three o'clock in the morning with a dream: "I had a cut on my heel, and when I pushed it, the heel fell off." *Free association:* "My Achilles' heel was lack of affection from my father. He could have done it, but he didn't. He couldn't stand up for himself, let alone for me. My mother tormented him. When he was reading the paper, I showered him with kisses to try and get him to respond, and when I woke up, I was furious at him and at my ex-husband. I was tempted to call my ex-husband, but realized there was no point to that." (The experience of intimacy had put her in touch with her anger at the deprivation of her self in relationships.) She continued: "Since I couldn't act out the anger that way, I got into a fight about parking the car and defaced the other guy's car a little bit, to get my anger out." I interpreted that the access she had obtained to feelings of intimacy had put her in touch with her rage at her father. Since a week had elapsed between this and the prior session, I asked her where these feelings had been all day. I also interpreted that her perspective on her father was that of a peer, not a parent. She said that until five years ago she thought she had the best father in the world.

In a following session, further focus on herself led to further awareness of her difficulties with her sense of self: "I was alone this weekend and felt okay. I saw the woman again, and by focusing on the here and now, I enjoyed it. I'm so sensitive to being taken over. It happened with my mother and it happened with my lover. I become an emotional slave."

I interpreted that the way she deals with how painful it is to focus on herself is to focus on others and then end up being an emotional slave. She overcame denial to perceive the reality cost of her defense. She replied: "I was thinking about my childhood and how different even then I was. I was very athletic and had a lot of ideas. Now I have no ideas. I have no commitment."

I again interpreted the need to defend herself against involvement in herself, and that focusing on herself led to difficulties in work, in ideas, in creativity, and in relationships. She replied: "The fear of failure stopped me. I had no burning desire and have no burning desire."

I asked, "Doesn't that give the texture of your life a kind of grayness?" She answered: "Yes, I don't feel engaged or connected. For example, I have been wanting to do over my bathroom and still haven't done it. Where did I lose the desire to create? With my husband and kids and no focus on myself? I never let myself become a part of anything."

In the next session, she focused again on self-activation: "**I've gone back to swimming, and I am doing laps in my pool. I've also gone back to my planting, which I love.** I'm feeling okay, but I begin to feel, is this all there is to life?" I said, "No, there is more to life; there is commitment to work and to relationships." She replied: "There is no other in my life. I'm feeling better than I have in a long time, but there is something missing."

Seventh Month

She Returns Again to Defense

In the next session, she focused on her sister's wedding in a fury about her sister's self-destructive behavior in not checking the husband out for his alcoholism. She had confronted her sister to no avail. She then returned to herself to talk about liking to be the pursuer and feeling uneasy when pursued, when the object focuses on her. After this session, she took a two-week vacation and returned for the eighth month.

Eighth Month

Interpretation of Relationship with Lover as a Defense Against Depression

"I realized when I had a good weekend [when she supported herself], I developed an enormous craving for my lover." I interpreted the self triad: when she supports herself, she begins to experience the negative voice of her mother and her dead self, and in order to deal with them, she reaches out for a mother in the environment—it's better to have a mother outside the head than to face the one inside.

She replied: "My lover is just like my mother. She tells me how wrong I am. On the other hand, she's loving toward me, while all the while she's putting me down. However, I am being more direct with everybody, and I am more direct about my sexuality. I could never call people before; now I can, and I can spend more time alone without going crazy. I'm more secure in my own feelings and thoughts." She began to tear and fell silent. I asked her what was going on, and she answered: "I'm thinking about how sad I was as a child. I was alone over the weekend. I put on my mother's ring for the first time in a long time. I lost one, and almost lost the other." (I suspected that this was acting out a fantasy of reunion with her mother but that she was too far along in treatment for it to take hold. However, I said nothing.) "When I felt bad, I had this fantasy of calling my lover, but I called my AA mentor instead (patient controls defense, depression continues). I felt lonely, unloved, and uncared for. However, I knew what to do about it. Why can't I have faith in myself? What I feel is 'poor me.' Then I get angry for feeling sorry for myself."

I asked, "Why the anger?" The patient replied: "Just because this was my mother. Although I can accept rejection better, I feel very sorry for myself. I am symbolically eating Mother's candy to hold on to her, but I don't want anything to do with her. If she were here, I couldn't fight with her; I couldn't win. It hurts. Where's the me? I sold out on myself. It's so easy to make Mother and my ex-husband the focus. I couldn't tell my husband I didn't want a baby, that I wanted to start business school. I couldn't express what I wanted. I tried to express it with Mother, but it always ended up in failure and defeat."

In the next session, the patient continued to focus more on her mother and did not defend, but now she developed a severe pounding headache as she came to the session. She said: "I feel angry—angry at myself and my mother. She pushed me to relate to my father. He explained that I had to behave because of her. I remember her rages. My anger went into being negative toward myself. Mother shoved me into socialization like a cat. I didn't know how to socialize. I was a hostile, angry kid. Mother took me to many psychologists. Never satisfied. I was not accepted by my peers. I had no port. My only pleasure seemed to be masturbation. I think I hated my mother, but my impatience and hostility were directed to myself. Today I'm not sure of myself. I know what I want and what to do. In the third grade I went to the dentist. He gave me gas, and I was vomiting. He made a sexual pass at me but I couldn't tell my mother. I had no rights with the dentist, like with my mother. Nothing I could do. So I lost. I have no recall of any intimate conversations with my mother.

"I'm having terrible trouble getting in touch with my feelings about my mother, and the headache continues. She was cheap, and I'm just as cheap as she was. I emulate her, but then I feel guilty. I'm cheap with myself. As a child, I saved my babysitting money to give her a gift, and then she attacked me. The will was being beaten out of me. My aunt gave lovely gifts. My mother never did. She was a manipulating bitch. I'm so used to being fucked over by her. I couldn't question her—it was no win. My grandmother was my only positive influence until I was 13. I can remember at my mother's grave feeling nothing." The patient is now back to facing the abandonment depression at the level achieved in the fourth month with the new addition of anger. Can she hold it?

Ninth Month

Rage at Mother; Headaches Continue

She began: "I'm preoccupied by people committing suicide. The suicide of myself to my mother. She was never honest. I wanted to go to one college, and she coerced me into another. The only one who let me know I was okay in the family was my aunt."

After reporting that she had broken up with a friend who was very critical of her, she asked: "Why do I need people like that?"

I interpreted that it was better to have a mother outside the head than to try to deal with the one inside the head. She replied: "I'm surprised when people compliment me. I'm detached. The last two weeks I have been detached, less in touch with self and in LaLa land. I don't like to be alone, and I want to get my act together. I feel hate toward my mother, who raged at me."

The patient then reported: "I visited my mother's grave, and I sobbed and said, 'You made it so hard.' Then I said to her, 'I forgive you.' I felt wholer—I felt right, not resentful, envious, expecting things. I felt free, more direct and accepting with other people. I feel clearer. [I thought, particularly with regard to boundaries.] It's a spiritual awakening. [I wondered if the splitting was promoting an escape into health to avoid working through the feelings about her mother.] Mother taught me not to trust men. All men want to do is screw you and leave you. I feel like the well with Mother is running dry, but on the other hand, as I talk about this, I have a severe headache."

In the next session, the patient remembered her behavior in high school! "I was selfish, pushy, competitive, and had no concern for others. This is when I most actively fought with Mother. I was selfish, angry, and hostile; disruptive; talking in class; fighting; always getting in trouble at school. However, when I went to college and got away from my mother, this behavior toned down. I guess I was angry without being in touch with it." Then she reported a dream in which someone else's father was having sexual intercourse with her. This isolated dream, coming out of nowhere, raised all kinds of questions about sexual abuse that have to remain unanswered for the present. But the patient continues to focus on the abandonment depression.

Tenth Month

Therapist's Vacation; Patient Returns to Lover

Most of this month was taken up by my vacation. On my return, the patient began reporting that she found things to kick herself for, and recently had started to experience severe rectal pain, as if two knives were penetrating her. I asked her about her feelings about my being away. She denied any anger. She said she felt that the rectal pain must be due to her emotions.

The patient reported a recent reunion at her high school: "I was told that I was the center of attention but didn't know it. I'm going back to seeing my lover again, but not doing the mother dance. We are more equal. I'm supporting myself with her. It started about a week before you went away. . . . I thought only about myself; I didn't validate others' emotions. Often I don't think about the consequences." Did the patient return to her lover to deal with the separation stress of my vacation?

Eleventh Month

Struggle to Stay with Memories, Feelings Regarding Separation from Mother and Abandonment Depression

The patient began: "I still haven't redone the bathroom. It seems that she is always there, but then my thoughts go to a wall, and I am paralyzed. I need the external force of somebody else. I never make a purchase myself without asking someone else. I have to act against the force pulling me back. I seem to be ruled by demons. I recalled my mother's dying and have thoughts about my own death. I've run up against a wall about Mother. When I was alone, I was afraid of death. Being alone was like being dead. I couldn't be alone." (The patient seemed to have gotten through a superficial level of the conflict with the mother and had come up against severe resistance to going deeper.)

In the next session, she said she had seen Bradshaw on television, which stimulated a great many thoughts and feelings about her parents and herself. First, she understood her father better, how he had never been loved, so that he could not love.

She realized more about her mother: "What she did was awful. Mother wrote my applications to college. She felt I couldn't do it without her. I was terrified about being told that I was doing the wrong thing. I hate her. She was so abusive. I feel upset when I leave here. I feel sad. I feel so protected with you. Father was there, but really not there. In high school, my father wrote to me: 'I'm glad you were born.' However, my parents cherished boys—girls are ordinary."

In the next session, the patient reported: "I block when I try to visualize Mother, and I have a severe headache. I saw *The Christmas Carol* and cried buckets over Tiny Tim. However, I identify with Scrooge. As a child, I had to be right. I even cheated on eye exams, but I never could be right. Decisions were so hard. I used to feel shame about not being right. This headache is killing me."

I asked whether this effort she was making to regain access to feelings about her mother might be a violation of her mother's taboo expressed in the headache. The patient replied: "I wanted approval but got none. Never good enough, and I never won. Every plan I made was not good enough. With Mother, I felt worthless. I tried to hide things I knew I'd get yelled at for. Mother used to say: 'You are going to kill me.' She raged at everything."

In the next session, the patient again reported severe headache: "It started on my way here. I cannot empathize with myself. I recall my mother's sister playing with me from age five to nine. Either I can't get rid of my mother, or I'm afraid of the void that would be left if I do get rid of her. When my mother punished me for doing right, I would go to my room and cry for hours."

I brought up again that taking her mother on in this fashion must feel like a terrible thing to do. "Are you bad for doing it?" I asked. The patient replied: "Mother used to say, 'I know best; do as I say.' I was terrified to be angry." She continued, "They all abused me." She reported that the headache was getting worse, as she cried with the pain.

"How is it that my mother's death gave me permission to divorce my husband and be a woman? It freed me. Mother screamed, 'You stupid; you cost me money.' She would yell, holler, and scream, 'Kill me.' I was ruining her life. She punished me for doing right. Mother convinced me that she was the only one who cared. Mother would show affection for me to others, when others were around, but not for me. But believe it or not, I still have Mother's furniture, and I still have her two master's theses."

The patient now went a little deeper into rage at her mother and the attacks on herself and ended up realizing that these were the ways in which she maintained her fusion with her mother.

Twelfth Month

Struggles with Memories of Self and Object, Particularly Rage

In the first session, the patient reported that a friend suggested that she come three times a week, and she asked me if she should. I asked her what she thought. She replied that she really has trouble committing herself to anything in her life, whether it is her work or her relationships, but that she is beginning to improve. She said that she is now working full-time, is able to overcome distance in her relationships, and can empathize with others. She used just to attack and distance, but now it was easier to be with her family, she said, but she was afraid that if she were to focus on herself she would not know what to do.

She then shifted to her mother: "I can't get angry at Mother." I interpreted that there was a taboo, that the relationship with her mother must be kept quiet. She replied: "When I talk about—when you talk to me about my mother, I get static and can't take it in. I remember rubbing her feet for hours before the TV. I had no choice." I related this to her struggle in treatment about having a choice to support herself. She continued: "Whenever I asked Mother for something, the answer was No. I'm terrified of men using me because of my mother." At this point, the patient was crying, and she said that the tears were anger. "I hate that S.O.B." (The anger of the abandonment depression came to center stage.)

In the next session, the patient reported trying to get her anger at the mother out by throwing eggs at a tree in the backyard. She then teared, talked about feeling deprived, growing up in such a hostile environment: "My mother got her ideas across through attacking other people, no love or warm feelings, didn't know what love meant; the anger is threatening. I put away Mother's pictures. I'm going to put away her dishes. I was always told I was wrong. Nobody said I was okay, plus any complaint, I was wrong. My father, my sister, and I were hostages."

In the next session, the patient said she had seen the movie *The Prince of Tides* and had cried throughout it without knowing why. She said: "Mother lied, had secrets, manipulated. I feel exhausted and numb. My father taught me not to fight, not to express anger. I feel crushed and dead. Also, my own voice keeps attacking me. It's a constant barrage 24 hours a day." I interpreted that there seemed to be a taboo about linking anger with her mother, that this was the Eleventh Commandment.

In the last session of the month, the patient asked: "When did I cut off and lose my sense of self? My difficulty facing my mother in the past is complicated by my difficulty facing what I did to my own children as a mother. **Today I went to a museum alone for the first time in 15 years.** I used to be afraid to be alone, but I loved being in the museum alone. When I was in school, my mother bribed me not to go on a trip by buying me a car, and then she ended up using the car herself."

Thirteenth Month

Continued Struggle with Anger at Mother Occupies Center Stage

She continued: "Mother used the silent treatment if all else failed. When badly hurt, I do the same thing. I can't talk. When I was in college, however, I was angry and obnoxious, a slave to my husband. On my trip here this morning, I focused on my anger at my mother. Why don't I stick up for me? I'm feeling sorry for myself, such a waste, being paralyzed. My husband was just like my mother."

I pointed out how she feels sad and then cuts it off. She replied: "The waste is sad, but I have to get over it. I cried a lot yesterday with my face in the pillow. My mother was always angry."

In the next session, the patient began: "I'm more in touch with what I want to do. I saw a TV commercial about supportive mothers and cried and cried. I had no memory of support by my mother. When I told my mother I was getting married, she didn't believe me, until my husband told her. I feel detached today. As a child, I felt rejected, but now I feel loved by my children and friends, and I can't stay with my feelings about my mother. Mother made me take ballet and all other kinds of lessons against my will and molded me, but I can't stay with it. I can't change the past, and I seem to be better." I pointed out that she seemed to want to use the present to defend against remembering the past.

In the next session, she continued: "I'm angry at my mother and at myself for letting her get away with it. I didn't realize how paralyzed I was. I cannot see myself shutting off feeling. My mother used to come home from work angry every night, but tell us she was sacrificing for us. As a child, I felt nobody cared about me, and as a child, I could do anything athletically; but as an adult, anytime I have to do anything new, I get terribly anxious. To do it, I have had to imagine I was someone else. I'm just beginning to get over it."

I interpreted that she was perhaps defending against anger at her mother, which had been on center stage, by her sadness with herself. In the last four months the patient has been able to focus on her self and the abandonment depression, which has uncovered her rage.

Fourteenth Month

The Patient Acts Out Her Anger and Then Detaches Feeling After an Incest Dream

In the next session, the patient reported getting tickets for a show for her friend without consulting her, and then being furious when she found that the friend was busy. I asked why she had not consulted the woman, and interpreted that she was having great difficulty getting in touch with her anger at her mother here, and that perhaps she was acting it out on her friend. She replied, "When I was angry at my mother, I could only go to bed and cry that nobody loved me."

I then interpreted that when she acts out with her friend, she feels strong and entitled, which is the opposite of the weakness she felt with her mother. She answered: "If I apologize, it's being a traitor to myself. I fought Mother tooth and nail but never won, and then guilt finally made me give in."

In the next session, she talked more about anger at her girlfriend, and then reported a dream: "I was making love to my mother, and I woke up and turned off the horrible thing. Mother was not responsive in the dream. I'm angry at not being acknowledged and responded to. Then I shut off completely. Was I abused by my mother? No. I always had a fear I was abused as a child. I feel 'poor me,' like a baby being tortured. Was Father supporting Mother behind the scene? He was such a kind person. I'm thinking more about my father, angry at his not standing up for me." The dream again raises questions about possible sexual abuse, but these cannot be explored at this time because the patient is detached and in defense.

In the next session, the patient reported that her feelings were cut off, and she's not supporting herself: "As a kid, I had been ornery. Every time Mother thought something was wrong, she took me to a doctor, and I recall the dentist making a pass."

In the next session, she reported being more self-supportive and in touch with her feelings and being easier on herself and on her friend: "I feel calm, like I'm on Prozac. I used to turn off a lot. I don't get upset with others as I did. I'm starting to see myself as a good person. I'm still having conflict with my friend over her sexual difficulty and her efforts to control me." (The defense has removed the anger and sexual problem from center stage.)

Fifteenth Month

Resistance and Acting Out with Friend and Children

The patient reported feeling good, clear, free, in touch with her feelings. This theme continued into the next session, which raised the possibility of a defensive flight into health following the incest dream. For example: **"I'm feeling more relaxed and better when I'm alone. I'm now working eight hours a day, relating better at work, supporting myself with my friend. I indulged myself for the first time on Saturday and just stayed in bed and read."**

She then talked more about her friend's sexual inhibitions. I pointed out to her her difficulty in accepting her friend as she is. She replied, "I don't feel the great love or the void anymore with her."

In the next session, she focused on her children's self-centeredness, lack of gratitude, and indulgence. I interpreted that she feels disappointment and anger at their failure to respond, but rather than set limits with them, she focuses on them to regulate herself and then becomes upset when they don't respond; and she does not set limits because it would interfere with focusing on them.

She replied about how strongly she had been influenced by her mother's saying no. In the next session, the patient continued to report feeling better, being more sensitive to her own needs, able to say No more easily, but continuing to press her friend for more sex and closeness, letting the friend know that her inhibitions prevented closeness. "She's loving but not demonstrative." I again interpreted her difficulty in seeing her friend as she is. She continued to defensively press her friend to resonate with her as a defense against the memories of her relationship with her mother.

Sixteenth Month

The patient reported an incident in which she was hurt, but rather than express it, cut off and joked: "Why can't I acknowledge being hurt? I look for it, but I can't feel it. I could never say I felt hurt. Anger was my response. On Mother's Day, I blocked Mother out, never had anyone acknowledge me as I am. I had to block out the hurt with Mother." [She was tearing.]

I interpreted that it was so painful to acknowledge her need for the other and the hurt when it is not met, that she cuts off all feeling and gets defensively angry. This led to the most painful feeling of the impaired self.

She followed through in the next session, reporting that she woke up in the middle of the night with a fantasy of "a disembodied heart trying to contract, but it couldn't because it was solid inside! *Free association:* "I felt scared, like I was losing my mind, afraid I wouldn't be able to find myself. There's nothing there. However, the rest of this last week I was more at ease with myself. As a child, 10 or 12, I spent hours crying, nobody liked me, nobody would care about me. In grammar school, I was a poor-to-average student; in high school, a top student—but not for me. But I love reading now; never studied because I wanted to; only now I read what I want; never felt liked by anyone; so terrified of abandonment, even by you."

I interpreted that the fantasy seemed to express her feeling about herself, that she had begun to express in the prior session what now came out in the dream and the fantasy, and that, as she gets deeper into her feeling, she feels frightened that I will abandon her. At this, she teared and said: "The inner core is rotten. I'm just getting to know me. You know, I used to like to take advantage of other people and their mistakes, to get away with something, but I find that I don't want to do it anymore, even though I am reluctant to give that up."

For the past six weeks, since the sexual dream about her mother until the last two sessions, the patient was more or less cut off from being able to link the feelings of her impaired self to her mother and seemingly escaped into health, and now, in the last two sessions, there was reentry, not through conscious images or anger at the mother, but through emerging images of the impaired self.

Following the last session, at which the patient was able to get affectively in touch with her impaired self, she had a repetitive experience with her friend, which she previously had denied. Her friend basically distances and puts her on hold. But rather than rationalizing it, she began the session by saying: "I felt hurt by her rejection, her standoffishness. It's clear to me that she sucks me in by kind words, and then she distances from me. And she says it's my problem, but I realize that it's not. I feel hurt, and I feel rejected, and I don't want to be in this game anymore. So I took off by myself and visited friends who responded, and I felt better."

To which I replied, "Because you're with people who like and respond to you." She answered: "It's so hard for me to say that." She then elaborated on how better she is able to activate herself; does not feel so guilty if she makes an error or mistake; and is trying to separate herself more clearly from her son, not waiting on him, making her own plans and expecting him to make his own plans. She then reported a feeling of loneliness in the context of seeing another woman who is buying and furnishing a house for herself, saying that she could not do that by herself, but that she could if she had someone with her. I interpreted that she said she uses others as a way of defining herself, and when she does not have another, she feels lonely. I pointed out that this feeling of loneliness may have as much to do with not having the other in her head to define herself as with not having a person in the external world.

SUMMARY

In 16 months, at once-a-week sessions, the patient has begun to explore the aggressive fused unit and its relationship with her impaired self, which has given her greater access to and use of her real self, and this has produced definite clinical improvement. Deeper exploration has been blocked, probably by dissociative defenses against probable physical and/or sexual abuse. This seemed to be emerging in the incest dream, which led to dissociative defense and flight into health. The latter issues remain to be explored.

6

The Guru and the Bed of Pain

Mr. B., 55 years old and red-headed, was tall, burly, and overweight. A well-groomed, successful lawyer, he had been divorced three times.

CHIEF COMPLAINT

In the setting of the imminent death of a close male friend and conflict with his closest woman friend, Mr. B.'s asthma symptoms, which had been controlled by medication, in the past year had become worse, and he was terrified that he might have a coronary occlusion and die. Several members of his family had died of heart attacks while in their 60s. He was in a panic, preoccupied with the fear of dying. He checked his blood pressure and pulse daily, and had his cholesterol checked regularly. He exercised three times a week; nevertheless, although on a diet, he was overweight.

HISTORY

History of Present Illness

He denied depression, but the affect of depression was probably absorbed by his somatic preoccupations. He did acknowledge, however, that he felt a lessening of his usual energy and sense of excitement in his work. He also acknowledged sadness over the imminent loss of his closest male friend, whom he had known for many years.

He complained of having had difficulties in his relationships with women throughout his life. At present he was seeing a much younger woman. He liked and was attracted to her, but admitted, "She wants emotion and commitment and I want mostly sex and I get angry at her demands. And as much as I like her, when she's not around, when I'm alone, I don't miss her and I feel fine."

He had been married three times, and in all marriages had functioned as a kind of Pygmalion with a younger woman. He would marry the woman and mold her, but after about five years, he would lose his sexual interest in her. During these marriages, he had had extramarital sexual liaisons. He always felt, he said, "I need an escape window. I don't like to be held down. I don't like to put my fate in anybody's hands. Anything that makes me feel bound frightens me. I always have to have an escape route."

Although his latest woman friend suggested that he come to treatment because of his conflicts with her, it was clear that these conflicts were not the main reason for his agreeing, but rather it was because of his underlying panic about his physical health and his fear of dying. He emphasized that he had stopped his sexual acting out in recent years because of his fear of getting AIDS. If he had not stopped acting out sexually, he probably would not be coming for treatment. He denied using drugs or alcohol.

At the age of 40, the patient had begun a course of psychoanalysis on the couch three times a week that lasted three years, but he said that he felt that it had not helped him very much.

Family History

The patient's father, who died when the patient was 19, was an immigrant businessman who was quiet and fairly affectionate, but quite distant. The mother, also an immigrant, was bright, well educated, and very active in political and religious causes. Both parents were successful, with the mother being the aggressive speaker up front, and the father the quieter and warmer intellectual who stood behind her.

Personal History

The patient, an only child, reported that at six months of age he was seriously ill with pneumonia and then had scarlet fever. At the age of five, he had a mastoidectomy, and his ear drained for many years. He also stuttered so badly as a child that he was almost incoherent.

At the age of seven, he contracted rheumatic fever and began to suffer with asthma, and spent the next year and a half in bed. The pediatrician told his mother that his prognosis was poor and that he might die. However, his mother was a fighter and refused to give in. She took him to Arizona, where he lived with her and a sister for a year; at the time, he still could not read or write.

He subsequently recovered, and at the age of 12 or so, returned to school, where he overcompensated for his long absence by becoming extremely competitive. He said that, as he entered adolescence, "I became a holy terror. I did nothing my parents wanted. I became a jock. And then I got into big fights with my father. I was at war with him most of the time. He was very courteous, strong, and gentle.

"I went on to college, where I became involved in music, and I also read a lot. Before my father died when I was 19, we had become good friends. My mother lived until age 69, but after my father's death, her functioning decreased, and I had to take care of her.

"As a student, I had a fantasy of becoming a lawyer, and fortunately I was able to turn my dreams into reality. What I did was literally to move into my fantasies, and I became extremely successful while still very young. I loved the excitement, and my success has continued to this day."

CLINICAL IMPRESSION

As the clinical picture unfolded, the key to the patient's intrapsychic dynamics emerged more clearly as follows: The prolonged period of illness, with much pain and a fear of death that could not be relieved by his doctors or parents, powerfully reinforced his feeling of abandonment. He felt helpless, hopeless, alone, terrified of dying. He dealt with those painful affects by giving up the emotional attachment of his real self to his parents, that is, by detaching affect and substituting a grandiose fantasy of the nice man or guru who gratified his grandiosity by focusing on and manipulating the omnipotent object to admire him. As he got older, he added workaholism and sexual acting out to his defenses.

We came to call this role that he played the guru—to defend against the fear of abandonment and death associated with his real self. He became a master at playing the guru for others, which brought him much narcissistic gratification. He was also aware from time to time of his having such underlying feelings of fear of death and void that he could not commit to a relationship with a woman except on a defensive level, and he eventually would lose interest. His fear of engulfment and death contested with his fear of abandonment in any real relationship. He also felt that although he was successful, he might have made better use of his creativity.

The confluence of four precipitating stresses uniquely upset this lifelong fragile defensive balance: (1) his age and the need to come to grips with mortality, (2) the life threat posed by asthma, (3) the impending death of his friend, and (4) the demand of his woman friend for closeness. All four stresses overcame his role-playing defense and threw him back to the fear of death associated with his underlying real self that he had spent a lifetime holding in check.

DIAGNOSIS

There are complex elements to this diagnosis. We will probably find some posttraumatic stress disorder dissociative defenses to deal with the early trauma, as well as the more obvious closet narcissistic defenses. In his relationship with others, he was always aware that, despite the surface appearance (i.e., he was focusing on the idealized other to help them), he was doing it so that they would admire him. We thus would have to call him a mixture of a behavioral closet narcissistic personality disorder and an intrapsychic exhibitionistic disorder. He knew that his grandiosity motivated the system.

INTRAPSYCHIC STRUCTURE

The structure was that of a grandiose-self–omnipotent-object fused defensive part-unit consisting of a grandiose self, "the guru," that focused on and manipulated the omnipotent object with the affect of being admired, adored, special, and perfect provided by that object. The underlying harsh aggressive fused unit consisted of an object representation that was uncaring, helpless itself, and withholding and a self-representation of being helpless, hopeless, empty, and powerless, with the linking affect of abandonment depression being led by the terror of dying. Important defenses were distancing in relationships, detachment of affect, idealization of the object, and acting out, avoidance, and denial.

THE TRIAD

The disorder-of-the-self triad operated as follows: If the patient activated his real self to work at a relationship, this would precipitate an abandonment panic and fear that he would die. He defended by idealizing the object and manipulating it to regulate the grandiose self. The panic and depression were further defended against by detachment of affect, workaholism, and sexual acting out. In his relationship with women, the detachment of affect defended him against the fear of death associated with commitment and permitted him to act out the guru role.

PSYCHOTHERAPY

First Month

Asthma and Fear of Death

Mr. B. reported asthma on exercise. Then his friend died, and he felt severe loss. This reinforced his feelings that he was better off by himself; he only wanted somebody with him occasionally, and he did not want them to bother him. He considered stopping the treatment, as he could do what he had done all his life, which was to escape into activity. "The actions cover up the feeling." I interpreted that this loss was so painful that he wanted to deal with it, as he had with everything else all his life, by shutting off the treatment and escaping. This explanation fell on deaf ears, and he decided to stop.

Second Month

Escape No Longer Works

Three months later, he returned and we began psychotherapy once a week. He began by saying, "Since the last interview, I fell apart. I got into more fights with my friend, Louise. I became actually depressed, unable to escape with activity. I began to have suicidal thoughts and felt that I was finished. My asthma began to act up even at rest. It saps my strength; I feel like giving up, and I have. But as much as I feel like giving up, I have enormous anxiety about opening up with you, facing that my life has been a failure. Why do I tire of any woman after five years? Why do I have to keep running?"

I interpreted the triad, explaining that his old way of dealing with these feelings was no longer working—the sexual acting out, the workaholism. And when he turned to face and explore what lay underneath, it was painful and he felt helpless and frightened (i.e., facing the abandonment depression and the fear of dying without his defenses).

He elaborated: "I feel guilty about manipulating women without feeling, playing the role of taking care of them but not feeling anything. What am I left with now? Have I ever conducted a real relationship with a woman? I'm like an incapacitated child locked in forever. I can remember rebelling against this at the age of eight. If I accepted what they told me, I would be dead. It meant death. I had to be free, to get out, and I rebelled."

In the next two sessions, he focused more on his physical state; the asthma was decreasing, his ability to exercise was increasing, and he had made **some more practical changes in his work and in his living arrangement.** For some time, he had been thinking about retiring, but said he did not know what to do. He discussed the possibility of teaching or writing a book.

(It seemed to me that although he did not say so, he was no longer as convinced as he had been that he was going to die of a heart attack.) He ended the session talking about how helpless he had felt as a child with rheumatic fever, how much his joints had hurt, and how afraid he was of dying. He said he thought that perhaps for him closeness meant dying.

Third Month

Interpretation of Idealizing Defense Against Painful Self

He returned to the theme of being close to a woman for five years and then having to get rid of her. He said he had recurrent dreams of death, from which he would wake up in a cold sweat. "Commitment and closeness seem to mean death. Self-activation leads to the abandonment depression and death. Even children growing, the passage of time, implies death. My anxiety about sickness, about bleeding to death, is enormous. I feel a rage against the sense of helplessness. Sickness means incapacity, restriction, being helpless."

I interpreted that the asthma attacks brought back the feelings of helplessness and fear of death he had had as a child when he was so restricted, and that these feelings were so painful that, in order to protect himself, he cut off feeling about his real self and stepped into a role that involved being macho and taking care of others, all in a state of emotional detachment. (Could the underlying mechanism here have been dissociation of the painful affective state with its self- and object representation and then the activation of the narcissistic defense?)

He responded: "The role that I play was so close to my real self that it seemed to work. In other words, as I began to act out these fantasies in the real world and they came true, they reinforced the role." (The role is that of a grandiose self being the detached guru, the caretaker of others in order to receive admiration from them.)

The patient then elaborated that playing this ego role, as he called it, tended to impair his perception of others since he was interested only in playing out the role and in their response to it. He said that the role playing worked better at work than with relationships. I suggested that this was probably true because work did not involve intimate relationships, that there was less emotional involvement. He asked: "How do I fight this role playing? Women are a fix for me. I remember as a kid being so frightened that I stuttered. I didn't learn to read until I was eight."

Fourth Month

Resistance

This investigation of the patient's defense (i.e., self-activation) led him to retreat quickly into acting out the role (defense), so that he came to the next four sessions reporting that he was escaping into work, he was seeing Louise more, and so on. He was also sleeping better. Could this be the result of therapeutic alliances being established?

At one point his fear of dying focused on the fact that he might have Lyme disease. He had this checked out and found that he was all right. He finished the month by commenting on his role playing: "I'm like a shark who has to keep moving in the water in order to stay alive"—to defend against his fear of death. (The triad: if he does not keep up defense, he will be faced with the abandonment depression and die.)

Return of the Fear of Death

The fear of death returned in nightmares of being buried alive or cremated alive, from which he would awake in a cold sweat. He said: "The final solution. The way I deal with the anxiety is to escape into reality through business, but I seem to be getting into deeper, darker passages. I am even more concerned about the helplessness than about death. I'm terrified of being dependent, I trust no one. I have decided to cool it with Louise and not see her so much."

Fifth Month

Therapeutic Alliance Starts to Become Established

In the next session, he reported dramatic improvements, suggesting further that the therapeutic alliance was beginning to become established. His anxiety was less, and he reported that he had not **seen a woman during the week for the first time in two years. "I feel I'm doing better and I don't know why. It started here.** I'm frustrated because I can't see the end process. I want to remember my dreams, but I am sleeping like a baby for the first time. I don't have any dreams. But I no longer am uncertain about living the next two years."(His fear of dying has decreased.)

In the next several sessions, he reported data that confirmed that reality limits were being set on the projected fear of dying and that the therapeutic alliance was beginning to be established. He reported a dream: **"I was a baseball player making a comeback and doing well."** *Free association*: "It was a happy dream. I was always interested in baseball as a kid. It's full of survival and optimism." He reported a second dream about two of his parents' oldest friends who had died recently. But in the dream they were vivid, strong personalities and he was visiting them. *Free association*: "They were full of life." He emphasized that he no longer was having fearful dreams. He no longer was overreacting in business deals; however, he could not control his eating.

Following that report, he had several bad nighttime bouts with asthma, and his fear of dying increased. He described his guilt over the fact that he could not reciprocate the strong feelings women had for him. He was pulling away from people in general and becoming pessimistic. He asked: "I am now free of commitment, so why am I not happy? Because for me commitment always equaled death."

He was afraid of falling in love. Commitment meant death. He was afraid of being incapacitated. He rebelled against the rules that limit and incapacitate. Accepting rules meant accepting death (as he felt it had as a child).

Sixth Month

Focus on Self Leads to Depression and Helplessness, and Memories Emerge

As he shifted his focus from his role playing to himself in the session, he became more depressed and helpless. Self-activation leads to the abandonment depression. "The last six to eight weeks I've become more aware of a lack of satisfaction. There is nothing I really want to do. I feel a great abyss. Where am I going, what do I do now? I can't go back, don't know what I want, I have no fantasies. You have taken away my fantasies."

I interpreted the triad: As he got away from the role playing and focused on himself, he felt more depressed and helpless, since his fantasies had always powered the role playing as a protection against these feelings. In other words, he had the fantasy first, and then acted it out. If he was not going to follow that old route, he felt a loss as to what to do.

He elaborated on these feelings in the next session. **"I really am doing much better. I've lost 10 pounds, the nightmares are gone, I'm not going to a funeral anymore. The asthma has decreased. I**

have changed from feeling strangled to having options. Where do I take it from here? The doom is less, but the relationship problem is still there. I'm even skeptical about my improvement. What is real and what isn't?"

Continuity began to be established as he continued the theme in the next session rather than resort to defense. He reported remembering a nightmare at age seven of being buried alive and a dream at age nine of lying between his mother's legs. He did not free associate to either dream. Then he reported a dream of Louise's closing in on him. *Free association*: "I had a fear of being strangled, I wanted out. I'm trying to be honest about this role playing. I can't believe psychotherapy has the impact it has. It's very unlike my previous analysis, which just didn't work. I'm suspicious, is this treatment real? I'm looking for confirming evidence that it's okay to feel better. Is my progress authentic or just more role playing?"

(It was my thought that his progress had to do with his shifting from acting out the role playing to focusing on the real self and getting support for this in the therapeutic alliance, which gave him more confidence that he could commit to treatment without dying.)

In the next session, he reported: **"I continue to diet. My symptoms continue to decrease. I'm doing well at work, but now rather than just plunging into the role playing** [i.e., acting out the grandiose self], **I am stepping back and observing myself."**

He confirmed the shift to the focus on himself by saying: "But I feel lonely, cold, directionless. Do I want to go out there with myself and give up the role playing? I've avoided real emotion and feelings about myself all my life."

Seventh Month

Commitment to a Relationship with a Woman Equals Death

The patient reported his guilt feelings about "manipulating women without feeling." He said: "When I get to like a woman, I lose all sexual interest." I interpreted that as he gets closer in a real way, he feels suffocated and trapped and so loses sexual interest. He reported: "I then begin to feel dependent on the sex, like it becomes all-consuming. The trap I'm afraid of; I'm afraid of becoming a slave to sex and then I pull away. Am I a sexaholic? I resent being a sex slave. The sex drive now becomes a cage, a cutoff. I want to, but then I can't, and I lose control"

Interpretation of Empathy Failure

In the next session, there was the first interpretation of an empathy failure that put on center stage his subtle idealization of the object, me. He began, "Sometimes I feel that you're not paying enough attention to me, and then I feel disappointed that what I'm saying has no value and I cut off feeling." I interpreted that he was exquisitely sensitive to my responses, and that if he felt I was not responding as he needed me to, he would feel disappointed and, left to his own devices, he would have to soothe these feelings by emotional detachment and retreating into cynicism. He responded: "As a child, I felt alone with my pain. Nobody could help me. I had to do it myself." I reinterpreted that his feeling about my lack of attention triggered the disappointment at being left to his own devices.

He "forgot" completely about the next interview and did not call; he told me it had completely slipped his mind. I said I thought his forgetting was probably due to the anxiety stirred up by my interpretation, which dealt with a disruption in his idealizing transference acting out. He was seven minutes late for the next session. My interpretation seemed confirmed by his opening comment: "I feel tired, there is no progress in trying to decide what to do. I had a dream that was an announcement on camera of my saying farewell to life. Nothing seems to work. I can't even feel depressed. I can't get myself to take notes. I'm looking for somebody to turn me on. But I don't want commitment. I'm the warrior with nothing and no one to fight. I'm more comfortable as a loner. Trying to develop the real me leaves me with nothing."

The interpretation is further confirmed later when he reported a dream; "I'm under a machine-gun attack, hiding behind a dead body." *Free association*: "I'm scared, I'm threatened, nothing has any meaning or interests me anymore. What am I doing with these women? I'm caught in limbo, I have no role. Psychotherapy helped put me in it and I'm mad at you for it. You've taken away my independence. You held up a mirror to me and turned the lights on. I blame both you and the process."

I then reinforced the interpretation as follows: His use of the role to protect against the fear of death if he focused on himself, and of his need for me to mirror him to protect against focusing on himself, had taken away his principal defense of playing out the role of the grandiose self, as well as his tools. As a result, he felt both angry and disappointed, but also at a loss as he focused more on his real self. I interpreted further that the giving up of the acting out of the role, the external reinforcement, brought him back to his real self and his fears of death, which arose from his fear of dying from his illnesses as a child.

I continued by pointing out that he was now in his 50s and the onset of his asthma symptoms had brought back this infantile fear of death, which would persist if he allowed himself to be his real self and did not play the role. He responded, "What is the authentic self for me?"

I again interpreted that giving up the role playing of the grandiose self and attempting to focus on himself here had flushed out his fear of death, which was associated with being his authentic self, and this was why he had such difficulty. This interpretation led to memories. He replied, "Doctors are part of this threat. It was the doctor who said I'd die. I remember their white coats when I was on the operating table. I remember the operation, at age five, my parents' leaving me on the table to be executed. They didn't tell me what was going to be done. Rheumatic fever at six and seven.

"I can remember lying in bed before age five and having a nurse and having almost to tie a string to her."

Eighth Month

Patient Improves After Interpretation

The genetic interpretation had its effect since he returned saying: "I have felt fine since the last interview. My nightmares are gone, but I'm mad because I'm dependent on you, and then I will be hurt again, you will fail me. Pain is the only reality. I can feel it, taste it, smell it. Physical pain, not the emotional pain. I denied that."

In the next session, he talked about having sexually acted out with another woman, but said it had no meaning. He then reviewed how 10 years earlier he had been in love with a young woman who had dumped him, and how shocked he was, but he also was afraid that he would have ruined her life if she had stayed since he would have lost interest after five years anyway. He pointed out that his cynicism was a defense against the disappointment. He withdrew from involvement, became secretive, and would not become close to anyone as a protection against disappointment.

On the other hand, he reported that he had not felt so well physically in 10 years. He then went on a vacation with another woman. He said the sex was good, but he again became annoyed at her seeking emotional connection and had trouble sleeping.

He reported a dream of choking: "Putting my finger down my throat to extract it and I woke up, it was so vivid. I'm so conscious of death, it's scary." This led to further sleeplessness.

Ninth Month

He returned to the feeling of living on death row, waiting for it to happen. I made a clarification between his infantile fear of death, which he projected on reality, and the reality of death, and said that he treated the one as if it were the same as the other, whereas it is not. I emphasized that he had soothed the fear of death by playing the role, and his shifting out of the role and focusing on himself here was bringing the fear of death to the surface for exploration, but that this was not the same as the reality of dying. He replied: "I used to feel as if I were living on borrowed time. My father's attitude was that the worst that can happen will happen. So he would give up, but my mother was a fighter and optimistic. My doctors were also pessimistic. And when I'm alone, I either fight like my mother, or give up like my father and prepare the shroud."

I suggested a third alternative, which was to attempt to explore these feelings about himself in his treatment. He returned with a dream: "I was chased by a mugger . . . he went off and then another came and then I got away." *Free association*: None. (I thought this was the patient's response to my interpretation that the treatment was stripping away a defense. Forcing him to face his fear of death was like being attacked by a mugger.)

He continued: "It's more clear to me that I function better at work when I am my real self than when playing a role. I used to feel that without the role, there was no me. I was a sexual role performer, and now I realize I don't have to perform, I can relax."

In the next session, he reported that he was **working all right, that he was using his time better, that he was not as worried about money, not as competitive.** "I used to have an inner terror I couldn't identify. Now I seem to be better. I came for relief here, I was choking to death. I can't believe this process works like it does. I'm amazed, and I don't understand it."

Tenth Month

Interpretation of Defense Leads to Memories of Fear of Death

He complained about procrastination, doing everything at the last minute, not being able to follow through. I interpreted that commitment to a woman or to a reality work task brought out the feeling of death, and he soothed himself by avoiding it and procrastinating. He replied: "If I don't juggle, I don't exist, I lose myself. I'm afraid that if I stop swimming like the shark, I'll sink and die. It's a kind of panic. I lived with fear as a child. I don't know the middle ground. At five, after the operation, Father was sure I wouldn't survive. I can remember coming out of the anesthesia in the elevator. A door opened and I opened my eyes; I was bedridden, swollen joints, deathlike. At eight, Mother again was told that I wouldn't live until age 15.

"We lived in a walk-up. My mother had an operation; it was botched up. I was sure she was dead. When I was eight, my father had his first heart attack, and when I was 19, he died. From six to seven, because of my swollen, painful joints, I couldn't move, and so later, movement, physical acts, even intercourse, all helped to confirm my existence."

I interpreted that the procrastination was to soothe the fear of death that would arise if he activated himself and committed himself to a task at work or to a relationship with a woman. This interpretation of the triad opened up the fear of death from ages five through six, when he actually was frightened that he would die.

In the next session, he elaborated on his memories of the fear. "I saw a movie about Egypt as a child and I had a fear of being buried alive in a sarcophagus. This haunted me for 20 years. And I had a confusion about what it would be like when I died. Would I be alive?

"From eight to 10, I had nightmares and conscious preoccupations with thoughts of being punished by being buried alive. Myself as an innocent victim. I felt suffocated, smoke coming out, a snake coming out of my mouth. A fear of being strangled. The role playing and the seduction are a way of proving to myself that I'm alive."

Following this, he reported a dream about a woman's chasing him, shouting at him, and his being mad at her. He recalled being sick at age eight and his mother's abandoning him. "After I was disappointed, angry, I felt betrayed. And this followed my fear of death."

This led to another dream of his mother's remarrying, in which he was preparing for the wedding and she was marrying an unknown man. *Free association*: "Mother never remarried. I had no great sense of loss in the dream. After Father died, I felt responsible for her because she began to disintegrate. I took care of her. I was supposed to put her in a nursing home, but I couldn't do it."

I interpreted that the dream was a response to the prior interview, his negative feelings about his mother about which he felt guilty, and so he did for her what she could not do for him. The dream was to get off the hook of being responsible for her.

He then mentioned that between sessions he does not remember the interviews. I interpreted that this perhaps was his way of protecting himself against the fear of death that would arise if he allowed himself to get in touch with these feelings about himself that arose in the sessions.

Again the patient missed the next interview and did not call. He said that he had no awareness that he was supposed to be here. (I thought it was a reaction to my last interpretation.)

Eleventh Month

Interpretations Continue

Efforts to explore his forgetting the interview met resistance. Then he reported that before when he was alone, he enjoyed the decrease in pressure, but did not particularly enjoy being alone. Now, he said, he actually enjoyed being alone. He then reported a dream about planning to remarry his first wife. *Free association*: "I worry about my health. If something happens to you, what happens to me? I remember that when my friend died, I felt guilty that I wasn't there at the moment. It was the same with my mother. I blamed my psychiatrist for the breakup of my first marriage because he got sick and was hospitalized."

I interpreted that his fear of being left was so intense that in relationships with women he had to blot out the perception of possibly being left by not allowing intimacy, which always involves the possibility of being left, and that with me he was similarly afraid that I would betray him by leaving him as he felt his mother had. He responded: "Twenty years ago, I had a real love affair. I really was involved and agreed to marriage, and then she left me and I was desolated."

Betrayal in Life Reinforces Affect of Betrayal from the Past

At this point, he was badly betrayed by someone at the office whom he had trusted, and he relapsed into depression. "I feel very vulnerable, can't even escape into sex, emotionally let down, it weakened my resistance." I interpreted that the betrayal at this time, when he was just beginning to understand his feelings of betrayal from the past, had pierced his role-playing defenses and reinforced the underlying vulnerability with its depression; that is, he was being rejected externally while he also felt rejected internally.

Twelfth Month

Betrayal Fosters Resistance

He continued to report depression over the incident. He had trusted this person and then was betrayed. This heightened his defensive cynicism. "People are unreliable. You can't trust anyone. I feel depressed and angry. Takes me back to the infantile situation. I feel helpless to do anything about it. I live only from day to day, but at least that's honest. I don't like being helpless and not in control. Between the ages of five and seven, after the mastoidectomy, I stuttered to the point of being incoherent."

I interpreted again that he had opened his feelings to this person as a consequence of his treatment in order to repair the anger and loss he had felt with his parents, and instead of getting repair in this relationship, the original abandonment was repeated, throwing him back upon his anger and depression.

In the next session, he mourned the loss of his role playing. "The role playing used to give me internal strength, and now it's been taken away. What is there, what should I do? I can't go into the role anymore, and real options seem so much more limited. I miss the comfort, it was my companion. Actually, because of this, my preoccupation with death is now no longer on center stage."

He continued to report in the next session that he felt numb, as if he had had an anesthetic, that he had no confidence in letting himself go and did not want to expose himself.

Thirteenth Month

Interpretation of Projection Leads to Improvement

He continued on the theme of his rage at the man who betrayed him, similar to his feelings about his parents. "I opened myself for another chance and he turned on me. Confirms that you can trust no one. I can't get rid of the anger and depression."

The theme of depression continued—dreaming about funerals, no interests, turning to death as an escape, giving up versus flight, like the role playing. "I'm faced with me, a void. Pain, fear, scared to death, surrender. Had to fight temptation to let go and give in to the pain and weakness.

"I escaped into fantasy when very young, at five or six. Underneath the roles was this huge, empty room." This led to memories of his ear draining for a year between the ages of five and six; his rheumatic fever at age seven, which kept him immobilized for six months; his stuttering from age five to age 10; his mother's illness when he was nine; his father's heart attack when the patient was 10.

I again interpreted the triad: as he focused more on himself, he seemed to see it as a void, an empty room, and though it was depressing, it opened up the opportunity to recapture some of the sense of self that he had lost.

In the next session, he reported feeling much better, probably as a result of my interpretation of his facing himself as not just a black hole, but as an opportunity for a new beginning, as well as for working through some of the pain from the past. He said: "Am I afraid to change? **I feel different now. I feel I can do what I want.** Between five and 11, my illness got worse, but I occupied myself with baseball and foreign affairs. I still think I can adjust realities to me, including aging and death. I don't trust reality. I looked at fantasy as a friend, a partner to my survival. Outside of that, I was helpless and couldn't do anything."

Fourteenth Month

Detachment of Affect with Women

He continued to report feeling better, but did not know why, which I used as an opportunity to interpret to him the difficulty he had in acknowledging that he felt better because of his own self-activation. He then asked, "Why don't I feel more with women? It's an emotional vacuum."

This led to a dream, "Somebody had been murdered. I knew who it was. I woke up with the sheets wet and scared." *Free association*: It was my health. Am I kidding myself? I've gotten better here, but how much is intellectual? Without the role, I'm nothing and lonely. There is a lack in me. I have no feeling for women."

I interpreted again that the way he dealt with his fear of dying was to cut off access to himself, and thus involvement with the other, and to step into the role playing, which was safer. The price was that in the real relationship, he had no feelings. And when he brings up his lack of feeling, focusing on himself, he frustrates the defensive role player, which then brings on the fear of dying.

He replied: "I can't go back anymore, it's almost impossible to scale that wall."

Fifteenth Month

Closeness Means Death

He began: "I've separated myself from the role in work and I am, therefore, much more effective. But the fear of death is all-consuming. I haven't let go of it. I'm also afraid of exposure, don't want to let anyone in. I have no feelings again for women. Nothing matters. It's only curiosity that keeps me going." He reported a dream: "There was a ceremony for the dead. Wrapping the body in a shroud scared me." *Free association*: "It was me wanting death as an out for the fear of death. It turned into an obsession with death. It scares me."

He reported another dream about a woman that he could not remember, and said; "When I get close to a woman, I pull out. I'm like the general in *Dr. Strangelove*. I deprive women of my essential self." I interpreted that he was fearful that if he allowed a closeness, he would lose all his precious fluids and die. I then interpreted that his sexual behavior defended against his fear of death because it confirmed in its intensity that he is alive. However, when involvement with a woman arises, he loses sexual desire because it brings with it the fear of death.

He responded: "My parents hugged me and loved me but they couldn't relieve the pain. I felt that my mother let me down. Love is bullshit.

"At age six, I remember a recurring dream of lying between my mother's legs. I felt good and protected. I can't identify love as a feeling."

Sixteenth Month

More Memories of Fear of Death

He continued: "At any possibility of involvement, I run away. I'm responsible for my life, but what have I done with it? I ran like a blind man. I used adventure and excitement as a challenge to escape. Being afraid of the feeling of void and vacuum and death. The past haunts me. I use it to avoid the future.

"Total identity is tied to the role playing, no existence without it. I go from external fix to external fix. Trying to contact real feelings, I experience fear, a vacuum, no echo. There is no peace of mind in internal reality. I don't even leave a shadow. I'm like footsteps in the snow. The last strong emotion of love was 10 years ago, and even that didn't lead to risking commitment. When I was five, during the mastoid time, I was sure I would die. For the whole year, I was frightened to death of death.

"I go from not caring to depression. Could I go back to age five, infantile? I had a pet then that I wouldn't let go. How can I at 55 go back to age five? It's a vacuum, a float, nothing there."

Then he reviewed his physical problems from age three through age seven—infections, abscesses, the mastoid draining, whooping cough, stuttering, rheumatic fever, and so on.

"When I was eight, Mother was hospitalized for a kidney infection. They took her out in a stretcher and I thought she was dead and I felt I had done it to her because I was sick."

Seventeenth Month

Resistance Again

In the next session, he talked about trying to get his act together, but as having no insight about himself. He said he felt as though he were in a vacuum, floating in ether, and for him no control also meant death.

He then missed the next session, and came to the following session again in resistance. "I run to the role player even though I know it's not the answer. I know why it happened, but it doesn't impel me to stop running to the role player. When I face the fact that there is nothing there, I come up against a solid wall. I've cut off real feeling with people more, not less. I'm very suspicious about the reliability of love. After the experience 10 years ago with the woman I loved, I cut off feelings with people, so that I never put myself in that position again."

I interpreted that the loss he experienced with the woman was a repetition of the loss he had experienced with his mother and father, as well as with the more recent loss of his friend. I then interpreted that he had been able to open himself up to the woman because she was so much younger and that having an enduring relationship was less likely. At some level, he must have known this, and then it came true. But it enabled him to feel more than he had before in his life. He said, "I was 50 and she was 20. Even then I had a fear that I couldn't follow through as a husband and I would do to her what I did to my first wife."

Again he returned to the same theme: "I focus on myself, I feel lost, hopeless. I begin to feel anxiety about losing control for the first time, vulnerable, unsure of myself, frightened. I feel like I'm pathetic, sick, helpless, inadequate, and afraid of death. I'm sitting immobilized as I did when I was age six. Then I escaped into the radio."

After three sessions of intense working through as a consequence of focusing on his real self, the patient reported: **"After the last session, I felt a lot better and was able to activate myself. I'm functioning 30 percent better on a realistic basis. I can make deci-**

sions. My perspective in decision making is different, more realistic. I began to feel there is a here and now. Felt more hopeful about situations. I used to feel hopeless. Now I'm more confident.

"Last week I was so depressed because I had intellectual insight without emotional change."

Eighteenth Month

Oedipal Conflict

This improvement continued and led to a new area of investigation, his sexual feelings for his mother. "As a child, I had a fear of relationships' being too much pain, no trust. I loved Mother, but was let down. My relationship with her was very physical, almost sexual. When I get too close to a woman, I pull back. I remember having sexual feelings about my mother at age eight, dreams of lying between a woman's legs. A physical sense of Mother, a closeness. I run away from closeness with women. When Mother got old and Father died, I became her father. It was mother's strength that got me through my childhood, her power."

He followed through in the next session, continuing to feel better, with two sexual dreams about women, which he had not had in a long time. "It was a deeper hurt with Mother, a sexual rejection by Mother. When I was an adolescent, I sought physical proof of women's affection. They had to respond to me sexually. I recall again the dream of lying between my mother's legs. In some way I feel my illness was a punishment for my sexual feelings.

"Since I started talking about this, I sense less of a fear of women and more of an ability to come out. When I was nine, Mother and I were alone in Arizona for two months. I was always physically conscious of Mother as a women.

"I didn't masturbate until 12. After I recovered. I became very physical and active and wouldn't slow down. Adolescent sex was to overcome feelings of rejection, to be accepted without pain."

I interpreted that his sexual relationships with girls in adolescence was to overcome the earlier trauma that sexual feelings with his mother led to pain and rejection, and thus the sexual act overcomes the trauma. On the other hand, a real emotional relationship brings back the fear of pain and rejection and he loses interest. He responded, "I'm anxious about whether I'm going to be able to function sexually with the woman the first time, a new woman, and then this anxiety goes away."

Nineteenth Month

Fears of Abandonment

He reported his awareness of the fact that he used his career to avoid facing his need to focus on himself and what he wanted to do. He reported he had not had a dream from which he woke up in a sweat in six weeks and had started to socialize more. "I cut my parents off when I was 14, I didn't share with them. The role-playing fantasy began when I was ill and became elaborated later. The sex wouldn't relieve the pain and it was to reassure myself, and I wanted only what I wanted. I enjoy my life and relationship with women, but I sense that there is something wrong with it."

I pointed out that much of his life revolved around the role playing in order to protect against the focus on himself, which led to a fear of death. He replied: "This fear has to do with more than something physical or traumatic. My mother couldn't stop the pain and then got sick and left me. Women are unreliable, you can't count on them.

"My first wife's leaving me confirmed my view. I met her at age 17 and we went together for five years. I never dreamed she'd leave me, and I took a long time to get over it. That divorce brought me back to Mother and her leaving me. I was then 30. Did I feel that Mother rejected me because of me and so did my wife, and therefore it's me? It was a fear of growing up."

At the next session, he continued: "When I have such comfort in my sexual role with women, why do I bother to work on it? Is it because of you? I say it's not because of me, it's because of you. What worries me is that sex runs out when I become involved. As if a monster sees the relationship as bad and turns me off. I'm more concerned about the sex being turned off than about the breakup. I'm afraid that I can't follow through with a commitment sexually.

"To me, relationship involvement means being dominated, abandoned, and dying. I'm constitutionally incapable of being faithful. If I could accept my role playing, I would be better off." I disagreed, saying that the problem was both what he does (i.e., being promiscuous with women) and, more important here, why he does it. In other words, it is defensive role playing. "The only time I've mourned a loss was that of my pet at age 12, and then in the last year, that of my friend. You can trust a pet but not a woman."

Termination

He reported feeling much better: **"I'm more at ease with myself. Certain levels of fear have been removed. I don't have to play the role to be a big shot anymore. And I don't get easily upset when frustrated** [when not mirrored]. **I handle myself better with people. I don't feel the need to play the role. I'm also not so worried about what I will do."** (In other words, he had more confidence in himself.)

"Why am I not panicking? I'm sleeping better than at any time in the last two years." I interpreted that the anxiety that kept him from sleeping was not due to reality, but to the degree to which it frustrated his role playing, and that his awareness of the function of the role playing decreased the anxiety and so made it easier to sleep.

I suggested that the reality problems persisted but the anxiety decreased because of his increasing awareness of the function of the role to defend against his fear of death. "I don't want to let go of the need for treatment. It's one place where I feel I can assess reality."

I pointed out that the issues that remained were his relationship with women and what he was going to do with himself. Would he continue at his present work or retire to do other things? He said: "Well, I feel okay about the relationship with women even though I can't be involved. And I also feel I can cope with the problem of what I will do. A little bit afraid, but I have to try it. A key question. Am I kidding myself or is this real? I don't seem any more to be the neurotic who moves into the house that the psychotic built, and I think I'd like to stop treatment." I agreed.

SUMMARY

The imbalance produced by the four precipitating factors—age, asthma, loss of friend, and the demand for closeness—had been overcome, and he had gained sufficient awareness of and distance from his grandiose-self role-playing defense and sufficient confidence in the capacity of his real self to use his real self to temper the operation of the defense. The mirroring interpretations had helped to redress this imbalance. They opened up his defenses and gave him access to the childhood origins of his current panic about death. The working through of some of this material relieved his anxiety and strengthened his real self.

At the end of the treatment, his symptoms had markedly decreased and his functioning had improved, but his intrapsychic structure had not changed. However, he had more awareness of it and managed it better. Shorter-term psychotherapy usually ends this way, with the patient feeling much better and not wanting to go further. There is no point in urging the patient to stay in treatment, as the dynamic forces are all against the therapist. If the repair has not been sufficient, the patient will have further trouble and return. For this patient, the profound detachment of the affect defense would be a serious obstacle to efforts at intensive analytic psychotherapy.

7

The Prostitute and the Game

I had treated Mr. C. for a number of years, long before I knew enough about the closet narcissistic disorder. My lack of knowledge and his detached intellectualized defenses became formidable barriers. I saw him once a week and tried to peck away at his defenses, but with only minimal success. Finally, he had to stop treatment because his work required him to leave the country. He had shown some symptomatic improvement. His workaholism and drinking lessened, as did his sexual acting out, and he had more capacity to activate his real self in some of his interests, such as photography and painting. There was no change in close relationships. Fate brought him back seven years later, at age 38, by which time I had learned about the closet narcissistic personality disorder.

His complaints remained the same: workaholism, depression, social isolation, drinking, homosexual acting out, difficulty in activating himself. He spoke with much more awareness of his profound sense of isolation and loneliness and his fear that involvement for him equaled annihilation or death. He felt that he had no boundaries.

I interpreted that it would appear that it was so painful for him to focus on this fearful aspect of himself that he protected himself by maintaining a distance from others to soothe the fear, and he tried to fill the loneliness with work, alcohol, and sex.

He replied: "I'm afraid of demands being made on me. I get frightened. I feel that the other person has ulterior motives and demands and will exploit me, and then what I do is show off to make the person interested in me. For example, in school I got good grades to please the teacher."

INTRAPSYCHIC STRUCTURE

The grandiose-self–omnipotent-object fused unit consisted of an object representation that provided admiration and adoration for perfect performance, and a grandiose-self–representation of being unique, special, and outstanding, with the affect of being admired for perfect performance.

The aggressive fused unit consisted of an object representation that severely and harshly attacked any efforts at self-activation and a self-representation of being like a prostitute—hopeless, helpless, worthless, and with the affect of abandonment depression. The prominent defenses were splitting, acting out, denial, avoidance, projection, projective identification, intellectualization, idealization, and detachment of affect.

The triad operated as follows: The patient regulated his grandiose self by (1) detaching genuine affect from the object, and (2) idealizing the object and performing perfectly to receive admiration. He avoided real self-activation in his relationships and work. The fragile nature of this defensive system was indicated by the fact that in accordance with the disorders-of-the-self triad, any move toward real self-activation triggered the aggressive unit with harsh attacking voices, and to contain his pathologic affects, he required social isolation, drinking, and workaholism.

The purpose of the grandiose-self–defense or "the game" was to defend against the pathologic feeling states of the "prostitute" (the impaired real self of the aggressive unit). The treatment would focus on interpreting this defensive link to enable the real self to form a therapeutic alliance that would bring the pathologic affects into the session to be worked through.

PSYCHOTHERAPY

First Month

Resistance

He began once-a-week therapy. In the first month, his usual defenses took over: avoidance of self-activation, avoidance of focus on the self, isolation and detachment, intellectualization, and denial of the self-destructiveness of these defenses. For this first month, he filled the sessions with detached intellectual verbalizations, mostly of his feelings that upon his return to the home office, the attitude of his co-workers had changed from one of being cooperative to being competitive, and that the company was letting him down.

Second Month

Mirroring Interpretation Leads to Impaired Self (the Prostitute) and Introduction of History

I interpreted to him that his disappointment in his co-workers' lack of response was so painful that he soothed the pain by avoiding focusing on it and detaching feelings, plunging into overwork, drinking, and sexual acting out. He responded, "Overachieving is a lie. Nothing is real—nothing is reliable. I can only rely on myself." This focus on his self led, in the next session, to an attack: "I couldn't bear to have anything good. I don't deserve anything positive." I returned to the work issue, saying that it seemed that performance was the only support for his sense of self and that his feeling that the business did not respond to it produced anger at himself and he felt worthless because of his performance. He replied that he had been so angry at himself over the weekend that he had come perilously close to crashing his car and killing himself.

I reiterated that if his achievement is not responded to, he is thrown back on his own feeling of disappointment and that there is no sense of self there. He confirmed this interpretation of the impaired self: "When I was away, I couldn't do what I wanted. Here I can't stand to be alone in my apartment. I can't stand me. Why am I so hard on myself? I've been doing more sex and drinking since the car accident. I don't think about myself, always others. As for myself, there is no one there, so why live? My mother had a void there, too; she was wrapped up in herself. My father had a sense of self, but no room for anyone else."

In the next session, Mr. C. reported that he attacked himself for efforts to self-activate. He continued: "When I was around eight, I decided that my parents were the children and I was the adult and I had to manage them. They were just not capable of liking me. I had to accept it and deal with them from a distance, so I gave up on them. My father was unpredictable and unreliable. My mother was harsh and punitive. Her mother was an alcoholic so she had to take care of her. My father liked the dog better than he did me. Both of my parents were very puritanical about sex. Father wanted me to share hunting and fishing with him, but I wanted books and movies. He thought I was a sissy. My mother is more like an ice cube, denies my homosexuality. If I so much as enjoy myself with others, the next day I feel exposed."

Third Month

Defenses Against Aggressive Fused Unit—Interpreted and Acting Out Confronted, Revealing Underlying Rage

In response to my interpretation that his busyness was an effort to fill the void left by the need to distance from the painful focus on himself and his relationship with others, he replied, "If I want to do the simplest things—learn to use the VCR, take a picture—I end up not following through and filling in with watching TV or drinking."

I reiterated that it would appear that the focus on the self was so painful that he had to avoid self-activation, as well as relationships with people, to protect it. I elaborated that when he activated himself, it seemed to bring on a profound self-hate attack, which led to the working, the drinking, the sexual acting out. Dealing with his painful feelings by drinking and sexually acting out competed with psychotherapy, keeping these feelings from being available in the interviews and thus was counterproductive. He had to control the drinking and sexual acting out if he was to achieve his goal. (This confrontation was necessary because the acting out posed a serious threat to his psychotherapy.)

In the next session, he said that he had responded to my confrontation with panic that I might throw him out. He then reported the following dream; "I was trying to get to the seat in the theater but couldn't, and two men said they'd show me but I'd have to do sex with them first. I said okay, but decided I'd run. I get in the back of the theater, and there's this body without a head, just genitals; it had holes for eyes, but it had an erection." *Free association*: "The images came from a movie I saw in which a man lost his girlfriend, who died, and he was trying to put the parts of the body back together."

I interpreted that perhaps he had experienced my interpretation followed by the confrontation as an attack, taking away his protections against his painful self, and that these feelings appeared in the dream and without them he would die. I elaborated that he had been able to deny the cost of these defenses against self-activation, but nevertheless, despite the fact that he denied it, the cost was there. My interpretation opened it up, brought it to his attention, and he panicked about what he would do without these protections.

He replied: "To be myself involves killing people. As a child I wanted to kill my brother. It feels like a big smiling thing totally involved with myself. Others have to get out of my way—a monster. When you want something, others try to take it away. Everything is calculated."

Fourth Month

Interpretation of Game Defense Against Impaired Self (Prostitute)

Mr. C. reported trying to control his acting out. He had felt disappointed in the lack of perfection of two young female visitors. This made him aware that when he feels people are not perfect, he cuts off from them. "I'm amazed at myself for doing this because I can see it cuts me off from enjoying reality. It's all right to demand perfection of myself."

I queried, "Is it?" I suggested that he may avoid the imperfection in others because it is a mirror that brings to his attention his own imperfections. He replied, "When my parents couldn't be parents, I switched to getting teachers' and others' approval."

I interpreted that he dealt with painful feelings of disappointment in himself and his parents' lack of acknowledgment by switching from that self-focus to a focus on the object to deal with these feelings of loss of the sense of self. He replied: "Myself equals killing people. I don't want to be with people, I just want to incorporate them. I want them, and their separateness makes it difficult. Wanting and not having."

I interpreted that he had retreated to this self-centered position to deal with the painful feelings about his parents' inability to acknowledge his difference and sense of self. He replied: "When I was in this foreign country, I did exactly what I did with my parents. I sought approval from others, not myself—decided I'd be the parent. I established the agenda for my performance. I did not submit to the others, but persuaded them to accept my agenda."

I suggested that he had made a virtue out of a handicap. If he had to focus on others, at least he could force them to respond to him, rather than the other way around.

In the next two sessions, he elaborated further: "I want to be with other people, but can't without distance. That's why I go out to eat."

I interpreted that he defends against his anxiety about being himself with others by avoidance, and so makes it difficult to get these issues out in the session. He replied, "I distance myself from reality as well as from others."

I pointed out that his workaholism suffocates his real self. Since he cannot express it in reality, he turns to fantasy for relief. He replied: "I go out to dinner to observe people rather than to participate. To relate is too scary. I can't tolerate the other's being separate. When I was away, in another country, I spent weekends without speaking to a soul. Not to escape is an effort. I have to begin by talking to people. I would like to support myself and feel myself completed. I'm afraid that if I declare myself with you, I would then fail in your eyes."

In the last session, he reported asking a friend to his home, which was progress for him. However, the friend talked about his own treatment, his own problem being himself, which mirrored all the patient's problems. "I saw it clear in him. I felt like I was losing my mind. I had all these insights, flashes, and ideas. Even flashes of lust. The more I am aware, the more I dislike life and hate coming here, but you force me to look at it more. The conversation with my friend brought to mind memories of my mother's crowding me out. I have to be alone, I want to run. I need breathing space. I can't have things my way, I have to get away."

This led me to introduce the "game" defense. I now interpreted that his fear of being crowded out and losing himself at the hands of his mother caused him to give up his real self and to activate the grandiose self to dominate her and become her parent. He reported that he had told his father, "You don't love me," and his father had said, "Of course we do, you are our firstborn." He added, "The only reason to love me—I was the firstborn."

After this interview, he reported flashes of some improvement—**flashes and bubbles of creativity. "I'm beginning to write notes, wonderful ideas, when shaving in the morning. It's like creative thinking using the unconscious.** Not my usual thinking"—his detached intellectualizations.

Comment

In these four months, interpretation of the idealizing closet defense overcame the defense and brought to center stage the impaired self and the abandonment depression. Unlike the prior patient, Mr. C. seemed able to stay with the impaired self and its affects.

Fifth Month

First Glimmer of Change; Working Through; Resistance Interpreted; Working Through Resumes

Mr. C. tried to remember his childhood, but had great difficulty. He said: "I remember my mother's harshness and her puritanical, vengeful attitude toward sex, but I can't recall either attacks or approval. I do remember being outgoing until age three or four, when my brother was born. I hated him and wanted to kill him. Father liked him better than he did me. Why didn't they love me? Must be something wrong with me. It's kill or be killed. I can't be involved because that's what happens—it's kill or be killed."

The last session freed up some self-activation. He now spoke affectively and enthusiastically, talking more about socializing.

He reported: "I feel more like a kid again. I'm not afraid to ask questions. I was talking to a woman, asking questions that I wanted to ask, rather than trying to create an impression. Then she responded, and my anxiety rose. I was afraid that she might intrude, make demands, want something, and then I had to stop being myself. I've been thinking about what I want to do and about whatever happened to that garrulous, friendly kid."

I interpreted the defense that the "garrulous kid" was buried to protect against the anxiety about the demands of others. He responded: "My grandmother felt that men should wait on women, take care of them. I was her favorite. The emotional demands were from my father. He wanted me to share his interests with him. Felt I was a sissy. Mother was neutral and unfathomable. I put myself in the closet, figured out the demands, and played off them."

I interpreted that the father was disappointed in the patient and the patient in him, and that it was all too painful so he put himself in the closet and began to figure out demands and strategies. He replied: "I deliberately disappointed him about going hunting.

Father had said I seemed to have some talent for shooting, but I wouldn't do it. I wanted to go to the movies rather than hunt. He asked me, 'What movie?' I said, '*Woman's World*.'" He said, 'That figures.'

"I was devastated. Not fair that he wanted me to be just like him, and I decided I'd show him by being the opposite. My parents also had few friends and were quite unsociable. I had liked talking to people. My mother's family had been outgoing." Here Mr. C. is working well on his impaired self. Will he continue in the next sessions or return to defense?

In the next session, as suspected, the patient defended against following through the exploration of the history of the impaired self by talking more about self-activation in terms of decorating his home. He said he wanted to dazzle people with it.

I brought up the fact that it must have been so painful to look at the conflict with his parents in the prior session that he had soothed the pain by avoiding it. He went back to describing his father as being always demanding, never satisfied, so that he had to manage him. His mother was inscrutable, unresponsive, and deeply selfish. I again interpreted that he actually had given up his sense of self and decided to manage his parents by impressing them even before he started school.

He replied: "The tales from my family of my friendliness had stopped by age three or four. I sought my father's approval and then hated him. I don't like to see him as self-centered." I asked why he closed the door on his father but still sought his approval. He replied: "I thought Father was more accessible than Mother. Even now, when Mother visits, I control the action, so I don't have to connect."

By the next session, his mother and sister had visited him, and he reported being frustrated, annoyed, and just wanting to get away and be by himself, and he seemed depressed. He reported compliant response to his mother's coldness, and I suggested that he had difficulty seeing her as she is in reality. He replied: "You make it sound like she's bad. It's wrong to think I should get even, it's not her fault. Can't be mean to her. Had fantasies of Mother dying in a car accident."

I interpreted that he protected himself against the disappointment and the anger at his mother by distancing, playing the role of a parent, at the cost of his sense of self and isolation. He replied: "Mother does things to have a firm control over me. She doesn't self-activate, because of its effect on others. She is a caricature. Her first act on entering my house was to clean the dirty toilets. There is no point in confronting her."

I asked where the idea of being her parent to deal with disappointment came from. He responded: "Her mother was totally dependent on her. My mother was the sober one—had to take care of everybody, and I had to take care of her. I had been Grandmother's favorite and took care of her. With Mother, I kept trying, but there was nobody there. Nothing was good enough or right enough."

I interpreted that he gave up his effort to communicate, to deal with the depression and disappointments, and distanced himself and became a parent.

In the last session, he talked about having played an audiotape for his mother to torture her. Then he raised the question: "How do you draw the line with people between being selfish and doing everything for them?" He continued: "I provide a setting for my mother to visit and then I want to run away. I'm afraid of their demands. I wish I weren't so threatened. I define myself in other people's eyes by my accomplishments. I show off to get a response, but it's not really me. At work I support myself to get what I want. With Mother, all I want is to get even."

Sixth Month

Defenses Against Acting-Out Relationship Interpreted, Leading to Aloneness

He began the first session talking about his impending vacation. He said he wanted to walk around in the outfit of a priest as a way to get the attention of others, which I interpreted as a reflection of his exhibitionistic defensive game.

He reported that a male friend had called to ask him out to dinner. "Why can't I do that? I start and I want to, and then I get afraid that I'll have to deal with the separateness. My sense of self only seems to exist when I am alone." I interpreted that he puts impossible perfect standards on others and devalues them, rejects them, to protect against his anxiety about self-activation in a relationship. "I'm so anxious about their liking me, I say to myself that I don't care about it and then I figure out what I want from them." I interpreted that he imposes an artificial figuring-out eye over a feeling that there is no eye. He replied: "I feel so alone. I felt so alone that I put on the priest's collar and went out to dinner to drink."

Seventh Month

Sustained Interpretation of "Game" Defense Leads to Deepening of Affect and Patient Agrees to Come Twice a Week

Our vacations occupied much of the sixth month. During his vacation he attended his 25th class reunion. At the reunion, he said he felt they were all judging him, but then he realized it was himself. However, he was unable to activate himself. "I couldn't force myself to talk to people."

I interpreted that since he had had relationships with these people, the reunion involved activating himself and brought with it the pain of rejection, and so he had to defend by avoidance. He continued: "My four years in college were a performance to get *A*'s to deal with the fear of being rejected rather than self-activation. That's my whole life. I told myself there was no real me." I interpreted that this was a way of soothing how painful it was to focus on the vulnerability associated with the real self.

He then reported that he was having increasing urges to do what he wanted; in other words, to focus on self-activation. I suggested that his track record showed that he had the strength to do it, that it was better to do it later than never, and that it was what could lead him out of this present trap. However, it did involve trying to contain, face, and deal with the painful feelings that emerged.

In the next session, he reported having investigated a new job and, at the same time, feeling this attacking voice in his head. He then went on to say that he had shown some friends his house, and although they had responded very well, that did not make a relationship. I agreed, and interpreted that it was a game in which he shows them how wonderful his house is and they respond, but he remains detached.

He replied: "At school I kept figuring out how to con the teacher in order to get good grades. I really wanted to read what I wanted, but I did the other. I tried to do some reading of what I wanted on the side. It was the closest I came to having a sense of self. I had a flash, over the weekend, of wanting to call someone, but I define myself so much by what others think. Should I rely on these bursts or are they escapes?" I interpreted that these bursts of self-activation are only one part of the sense of self that he had had to forgo in order to protect himself by focusing on others, and that he had ended up on the treadmill of workaholism and drinking, which drowned his sense of self. He replied, "I was very outgoing until I was about three when family tales report that my spontaneity stopped. Mother used me to show off—I was a precocious reader." I asked whether this was how he learned to substitute showing off for relationships.

In the next session, the patient again reported more self-activation, saying that he had invited friends to his home, socialized, and enjoyed it, but when they left, felt alone and nostalgic (the triad in action). I emphasized that he was acknowledging the pleasure of relationships, and then the feeling of loss recurred, and that perhaps he had to deny his need for relationships in order to deal with the vulnerability of feelings of loss. He continued: "I feel I'd be judged by others and couldn't control it. To relate is to give up something important—to control what people think of you, otherwise they would find out what you are and hate you."

More memories emerged: "I was to be a showpiece for Mother, to make up for her marrying beneath her. Her mother was an alcoholic and her father died when she was very young, and I did perform. I got all *A*'s. Mother was the strong, the cool one. She never acknowledged my grades. No matter what you did, it was never good enough, and at the same time, I loved both reading and playing the piano."

In this session, he asked: "How did I get to where I am, to being just a performer and an achiever? It's such a waste. I can remember in school wanting to be a doctor." At this point, he began to cry for the first time as the affect broke through.

He continued: "I wanted to have relationships with people, but I had to be an overachiever. Then I drifted into my present work and started to make a lot of money." I suggested that his self-activation and idealism had been sacrificed to the achiever. He said, "The achiever protects me from my parents' attacks."

Since a lot of his denial had been overcome, here I raised the possibility of his coming twice a week rather than once a week, to which he agreed.

He began this session reporting being angry and disappointed in me for not backing his wish to be a doctor, and that this put him back on the achievement track. I suggested that when I did not respond in the way he felt he needed, he would become disappointed and angry and had to soothe his feelings by distancing himself.

He said: "Father liked the dog more than me. I tried to make myself perfect in every way, but they didn't like me. I hated my brother. I wanted to be a doctor in college, but it disappeared. In college I couldn't make friends. I was afraid they would find out what I was like and reject me, and my homosexuality was involved. A fear I wouldn't live up to their expectations. I was disappointing him."

Eighth Month

Momentum Deepens Memories with Affect of Origin of Game to Defend Against Loss of Grandiose Self

He began with a dream: "In my apartment—full of empty rooms I hadn't seen before, what could I do with all that space? Then I was in an Italian town with my grandmother—a woman was astride a man, killing him, hitting him. He got up and hit back, and then I told my father about the dream." *Free association*: "I think I had the dream so I'd have something to tell you. This image of a woman attacking me in the night, stabbing me. I wish sex was never an issue. My grandmother was as selfish as my mother, but she indulged me, and she was more expressive and outgoing than my mother. My mother was very disapproving. I liked my grandmother, she praised me. I could do no wrong. The first year, I was alone with my grandmother and my mother, my father was away at war, and he came back when I was three."

In the next session, he did not return to this theme, but defended by talking about his fear of being alone in his apartment. "Why can't I stay home at night?" I interpreted that it would reinforce his loneliness and the need to face his feeling about himself.

He said: "I have to keep busy. When I am alone, I feel there isn't any me—there's nobody there. My grandmother and mother ganged up on me and made me into a queer. I was outgoing with them. My grandmother idealized me and I felt wonderful. My brother was born a year after Father returned. Father didn't think I was wonderful." I interpreted that it was in that year that he had lost his sense of being special and unique and had tried to recapture it later by playing the achievement game and getting admiration, and at the same time protecting himself against feelings of loss.

In the next session, he reported that the funeral of a friend's mother had brought back thoughts about his own mother—sadness about the lack of communication. He told how he had disappointed his father and how he felt guilty, and he said that it was not their fault because they had problems. "I am as sorry for them as I am for myself." I interpreted that it was so painful to explore this that he avoids exploration as a way of dealing with his guilt. I explained that the purpose of exploration is not to assess blame, but to try to resolve his difficulties with himself and his relationship with others.

He then returned to that early period before his father returned: "I was spontaneous and outgoing and aggressive." I interpreted that there were two traumas to his sense of self—his father's return with a negative attitude toward him and the birth of his brother. He replied, "I must have thought it was my fault." I interpreted that his father's envy of his relationship with his mother and his father's passivity focused on the patient's homosexuality. He replied, "So I hid my feminine actions and I hid being spontaneous and I had it buried in loss and disappointment and compensated by mastering the achievement game."

Working on his impaired self and the abandonment depression triggered the defensive part of the triad. He began the next session by defensively saying that "all that stuff" brought up in the last session was very academic. I interpreted the triad: it was so painful for him to look at his feelings of loss and disappointment that he defended against the feelings associated with it by detaching and intellectualizing.

He returned to the theme: "I feel ashamed and hurt and rejected by Father's rejection—calling me a girl. I rebelled and buried my real self. I still wanted his affection. I hated my brother, the dog, anybody who got it. I tried to embarrass my father. I was the bad seed. It was terrible, but I enjoyed it. On the other hand, I also liked Father, but he wouldn't like me, so I got even."

Comment

After eight months, the vicissitudes of the triad were illustrated—interpretation of defense leading to the abandonment depression and impaired self, which led again to defense, which was again interpreted.

Ninth Month

Transference Interpretation Deepens Analysis of Vulnerability of Impaired Self

After a visit home, he reported that his parents were always judging and criticizing each other: "In New York City, I'm isolated, but I'm protected." I interpreted that a relationship with others leads only to disappointment and rejection, but that he still wished to relate. He replied: "I ought to be able to enjoy people as they are, but it all ends in sex, death, and annihilation. People will expect me to have a self and drop me when they realize there is no self—be disappointed. How did I survive these pressures?"

I interpreted that he did so by giving up his sense of self because of disappointment, and also by giving up real relationships and substituting the achiever and performer. He replied, "It's like saying you can't touch me."

The focus of his impaired self led to his description of a defensive dream in the next session. "My parents were in a retirement home. My father was dying. Everyone was very calm. My grandmother and mother were there, and I just sat there." *Free association*: "The dream was nice."

I interpreted that the dream was a reunion defense to deal with the disappointment expressed in the prior session. He had experienced more feeling and felt like a fish out of water when relying on feelings. He replied, "I play the same game with you as with others. Perform for approval."

I interpreted the transference acting out: He had the same anxiety with me as he did with others. If he were to open up, he would experience rejection of the inner monster, and so he defends by attempting to get approval by playing the game, but in doing so, he just digs the hole deeper. The dream expressed his wish to recapture the special self he felt with his grandmother, which he had lost. He said, "I not only lost center stage with my grandmother and my mother, but I also had to make my father feel better as well."

He reported showing some photos he had taken to a friend. His friend's response was very positive, but the patient devalued his remark. I interpreted that he was so sensitive to rejection in relationships that he protected his vulnerability by devaluing and being cynical about his friend's remark.

He said, "The last thing I do is admit that these sessions influence me." I pointed out that he was doing to me exactly what he did to his friend. He was devaluing what goes on in order to avoid the pain of focusing on himself in the relationship to protect against disappointment.

This interpretation of transference acting out evidently got to him because he "forgot" the next session. In the following session, he responded: "I forgot. I was working, and I wasn't aware what made me forget. I often can be direct with friends, and sometimes I can speak about myself."

I interpreted that I suspected that he forgot to deal with how uncomfortable it was to experience those feelings. I asked what had happened to his feeling about being rejected by his father and having to be an extension of him and his mother. He said: "With my parents, it was total rejection or total absorption by them, but with friends I don't feel this. I relate to my friends more in a real way; I want something from them, not from my parents."

In the next session, he reported: "When the others demand, I feel smothered. I want to run away or analyze them. I should try to stay with myself."

In the next session, he focused on the negative voice that tells him that he does not deserve to feel good about himself or with others, that when he feels good, it is fake, to get away from being depressed. The voice says, "You don't have a self and are stupid." He reported being at a party where he felt panic that he would look like a fool and be rejected.

In the last session, the patient reported: **"I get more ideas when I focus on myself** than on others. **I did so and did well and felt positive about myself,** and then I felt like drinking (this triggers the triad). When I focus on myself, it brings with it feelings of loss, rejection, being on thin ice, seeing the other person as thinking, 'This is not what I expect from you.'"

I interpreted the triad: If he focuses on himself, he will be rejected. He projects this inner thought on others to deal with it, but otherwise silences it by being a workaholic and drinking. He replied: "I want to stop going out to dinner and drinking every night. It avoids being myself and feeling a need for others. In school, when I knew I couldn't succeed, I played with the situation and always did well." I suggested that this was the same game as that he played with his parents. He replied, "Since I felt they wouldn't like me no matter what I did, it was a relief to not want to be liked, so I could play the game." I interpreted that it was too risky to even take a chance.

Tenth Month

Analysis of Fear of Intimacy

The patient reported a dream: "I was seeing a woman psychiatrist, but there was a man there who was dangerous." *Free association*: "The man in the dream was you. You're helping me get better by helping me to focus on myself, so you are a threat. I have to get rid of you. My game of performance doesn't work here. **I'm focusing more on myself at work.** Worrying less about others. I deliberately behave in a way not to get approval in order to get it."

Then he sighed and asked, "How do you stand listening to this all day?" I pointed out how harsh his attitude was toward his own feelings. He responded: "I feel sorry for myself. I want to share, but I can't focus on myself to put myself on the line. For example, you'll recall my former boss. If he really knew me, he wouldn't like me. If a person didn't reject me, I would think he was pretty stupid."

I suggested that he seemed to recognize only two options, rejection or isolation from others, but also that these feelings were related to how he feels about himself. He defends against these negative feelings about himself by putting them on others. He responded, "We have been through all that." I suggested that being through all that was painful, and that this was his way of defending against it by dismissing it.

He continued: "Grandmother made me feel okay, but not my father. My father needed me to be an extension of his self. It was my fault that I didn't fit it. Father was the center of everything so I am nothing. I solved the whole thing by putting it in the closet and becoming an achiever."

He reported having dinner with a colleague, throughout which he analyzed him. I suggested that perhaps he had been upset by the prior session and had soothed it by stepping into the old role with the friend. He replied, "I wasn't that upset." I again pointed out his denial, and he sighed deeply, as if he were carrying a big burden. I interpreted that perhaps he sees me as demanding that he forgo this role and look at his impaired self.

He said: "I am afraid of others. I'm afraid they will grab me. Or am I afraid of myself, that I will explode? The fear is quasi-sexual. A man poked my arm and I felt fear and wanted to run away and scream. It's as if he will do something sexual to me. The fear does not occur if I know the man is homosexual. I also have this fear with you. Could I have been sexually abused as a child? I remember being in bed with my aunt, but nothing more."

In the next session, he first was angry at himself for looking for someone else to blame. I pointed out that he no sooner focuses on himself than he turns around and attacks it. He then recalled a sexual incident with a priest. He had confessed masturbating, and the priest asked him to remain after his confession. The priest then asked him to take his pants down. He complied, but the priest did nothing, which disappointed him. He said, "I am afraid of being touched by anybody I know. My parents and the priest distorted the role to gratify themselves, like kids."

I interpreted that when he was a child, the people in power coerced him to give up himself. He replied: "That's why I have sex with strangers. It doesn't involve me. The closer the other person comes, the more I feel smothered, the more I need distance." This awareness activated the triad, and in the next two sessions, he retreated to defense, talking about work and his disappointment in a girlfriend from high school. In the following session, he talked about being terrified at looking at female nudes: "A fear, revulsion at the pubic area." He then discussed his hobby of making slides of paintings and projecting them, and how, whenever he does so, he is barraged by a constant attack, his mother's voice asking why he is doing it. "As soon as I have a creative impulse, want to do something, there is this attack [the triad again]. I have this picture of my mother, which I want to blow up, in which she looks like a cat. The attacking voice says, 'I don't want you to do anything but be there for me.' It's really my father more than my mother. I have this wish to be cuddled by a homosexual man."

When I interpreted that he had a wish for closeness, tears came to his eyes. He said: "I wish there were no sex, it gets in the way. I saw an attractive woman and the voice said, 'You don't deserve to feel that.'" The patient looked sad. He said, "I don't call people by their first names."

I suggested that this perhaps was too intimate, that either there is no self or everything is an extension of the self.

Eleventh Month

The Game as Defense Against Feelings of Hopelessness and Helplessness

At the first session after my vacation, he began again in defense, intellectualizing about work, as well as his coming vacation in four weeks.

He missed the next two sessions, ostensibly because of his work. In the next session, he focused on what he might want to do: "I always wanted to be a doctor and a psychiatrist. In the eighth grade, I read *Interpretation of Dreams*. My mother called it filth and took it away. At age 10, I had my appendix out. Since I wanted to be a doctor, I liked the hospital and people were nice to me. I did it all by myself; Mother and Father were called only after I was in the hospital. My father liked the dog more than me, and I had to compete for Mother's attention, but never got it."

He then returned to the fact that with his grandmother and mother, he was the only child and the center of attention, and to the loss he experienced when his father returned and his brother was born.

In the next session, he complained bitterly about the change in the atmosphere at his work, which in a way resembled the disappointment he had experienced at the age of three. He had been doing very well and was a favorite at work before he went away, and when he came back, it had all changed. Now, he said, he must look for another job.

I used this as an opportunity to point out that the reason he was in this situation was his difficulty in focusing on himself, and that if he wanted to change the external, it would be vital to be able to resolve this difficulty because that was the agency for change. He replied, "I remember being special to my grandmother without having to do anything for it."

I interpreted that he had lost this and repaired it with the game of being an achiever. He replied: "I saw relationship as competition, but couldn't connect with my parents no matter what and get their acknowledgment, but I could get it from teachers by doing well."

I interpreted, again, that he gave up his self with the parents because he felt the situation was hopeless. He still feared that if he were to open himself up in a relationship, he would be exposed to hopelessness. He replied: "I didn't exist for them. They didn't like who I was. If your mother doesn't like you, how can anyone else like you?"

In the next session, he again asked: "What do I want to do? I think of giving a party, but feel the others will reject me for being a faggot. My peers made fun of me for being a sissy. Father wanted me to be a hunter and fisher, and I wanted to see movies, like *It's a Woman's World*. Did I do it to get back at him for rejecting me? He wanted me to be a man and rejected me. I'll get even by being the opposite. I wouldn't have been such a sissy if they hadn't teased me. Wouldn't it have been a tragedy if my whole life had revolved around this?"

I interpreted that the tragedy was that he sacrificed himself to revenge. I told him that the vengeful façade works, but the painful self persists, as seen in his reaction to giving the party and in his workaholism, drinking, and isolation. He continued: "I'm happiest when I can be the devil's advocate, getting even with the parents. If I were not getting even, why would I be homosexual? My mother wanted me to be her little boy. If I'm like a girl, I can't be her little boy. I escaped from being what Mother wanted."

I interpreted that he used his sense of self as a vehicle to express his anger, and also probably to deal with the feeling of helplessness with his mother. He replied, "I was always afraid that what I wanted would be taken away."

I interpreted that the fantasy was a defense against exploring the painful self that existed under his revengeful self. He asked, "What will happen?"

I interpreted that he was afraid of losing again if he were to explore that devil's advocate self. He said, "I can't control people's leaving."

I said, "No, but you can repair it. You get stuck in the effort to repair." He said, "The devil's advocate combats the negative voice."

In the last session of the month, he was in defense, which I interpreted as a reaction to the prior session. He said: "No, it's not just the last session. Since the last session, I've had two rejections at work and my mother's visit, the three of them together cut off all feelings." He then reported a dream, in which his mother had a bald spot on top of her head. *Free association*: "Mother is just like me. I was with her. I wanted to punish her by forcing her to do what I wanted, which is the revenge, but I tried to treat her as a person rather than as a target for revenge."

Comment

In the last three months, the patient explored more deeply his narcissistic vulnerability and his defenses against it, particularly the closet narcissistic defense. He now applied it to the treatment—performing for my admiration. I continued to interpret the defenses of the triad, which brings him back to the impaired self, and the abandonment depression, specifically his feeling of hopelessness.

Twelfth Month

Loneliness and Losing His Job

The patient reported that he was depressed after the family visit. His mother was impenetrable and cut him off, but he still kept trying with her. He said that it made him sad and he sought comfort in crowds at bars. After the visit, he went out cruising and drinking. He then said that he was going to try to write, to do what he wants to do. "I can't just go along at the job. I'm disappointed at how I've been treated, and I have to look out for myself."

There followed a three-week business trip overseas, which continued the same theme of isolation, difficulty with being close to his friends, and turning to drinking and sexual acting out. However, for the first time, he identified feeling lonely: "I felt so lonely I couldn't stand it." He then said he had been asked to leave his job by the end of the year. I offered my condolences and he discussed some tentative plans. He was relieved, he said, because he disliked the job, and even looked forward to other opportunities. However, he was very anxious about his financial future, although he had more than enough money.

In the next session, he returned to the feeling of loneliness. I interpreted that his difficulty in focusing on himself had come to the fore and brought on this extreme feeling of loneliness, which he tended to soothe by drinking and sexual acting out, and, therefore, they were not available in the interviews. I suggested that he would have to control these activities to be able to work on them in treatment. In the last session of the month, in defense he reported showing a woman friend his art objects in order to receive her approval; he felt that he was doing this because in this way he gets the approval without having to put himself on the line.

Thirteenth Month

Interpretation of Game and Detachment Defenses Against Hopelessness

As the patient made efforts to control his defenses, the underlying anxiety and intense loneliness and isolation continued to surface (the triad of the disorders of the self). He reported, "This weekend I panicked. I felt so alone at the thought of what will happen to me."

This took place in the context of his losing his job. I interpreted that he must discriminate between the external problem, which is what to do about his life now that he is losing a job, and the internal problem, which is that focusing on himself interrupts the focus on others and reinforces anxiety about managing himself on his own.

He responded, "I've found a couple of book topics regarding my work that I want to write about." He then returned to the terrible feeling of panic and aloneness he experienced when a friend left his apartment: "I have nothing. I can't say goodbye to people. I say to them, 'See you later.' When I have money to travel, then I can always see people again. I can't bear the idea that I can't return to a place.

I have this urge to make everything familiar. I'm afraid I'll end up as a bum with nobody wanting me." He elaborated on his separation anxiety: "I left graduate school after the first year. I had a panic that I would not be the best and, therefore, I would be rejected, and even so, it wasn't me. I joined the Peace Corps for two years. On my return, I got an offer of a job and I rejected it." He then reported that he had decided to activate himself at work and to challenge the board's right to fire him; he became obsessed with the idea, and he began to feel high and all revved up.

I interpreted that although externally this might be a good thing, internally it sounded as though he were back in a narcissistic game. He replied: "But I'm still all alone, afraid to be close to people. When somebody, a man, gets closer to me, I want to find fault with him. If he gets to know what I'm like, he'll reject me. My challenge is supporting myself. It's very hard to persist, hard to do. I need a cover under which to hide. I have to drink or eat or go to a movie. I can't keep myself out there. I want to be accepted by others, not have to negotiate for myself."

I interpreted that his friend's rejection was a repetition of what had happened to him as a child when his father returned from the war and he felt rejected by his parents and had lost his loving and adoring grandmother. I said that he had to wall himself off, detach from feeling, to deal with the feelings of loss and the anxiety about focusing on himself and to protect himself against rejection.

In the next session, he mentioned that he was avoiding writing to a friend. "I feel too exposed and would be disappointed in him."

I interpreted his vulnerability to rejection whenever he attempts to activate himself with another. He replied: "My grandmother thought I was wonderful. Then I lost it with my parents."

I suggested that his grandmother's "wonderful" was not a response to him as an individual, but rather an effort to idealize him, and then when his parents came along, they attacked him. The underlying sense was that there was no external object that could respond with appropriate acknowledgment of his real self. He said: "My main thing is to get others to say I'm okay. If I focus on myself, I will be punished and fail."

I interpreted the triad: if he activates himself, the parents attack.

In other words, he lost his grandiose self with the grandmother and then his real self was attacked. He said: "My success was very important to my mother. She used it for her purposes, but she disappointed me. I wanted her to be nice to me and take care of me, but she only thinks about herself."

In the next session, he again focused on how he dealt with separation anxiety and feelings of loss by saying he had had a visitor to his apartment. After the visitor's departure, to recapture his presence, he kept focusing on a note the visitor had left him. He continued, "My mother was not interested in me, but was interested in herself."

I again interpreted the triad: he managed his depression, anger, and disappointment with the mother's lack of acknowledgment by disconnecting feeling and entering a narcissistic game at the cost of isolation of his self, substituting being admired for emotional connection and sharing, and this problem in relationships was similar to the problems with self-activation. He puts his real self in the closet because it brings on the feelings of loss, and he attempts to recapture the grandiose self by playing the narcissistic game.

In the next session, he reported writing to his friend, and then becoming very depressed and going out to drink and cruise (the triad again). He reported: "I had expressed myself fully, whether he accepted or rejected me. I'm enraged at my company for firing me. I started to write. I'm full of memories, but how will I say it and express it?"

He then reported: "I'm depressed and inadequate, nothing special about me." In other words, he expressed his feelings of loss of the grandiosity.

I interpreted that this feeling was a replay of the past in his head and that the way to deal with it was to do so in sessions rather than through drinking and cruising. He described the triad: **"I spent three hours writing what I wanted to say; in other words, focusing on myself, not others.** Then I attacked it, got cynical, had no self-confidence, scared to focus on myself. What if they don't like it?"

In the next session, **he reported being at a meeting where he spoke up. "I would never have done that before."** Then he again went out to visit bars, this time to not be alone.

I again interpreted the triad: when he activates himself, he feels depression and the loss of the feelings of grandiosity and specialness, and he goes out to defend against these feelings of loss. He replied: "The bar search is for a series of potential audiences and to make them like me."

I interpreted, "As you were able to do as a child with your grandmother." This led the patient deeper in the next session. He reported: "I was out over the weekend drinking and cruising, and I heard this attacking voice, my father's voice, wanting me to be like him. I felt hopeless. I remember one time my father called the dog a bum for wanting sex. The dog was trying to be himself. My father attacked, with cold contempt, both the dog and me."

I again interpreted his efforts on the previous weekend, in trying to activate himself, had led to the father's attacking voice, and so he drank and cruised to quiet it. He replied, "I had suicidal thoughts and I was very depressed."

I again asserted that if he could control the drinking and cruising, then perhaps he could work through the hopelessness here. He reported: "To not be an extension of my father would be disloyal, the coldness similar to that of Mother. I can't connect with her, something not there, didn't get to that person, but it's your fault. I feel it's not my fault; let me alone."

The patient was weeping. "I cried and told my parents that they didn't love me. Father said, 'Of course, we do. You're our oldest son.' In other words, the only reason they loved me was because I was their son, not because I was who I am. So it was hopeless to connect. I dislike you for doing the same thing as my father, fitting me into your scientific theory. I have to do what you want. I don't want to do what you want."

I interpreted that this latter feeling seemed to spring from his sense that no one could be interested in him. It all has to be manipulation. I pointed out that I have no personal stake, that I'm responding to his difficulty and his vulnerability, and how he uses that is up to him. I then suggested that this means allowing a connection with me and facing the hopelessness about the voice of his father. The patient asked, "What is me?"

In the next session, he continued: "Life consists of people manipulating to get what they want. I can't believe anybody could be interested in me. My mother's siblings and their children are all ne'er-do-wells and she takes enormous pride in my success. I thought my father's disgust was with sex; I now realize it was with me for being me. I had a peculiar experience. I was reading, interested in it, and I heard this voice say, 'Go jerk off.'"

I interpreted that activating his self by reading created anxiety that he wanted to soothe by masturbation. He replied: "I hate being alone, because I can't decide what I want to do. And then I have to drink and cruise."

I interpreted that the workaholism avoids self-activation, which is the linchpin of the narcissistic game.

Comment

In the past two months, the expression of the triad has become clearer and clearer, and the interpretations of the defenses have led the patient deeper into the abandonment depression and toward the genetic origins of his impaired self and the depression and the attendant feelings of hopelessness.

Fourteenth Month

Exquisite Vulnerability of Wish for Closeness and Defenses Against It

In the next interview, he reported reacting to my comments about connection as a demand: "I'm upset by your saying that I have to connect with you. You're demanding something of me, fitting me into a category of yours, and if I don't, I will disappoint you. I have to be an extension of you." He then intellectualized, "Before, I wanted to be interesting and make you like me, and now I'm disappointed."

I interpreted that he had experienced my comment about connection as a demand due to his extreme vulnerability, and that when he, as a child, had moved from the admiring grandmother to the parents who wanted him to be an extension of them, he buried his self and his connection with others to deal with the painful affect and substituted the narcissistic game. In psychotherapy, he has had to face these buried feelings of vulnerability in order to recapture his real self and to find acknowledgment of his real self, not admiration of his grandiose self. He replied, "I'm beginning to feel that my job isn't everything."

In the next session, he reported retreating to defense by drinking and cruising: "I did it deliberately to make you angry, so that you would kick me out and so I could drive you away."

I interpreted that, in the prior session, he had opened up his wish for closeness (i.e., self-activation), and with it his exquisite vulnerability and loneliness (abandonment depression), and that he had acted out to create distance and reestablish inner equilibrium (defense) (the triad). He responded: "After the session, I wrote my job resumé, this time expressing myself, not just trying to please. I want to make you into a negative, punishing voice."

I interpreted that he protected himself against the vulnerability by creating distance and then externalizing an internal negative voice. He said, "It's true, you do acknowledge me, but not in the way my grandmother did. Why do I have to be so dependent on others?"

I replied, "Because evidently it's too painful to focus on yourself. It blends right into the negative voice." He said: "I have to convince myself that if I do focus on myself, bad things won't happen, I won't be punished. The voice is total, absolute, complete, very depressing, but I can rebel. I can tell you to drop dead and then rebel. The voice calls me a fag."

In the next session, he reported two dreams of disaster. In one, a doctor told him that he had AIDS, and in the other, a giant ocean liner was tumbling toward his office building. *Free association:* "My position in life is being threatened."

I interpreted that if he focuses on himself, as he pointed out in the last session, the negative voice indicates cataclysm and death.

He returned to his resumé: "Shall I play the game or be truthful? The voice attacks everything I do." He then reported that he had been to the dentist and that the technician was pregnant, and the contact, he said, felt very nice. Then he had a fantasy of doing a painting of her being forcibly aborted.

I interpreted that the experience with the technician evoked feelings of closeness and connection of the first two years and then the feelings of loss, and that he handled them by this rebellious fantasy. He replied, "So what?"

In the next session, he reported that he was very depressed at seeing how some friends were able to activate themselves, which he could not do, and that he had feelings of loss and being all alone. However, he said, it was a demonstration that he could be with someone without being afraid of being taken over. A long silence followed, and then he reflected on his defenses. "I've been so unreal. Others are so in touch with their selves. In my need to not show, to keep removed and controlled, I isolate myself from people." He was now weeping. "Where do they get the courage to take chances?"

I questioned, "Why can't you? Why assume defeat?" He continued: "With my mother, there was no response to self-activation. The relationship was absolutely confining. Father wanted me to be an extension of him. Mother was weirder, wanted me to be hers, a possession. My maternal grandfather died when I was 12. Mother smothered me, showed me off." I suggested that with his mother there was no room for his own self-activation.

In the next session, he talked about worrying that if he were to write a book, it would be confining.

In interpreted that this anxiety seemed to be that if he were to commit himself to his work, as well as to relationships, it would be confining and restricting rather than fulfilling. He replied: "I never committed myself to what I wanted to do before. I envy intimacy and the life a friend of mine has. I volunteered for the Gay Men's Health Crisis clinic. I always thought doing for others was important, helping those who are less strong. As a kid, I was protected from my peer attackers by an older boy. He was poor, and he was good to me." At this point, the patient was crying. "I had a friend in the Peace Corps. People who like you for yourself, it's a wonderful feeling."

Fifteenth Month

Image of Impaired Self as Prostitute Emerges

The patient began the session by announcing that his long-planned six-week trip to visit the capitals of Europe and Asia would begin in two months, and that he would then write about it. This trip would come at a crucial time in the treatment, as he was allowing a relationship to develop and his vulnerability to be exposed. However, he had lost his job, and the trip was his effort to cope with the loss, so I decided not to intervene at the moment.

In the next session, the patient reported that he wanted to tell his superiors that he was going to be writing a book, rather than looking for another job, which they were paying him to do.

I asked him why he felt the need to tell them. He responded that it was his fear that if he did not toe the line, he would be abandoned. Then he talked about how he does not follow through even with his artistic ideas. I pointed out that he does not even investigate why he does not follow through. He replied, "I want to do three projects and can't decide, and then I end up doing something else."

I asked, "To avoid the attacking voice?" He sighed, and I pointed it out and asked if he were depressed. He replied, "There's an enormous pressure against activating myself."

I interpreted that it sounded like a rationalization about the difficulty of facing depression associated with activating himself. He replied: "Work takes care of it all. I don't have to focus on myself in work, and it provides me with a lot of money for the rest of my life."

In the next session, **he reported an orgy of self-activation—writing, buying a computer, working on his art—and how, although the attacking voices appeared, he can really do what he wants to do.** He seemed quite elated that he had enough money to live, and he even went to the gym.

In the next session, he returned to feeling exposed, with no sense of self with others. He said that he was with a couple and enjoyed their company, but that he could only take so much and had to be alone to repair it. "I can't be me, just like with my father. I never wanted a female therapist because of my mother, who was so controlling and manipulative."

I interpreted that his mother had ended up being the center because of the loss of his grandmother, and that here with me, his fear of being an extension of his father was rationalized as my wanting him to fit into my therapeutic scheme rather than my supporting his self-activation.

In the next session, he reported his anger at being rejected by the company and that he had gone out and picked up a man for sex: "It's all a game to show I'm in control." He did this in order to deal with the painful feelings about himself, a sense of helplessness with regard to the company. He said: "Rejection by the company signals to others that I'm bad and at fault, even though I'm glad to get out. I don't like to accept homosexuality. I wish I weren't sexual at all, like a kid. I don't feel sex with men I like."

I pointed out, "Or with men with whom you have sexual relationships." He continued: "I can't stand to be homosexual, not fair, feels unnatural, can't stand not being perfect, being dysfunctional."

In the next session, he reported going to a meeting at the Gay Men's Health Crisis clinic, where he spoke up. He said, "I felt like I wanted to talk to people as I did as a child." And then, he said, he felt exposed and naked and retreated and the voice attacked him. He turned to me and asked, "Will it go away?" I said I wondered why he turned to me rather than investigate this voice.

In the next session, in a very dramatic form, his impaired real self emerged in the following dream. "There's this Indian woman in a sari, then a prostitute, very sick, has AIDS and is trying to get a customer, and I thought how pathetic." *Free association*: "That person was me, trying to get people to like me, but it's a hopeless task as no one would. Before this session, I stopped cruising and had dinner alone at an Indian restaurant."

I pointed out that it seemed at the moment that it was too painful to stay with this impaired self here, but that the dream was the self feeling that the game defends him against. He replied: "With my father, there was nothing wrong with me except me. I have to be an extension of them—no one out there will acknowledge me. My company now reinforces it. I can't cure it because of you. I can't be like them. I can't put on a mask, but what do you do?"

I asked why he felt so helpless. He replied: "I was so dependent on Mother, who was so frugal. I would deny the dependence and figure out how to get what I wanted from them. I had a lifelong daydream of someone dying and leaving me all the money so I could be myself."

I interpreted this as a fantasy of his mother's acknowledging him so he could be himself. He said: "My mother liked to bake cookies. I'd take them and hide them and not share them."

In the next session, he reported a dream in which there was a sexual acting out. *Free association*: "I'm not what my parents want me to be and there's no way to remedy that. Mother wants me to be something and will smother me, so I'll be the opposite. Instead of being a little boy and smothered, I'll be a little girl. Mother was so censorious."

I interpreted that after the prior session, he was feeling angry and smothered, and rather than act out as he had before to defend, he controlled the acting out as a revenge, and it was expressed in the dream. He replied, "Where do I go from here?" I again asked why he felt so helpless. In the next session, in reporting a contact with a new friend, an older man, his vulnerability and anxiety rose. "I felt he wanted to take over my freshness and innocence. I wanted to run and hide. He sees my façade, not me—he takes certain things away from me. Every human relationship is predatory."

I interpreted this as a projection of the internal voices, which overwhelm his external reality, and pointed out that his attitude toward them was important. Are the voices a projection or reality?

In the next session, **he reported that he had written for one hour and that he has to get to the point where it is natural, like dancing.** "Why can't I do what I want to? I feel so selfish. Feeling myself brings on thoughts of killing my brother or being an extension of my parents."

Sixteenth Month

Fear of Engulfment of Self in Transference and Other Relationships

The patient continued: "The voice attacks me at every turn. Whenever I feel I've won, I'm attacked by the voice [the triad]. It never stops. I challenged it all day by painting. And then I went out and drank and started to cruise around. I was enjoying the painting and then I felt, is this all there is?"

I interpreted the difference between grandiosity and real-self–satisfaction, that when he activates his real self, he feels the loss of his sense of grandiosity, and through the grandiosity, he must be perfect in all his actions, as well as in relationships, so that real-self–satisfaction represents a feeling of loss. He replied: "I have to get away from myself. The drinking is self-obliteration, and the sex also."

I then interpreted the triad: he focused and supported himself and then he joined the voices and attacked himself. He replied: "I have to obliterate myself perfectly. After, I feel it was a terrible waste."

He began the next session by offering me a copy of a videotape of the performer Divine in *Pink Flamingo*, saying that few copies were available and these were very hard to obtain. I acknowledged his wish to share this with me, but said I felt it was most important for his treatment to understand why he wanted me to have it and that it would be inappropriate to his treatment to take it. I explored his reaction to my turning it down, but he denied any disappointment.

He continued: "I'm doing my artwork, and the voice is attacking me every step of the way, but I force myself. I spent the weekend with my sister and her family, and I felt closed out of something wonderful. Later, I thought of giving up my apartment and living in the country and writing my book. Then a neighbor came to my apartment. I was frightened and afterwards I cruised. But I like people and I would be very lonely in the country."

He then reported two dreams. In the first: "I was climbing a stairway to a ladder to see something, and it got smaller and thinner, and I couldn't take it any longer. I felt claustrophobic and slid down." In the second dream: "I was in a convertible, entering a tunnel. Huge fans fell in slow motion. I had to be careful. At the other end, I couldn't dodge and had to go straight through. Then I was in a hospital bed next to an old woman. A visitor was saying, 'Why don't you talk to her?' Then I was looking for contact lenses that belonged to the cleaning woman, and I took them to her." *Free association*: "The climbing and going through the tunnel were being myself. I didn't want to be. The top of the ladder and things falling down were the voices trying to stop me. Today I felt less anxious and there was less voice attacking me. I felt more adult about—I felt that you're supporting me and that I'm changing."

I interpreted that the dream was about treatment, and that if he activates himself and his relationship with me goes well, he will feel suffocated and have to climb down. Giving up the game and relating to me without it evokes his anxiety about being an extension of me as a symbol of his mother in the dream.

In the next session, he responded to the interpretation, saying: "I want your approval. I wasn't disappointed about your not taking the tape because I ought to grow up. I wanted to show off for you, the same as the bar hopping. I want to be noticed and liked."

I interpreted that he did so to defend against his impaired, vulnerable self. "I have to be an extension of the other but I can't, so I fail."

I interpreted that, in other words, he loses his sense of self either way. And the drinking and cruising and workaholism are to keep these feelings buried. He responded: "But I like people. I'm longing for a relationship with others. I love Monet's painting where there's a perfect balance between the individual and the group, and they're all mature adults, integration, sex and nonsex. My brother tattled on me to my mother and I wanted him to die. When I was 10, I disliked a woman in line and I kicked her twice. It's egoism. Your self can get out of hand. I can't communicate, but I can't bear to be left. I desperately want connection. Makes me think of my grandmother."

I interpreted that it was either total connection as with his grandmother or no connection at all.

In the next session, he reported having taken a test for AIDS. "If I have it, I feel you will reject me."

I interpreted it as a stigmata of his impaired self. He said: "Why can't I stand to focus on myself? I was doing my thing around my house and felt enjoyment and calmness, and then I wanted to show off, wanted to attract people."

I interpreted that if he focuses on himself, he feels anxious and rejected, and then activates the game in order to soothe these feelings. He said, "If I support myself, I'm childish, selfish, and wrong."

I differentiated for him healthy and pathologic narcissism. He replied: "It's bad to be yourself, because you're not part of them. I hate my parents, so I play the game for them to admire me. The bar hopping had nothing to do with sex, just wanted them to like me. A neighbor expresses interest in me, and what happens? I wonder, what does he want? I feel claustrophobic, want to run away."

I interpreted this as a fear that his neighbor wanted him to be a part of him. I asked him why he had so much difficulty investigating this impaired self. "What's to investigate?" he asked. "The voice attacks me."

Again I pointed out that he accepts the perspective of the voice—that is, he is unable to relate and he cannot be part of his mother or his father, so it is hopeless. He replied: "I always had the sense that my parents could turn off the food. At college, I felt that if I didn't get *A*'s, I would be fired. I feel the same way at work. It's perform or be abandoned."

He mentioned his upcoming trip 10 days hence, pointing out that when he makes a trip alone, he feels more detached, more depressed. Having an objective helps, he said, but it also creates problems with focusing on himself and relationships with people. He had planned the trip to cope with his firm's rejection. We explored his various other alternatives, including the fact that he may have planned the trip as a resistance against his treatment. He said, "I want you to be my grandmother and admire me."

I interpreted that he vacillates between fearing that he has to be part of someone else and wishing to be part of someone else, as it was with his grandmother, and then playing the game to win admiration as a defense. He said: "I've had two contacts with people; both of them initiated anxiety and fear that they wanted something from me. A woman told me that I looked nice with my contact lenses, and I automatically pulled back; the same thing happened with a man who tried to help me with my art. I fear they want to take, extract something. I can't think I'm liked for myself."

SUMMARY

In 16 months, once a week for seven months and twice a week for nine months, the patient demonstrated clearly the triad of the disorders of the self: self-activation–pathologic affect–defense. The mirroring interpretations of the idealizing of the object to regulate the self enabled the patient to begin to form a therapeutic alliance, to control some of his acting out, and to begin to explore the pathologic affects associated with his impaired self. This led to another level of defense—the attacking voices and the feelings of hopelessness and helplessness if he focuses on his real self. These must be worked through before he can move deeper.

8

The Puppet on a String and the Whim of Iron

Mr. D., a short, obese, dark-haired, 50-year-old married businessman, came for psychotherapy after a heart attack with the following complaints.

CHIEF COMPLAINT

"I'm hanging on to a bad marriage because I'm afraid of being abandoned [he had been involved in codependent groups and conferences and had read several of my books]. I abdicated to my mother, and I have since abdicated to two wives. I have sexual trouble with intermittent impotence. I feel chronically depressed most of the time, lost, no identity or sense of self."

HISTORY

History of Present Illness

"When I was in my 30s, I was a heavy drinker, but except for an occasional glass, haven't drunk in the past 15 years [a claim to be viewed with caution]. Now I escape into being a workaholic, into sleep, and into overeating. Before my heart attack, I was 65 pounds overweight, and I since have taken off 40 pounds but I am still roughly 25 pounds overweight.

"I procrastinate when it comes to my responsibilities. I let things go, and then I try to manipulate. I don't pay bills. I allow my wife to overspend so that now I am in debt. I feel so frustrated about myself. I can remember as a youngster wanting to be a writer and wanting to be creative. I've been in marriage counseling for several years with my wife, but without much success.

"I have been married for 16 years. My wife is 44, suspicious, demanding, angry, critical. When she gets upset, she attacks my inadequacies. I feel hurt and withdraw, feeling she is not fair. Two years ago, she ordered me out of the house at knife point. She also drinks too much. My trouble is that I allow her to do these things. She is suspicious of my having affairs, which is not true."

Family History

The patient described his mother, now in her 80s, as extremely domineering, guilt evoking, and enmeshing, but very stingy and angry.

"She required me to toe the line at all times. If I didn't, she would beat me with sticks. I disliked her and fought with her until I was about five, then I gave in." The patient reported that he had trusted, admired, and respected his father and had a lot of fun with him. "He was optimistic—I did things with him." He died when the patient was 21, and the patient became very depressed and buried himself in work. The father, however, had been rather passive and went along with the mother's domination. He was a close friend, but he did not help the patient with his mother.

Personal History

"I battled with my mother and had rages during which I broke things until I was age four or five. An only child, I can remember that I couldn't wait for my father to come home. Years after that, I stopped fighting, and had no choice but to go along. While in grammar school, I was extremely unhappy at home; my mother raged at me. She raged at my father for not being around, for drinking. There's a possibility that he was an alcoholic. He was angry at her most of the time.

"In grammar school I was interested in debating and dramatics and had many friends. I then went to a prep school, and had the first glimpse of a sense of self. I was able to achieve academically by doing what I wanted. I got into debating and drama and it was the most fulfilled I've felt in my life. I felt like I wanted to be a contributor. I was playing a role that gave me satisfaction. I dated some but had no sexual relationships.

"Both parents wanted me to go into business, and though I wanted to be a writer, I went along with them and became a grind proving myself. For the first time, I got very good grades. I was president of the dramatic society, but I did resent the grind of study.

"In graduate school for an M.B.A., I had an enormous amount of anxiety, but I found a mentor who was a big help and I continued to be a grind. After graduation and while getting started, I got married, at age 23, but had great trouble with my wife. I saw a therapist, who told me that he thought she was psychotic and that I should divorce her. In the meantime, we had two children. I finally did divorce her. I married my present wife 16 years ago."

INTRAPSYCHIC STRUCTURE

The patient's intrapsychic structure consisted of a defensive, fused, grandiose-self–omnipotent-object unit, which consisted of an idealized omnipotent-fused-object representation that offered admiration to a grandiose-self–representation for fulfilling the expectations of the object representations by perfect performance. This was a brittle, fragile defensive structure based on a fantasy projected on the interactions with his mother, and underneath it was the most dominant, harsh, aggressive underlying fused unit with a severely harsh and attacking object representation and a self-representation of being inadequate, bad, fragmented, and empty, with an affect of fear of engulfment and abandonment depression, a lack of a sense of self or identity. The impaired real self was a dramatic factor in the difficulties in activating the self and taking responsibility for the self.

The triad operated as follows: self-activation was avoided and the abandonment depression was defended against by detachment of affect and intellectualization and by idealizing the object and complying with its expectations without any affect. The underlying motive for this theme was that if the patient performed perfectly, he would receive the admiration necessary to regulate his grandiose self. Real-self–activation led to abandonment depression.

CLINICAL IMPRESSION

The diagnosis of closet narcissistic personality disorder of the self seemed clear, with defenses of alcoholism, workaholism, obesity, detachment of affect, idealization of the object, and intellectualization. There was the possibility of a posttraumatic stress disorder as a result of physical abuse. There also were some indications of a good prognosis in his good relations with his father, his outside interests in writing and dramatics, and his high level of functioning. These were, however, counterbalanced by his two marriages to attacking women, which suggested both physical abuse as a child and an identification with the aggressor defense—that is, he was compelled to marry attacking women to externalize the internal attacking object representation. I suggested that he start once-a-week sessions.

PSYCHOTHERAPY

First Through Eighth Month

Interpretation of Defensive Focus on Object Leads to Real-Self–Activation, Affect, and Memories

In the first therapeutic session, he elaborated on the theme of focusing on the expectations of the object to defend against feelings of inadequacy of the self as follows: "I have a chronic sense of being inadequate, of not achieving what I want. I am overly committed to very long hours, many obligations. I'm unable to say no, so I'm not able to keep to the schedule" (i.e., expectation of the object).

"I'm on this treadmill; if I could only perform, I will feel all right, but when I say no to an expectation, I feel inadequate and empty. On the other hand, I neglect my responsibilities around the house. What do I do about it?"

I interpreted that it seemed as if he felt the need to focus on others to soothe his painful feelings of inadequacy about his self, but when he turned to focusing more on his self, he felt helpless. I wondered why.

In the very next session, he mentioned **efforts to active himself, to try to organize his day better**, but, illustrating the power of defense, he said: "I have so many obligations that one obligation interferes with the other, and I seem to always escape into these activities. I don't know how to be honest with myself. For example, I didn't publish four articles I wrote because of my wife's complaints of how much time I was putting in at work. I'm under constant criticism from her. Why can't I be myself? Why can't I support myself with her? I'm like a soldier who does his duty. I was an average student till prep school. My idea is that if you are gong to do something, you must be a superachiever, and this began in graduate school. I had been a disappointment to my parents in grammar school."

I again responded with a mirroring interpretation of the defensive part of the triad, that it was so painful for him to focus on himself that he soothed it by running on the treadmill of the superachiever.

He said: "Why is it I give up myself? I have an absolute surrender to authority. For example, I had a good research idea that I gave up because the authorities disapproved of it. I'm mad at myself for doing this, and for putting up with my wife and her attacks." He elaborated further on my interpretation by taking a first look at the impaired real self. "If I look at myself, at what is down there, it is a hollow man—an inner failure."

He then reverted to focusing on the object—his wife's attacks, her suspicion of an affair, his arguments with her over whether she was right. He spoke of being afraid that she would make another suicide attempt and that he would not be able to tolerate the guilt. His wife's problems and her attacks reinforced his defensive focus on the object, and they became a prominent theme in the treatment.

A voracious reader, he reread one of my books to get an intellectual grasp on his problem, which evoked two memories: (1) at age four or five, he broke his mother's favorite vase; (2) at one point, she punished him for drawing on the wallpaper, and in a rage at her erasing his drawing, he hit her and she fell down the stairs. These memories, however, were without affect. In another session, when he again complained about letting his wife get under his skin, I again interpreted that his need to focus on others was a way of regulating himself. He replied that he felt guilty about not seeing his wife as a person.

He recalled that as a child, after the age of four or five, the only thing he felt was guilt, no anger. His mother used to threaten him with abandonment for "bad behavior." "There was a prison in our community, and she used to say that that was where I would end up if I didn't do what she wanted, or that she would send me to an orphanage where bad boys were sent."

He continued to recount his efforts to "reason" with his wife. I thought that his passivity and his difficulty with setting limits on his wife's attacks so reinforced defense that they had to be dealt with at once. I questioned why he engaged in these discussions with his wife rather than set limits on them, since all they did was escalate the argument. He responded that if he did that, he would feel guilty. (The triad: if he activated himself rather than follow her expectations, he would be overwhelmed by guilt.)

Nevertheless, he did activate himself to set limits on these arguments, and reported himself as feeling isolated, depressed, and guilty. However, at the same time, he brought up another facet of self-activation, his interest in writing. He said that for years he had kept an unfinished novel in his desk. He then introduced for the first time the fact that he related to his partner in the same way as he did to his wife—his partner made extreme demands to which he acceded rather than set limits.

Affect and Memories Emerge

These small efforts at self-activation, even though partially based on compliance in accordance with the triad, led to an increase in anxiety, insomnia, and the emergence of some memories. He asked: "Why am I remembering going home in terror with a report card at the age of six? I was never allowed to be myself. However, I did like to paint, and they did support the painting, which became an escape from the performing world. When I was a kid, my parents would not let me have a dog, so I painted one when I was nine. I played the violin in high school and college. I also did acting as an escape, but my parents discouraged these artistic activities as they were not practical. Even performance at school became an escape from home. My parents gave me an ultimatum—go to college or get out. I have the same feelings on Saturday nights at home with my wife as I did when I was home with my parents at age eight. At age eight, I was in a panic about being sent to camp, and the panic was so great that it caused me to fight them, and they finally didn't send me. **I feel now that I am sort of going back to the artistic pursuits and also seeing things in my wife I had not seen before.** She's practically like my mother, and I have to perform for her the same as I did for my mother."

The patient's wife reacted to his self-activation at home by attacking the treatment, saying that I had missed the diagnosis and was being very destructive to him. He first objected, but then began to wonder if she might be right. He picked up this defensive shift of the triad from self to object and said: "As I think about what I want to do, to be myself, as I am thinking about it, my thoughts shift from what I might want to do with how others will see it." He reported having had dinner with his mother, who either told him what to do or ignored him. He added, "How did I survive my childhood?" He then linked his wife to his mother, saying, "I'm the one who is always wrong."

Still focusing on the defensive acting out with his wife, I suggested to him that he had had no choice about his mother, but he certainly had had choices about both of his wives, and that he seemed to feel the need to choose wives who would attack him. This comment seemed to stun him.

In the next session, in the context of having to prepare a lecture, he reported the following dream of anxiety about grandiose-self-activation. "I was on stage—I couldn't remember my lines—I was blank—I couldn't speak—I was put on stage without preparation—I woke up sweating." *Free association*: "In graduate school, I had this dream three times a week, and afterwards two or three times a year, and I have only had it once or twice in the last 10 years. When I give a lecture, I take 10 hours to prepare it even though I know it. I do it so that nobody will ask a question that I can't answer. I have to be perfect." I commented that it appeared that the dream expressed his terror at not being able to perform perfectly, and at the same time I wondered if it might not also be a reaction to my comment in the prior interview.

He reported in the next session that, with regard to the lecture, **he had given up the hours of preparation and had experimented with speaking spontaneously**. He said that he did quite well and felt that maybe, just maybe, the dream would not recur. (He had shifted from the grandiose self to the real self.) Then he elaborated: "I'm so mad at myself for having to perform—how much of life I have missed—the anxiety—the stage fright—the insomnia—'Never get caught with your pants down.' I really didn't see all this, and particularly how much I focused on others, until the last two weeks."

This led in the next session to some memories: "My father was an alcoholic, my mother a rageaholic. Why did I have to play the role of a man servant to a rageful woman? Mother invented rage. She used a switch on me before I was four. I remember the fight with her when I was four and then she beat me."

In the next session, **trying to think about what he wanted to do (i.e., real-self-activation)** led to painful memories: "In the third year of prep school, I didn't know what I wanted—Mother demanded that I commit to graduate school or she would stop paying for my education. My father left her around this time. My mother crushed all my efforts at other activities. I had been interested in writing, maybe advertising. My parents told me to forget it. I was attacked for any extracurricular activities. Although I was in the top third of the class, my marks weren't good enough. Fortunately, I befriended an older friend of the family, who became my mentor and directed my true interests. By the third year of college, I was committed to graduate school. But when I began, I started to overeat. I was able to control my overeating throughout school, but it returned after graduation. I want to get back to the feeling I had about myself around age 20." He continued: "I put myself on a diet, and I realize that I have to stop reading psychiatry, it is all intellectualization. At the same time, I am feeling more and more depressed, angry, and restless. As a child, I fought my mother, I was full of rage. When I was six or seven, the punishment changed to being severely physical. I gave into terrorizing threats of abandonment."

My initial interventions were on the defensive idealizing of the object and the acting out with his wife. I deferred interpreting the intellectualization until later. These interventions led to some self-activation with her, more affect of depression, and some memories. With this patient, one has to be careful to try to distinguish between compliance and genuine therapeutic movement. The patient seems to have picked this up himself in his comment that the reading is all defensive intellectualization.

Increasing Depression Leads to Change to Twice-a-Week Therapy After Seven Months

In the next session, he reported that he leaves the interviews with "a grenade that's been dropped that later explodes between the sessions." He came to realize his family's pathology and questioned: "How bad am I that I need these people? Why can't I change my pattern? I don't know what to do without the treadmill, but I keep trying to get off it. **I'm changing my behavior in the office—not complying with my partner's or customers' demands—and I am not going along with my wife's attacks, but I feel more and more depressed.** Why do I need this?"

He then recalled a memory of having a food allergy at age five that led to a severe diet. He could not stay with his peers, but had to be picked up for lunch by his mother. He fought the diet. He could not have sweets. His father supported the rebellion, but his mother attacked him. His mother humiliated him by calling the mothers of all his friends to tell them that he could not have lunch with their children. His deepening depression gave us an opening to explore his coming more often, and he agreed to change to twice-a-week therapy.

More Real-Self–Activation Leads to Depression, Rage, and Anxiety

In the next session, **he reported having firmly set limits on his wife's behavior by maintaining that there was no affair, and that the problem was hers.** She responded by telling him that her therapist had said that the patient was a tower of evil and that she should leave him. The patient continued: "The most chilling thought to me was the realization that this was her hallucination. I feel upset and hurt for her. What pain she must be in to see things that aren't there. It leaves me feeling gray and empty."

I raised the question of why he thought he had gone along with her behavior. He replied: "It was a fear like that I had with my mother, whatever she said was true, a fear of the switch. And not only with my wife, but I see the same thing happening with my partner. Why do I need an attacking woman whom I have tried to defend myself against? Now, instead of focusing on pleasing others, I want to be left alone and to do my thing, and I am not so driven to please. It seems to be a dramatic change. For example, with my lectures now there is no elaborate preparation, but I begin to feel both anxious and guilty."

In another session, he reported that at a very important lecture, rather than go through obsessive preparation, **he spoke spontaneously and got a tremendous response from the audience**. Following the triad, this activation of his real self produced enormous anxiety and self-attack: "All weekend after the talk, I felt anxious, felt I blew it, it wasn't right. I wasn't in control. What is this false self?" I suggested that it was not his false self, but his real self. He had done what he wanted to do and now was attacking it. Why was that?

In the next session, he continued to demonstrate the triad by the shift from focusing on the object to focusing on the self, increasing his depression, frustration, and anger, but he contained them in order to explore the problem with self-activation. "I'm depressed, the old ways don't work, I'd rather do nothing than function. I'm just not self-motivated. I'm beginning to see that the reason I read psychiatry is to prepare for my performance here with you as I do with others. [Again he notes the transference acting out of compliance.] When I focus on myself, I feel so guilty. My mother said that disobedient boys went to prison. I was constantly threatened with military school. 'You will obey or be broken.' I was not allowed to be myself—I became the world's greatest mirror—I was told how to be. Before age six, I fought with my mother, and after that I gave up."

His self-activation stimulated a triadic dream about how self-activation leads to disaster, based on a memory of a real event that occurred when he was three and a half. "I'm in nursery school and I love playing with this big St. Bernard dog. I sneaked into the doghouse, and the dog blocked the entrance, so I couldn't get out and I fell asleep. When I awoke, I came out to a bedlam—I was missing—they called the police, who questioned me. I thought to myself, 'Why are they doing this? What is all this upset about?' There was a motorcycle and I focused my attention to it so as not to listen to them. I thought I would love to get on that cycle and go." *Free association*: Is this how it all began? It's a story Mother used to tell but I didn't remember. The police told me how bad I was. In the dream, I did what I wanted, I was happy. I still feel upset by the dream. Depressed, agitated, afraid I can't handle the four horsemen of the apocalypse [his reading again]. I'm afraid of what's down there. I've been to all the codependency movements, I've listened to Bradshaw. I knew it all, but I couldn't do it."

These efforts to self-activate in the next session led to memories of earlier efforts at self-activation. "During my senior year in college, I reached a peak, I had a lot of activities. I lost 55 pounds. I was editor of a literary magazine. I wrote plays. I was the president of the dramatic society. I started a literary journal. There were no negatives, the world was a joy. I was doing for myself, not others. Where did this negative come from? Why do I need critics? It's very depressing. I suspect that graduate school began the submersion in others. Only performance counted or it was death. I was afraid to make a mistake. I was driven to perform in order not to feel guilty about incompetence."

He then moved deeper into memories about this defense: "I recall this wintry-void feeling as a child. I also recall the reward for playing the role for my mother. Was I performing for approval to fill the void? How do I retrain that? Must I be stifled because I was deprived? When does the approval of others become self-esteem? Why do I forget my own agenda when under pressure by others? Self-sabotage leads to self-loathing. I'm still continuing to revamp my schedule to suit myself, but I also keep slipping."

His wife continued her attacks, and in response to them, as well as to the explorations in psychotherapy, he regressed to attempting to "reason with her." I pointed out to him that he seemed to feel a need to see her in ways that were not consistent with her behavior. She had never been able to reason about this issue, and his trying to do it with her gave credence to her behavior. I wondered why he felt the need to do this.

He returned in the next session with the feeling that my comment had been an attack. "You seemed to be saying that I was gong along with my attacking wife! I realized finally that you were saying that I needed someone to pass the buck to. Both of my wives were dominating, critical, and couldn't be pleased." I now followed through with an interpretation of how painful it was for him to see his wife as she was, and that he soothed the pain by projecting a fantasy on her. I reinforced the interpretation with the story of actor Joe E. Brown's role in the movie *Some Like It Hot*. Brown takes Tony Curtis, who is dressed as a woman, to the yacht to visit his mother. He is enamored of the woman he thinks Tony Curtis is. Curtis tries to dissuade him, and when he is unsuccessful, he whips off his wig and says, "And besides, I am a man." And Joe E. Brown answers, "Well, you can't have everything."

At this point, the patient recalled a neighbor's three-year-old grandson who is quite uninhibited and spontaneous but totally undisciplined. This stimulus reinforced the session and stirred up memories. The patient reported: "I'm beginning to lose the numbness and to remember the past as I see this boy, who is a basket case. At four and a half, I was a model child. I wore a bib when I ate because Mother didn't want my clothes soiled. Why was I so model? What went into training the dog, meaning me, to jump through the hoop? One time I accidentally pushed a saleswoman when we were in a store. My mother and father took me home and beat me with switches until I was red. I was frightened and choking and the beating didn't stop. [He now described dissociation to deal with the trauma.] As I left my body, I wondered, in a state of emotional detachment, how this thing would end. I felt rage and fury. I can't stop these memories. The humiliations. I was strapped in a chair for spilling my milk. 'Don't get dirty' was emblazoned on my brow. Mother forced me to repeat in company, 'Children are to be seen and not heard.' It was humiliating. Before that age, I was able to express my anger. In one outburst of rage at the top of the stairs, I tackled my mother and she went down the stairs.

"I can remember shouting at her, 'I hope you die, I hope God kills you.' I can recall the fury at being beaten. She slapped me in the mouth, almost tore my head off. I defiantly repeated, 'I still hope you die.' I was picked up and beaten by a switch again. When my mother was hospitalized, when I was age six, I told the babysitter that I had done it and she wouldn't get well.

"This must be where my omnipotence began. I felt very guilty about wishing my mother dead. When my mother returned from the hospital, I was sent to my grandmother for several months. I was delighted. I felt my grandparents understood me and I could be myself—I loved it. I didn't want to return home."

Interpretation of Resistance of Shifting from Past to Present

In the midst of this painful recall, the patient abruptly stopped, became resistant, and said that these memories had nothing to do with him in the present or in the future. I suggested that it was so painful to recall how humiliated and bad he had felt with himself and his mother, he soothed himself by downgrading its importance, but that, on the other hand, these memories emerged as a part of his effort to focus on himself in treatment.

This led to further memories: "I had to be in bed at eight o'clock every night until age nine. I felt isolated—like in a cell. I could hear the kids playing. I could hear the Good Humor truck, but I wasn't allowed out. If I wasn't asleep by nine, I got a phenobarbital. I learned to be invisible though present. I still could make myself invisible—just blend in. I wrote a story that I thought was about my wife, and I later looked at it and realized it was about my mother. Nobody trusted me. All decisions were made for me. I was made to feel a selfish ingrate for not accepting this guidance. I was taught that achievement was happiness. I was not allowed to explore myself.

"From six until I was 12, I was on a strict diet that made me a stranger among my peers, and they made fun of me. When I would try to escape from the diet, my mother would attack me, saying, 'Look at all I'm doing for you and you sabotage it.' Then I felt guilty and tried to please her more. I never felt abused as a child because there was no need to feel abused—only a mirror—I reflected what my parents wanted. There was a constant threat of boarding school, state reform school, and so on. Now I have to get off this treadmill and invest in myself and forget the past."

I again interpreted that this was his effort to soothe the pain about remembering the past, but also that recall of the past was essential to recapturing his sense of self. He responded, "I used to feel guilty if I were myself, and now I feel guilty if I'm not myself."

I responded with an interpretation of the transference acting-out compliance. I asked, "Is it possible that it's so painful and difficult to focus on yourself and to recall these painful memories that one of your ways of soothing it is to focus on what you see as my expectations as a way of protecting yourself?" Was he activating himself because he wanted to perform for me in order to protect his grandiose self?

The patient responded to my interpretation as an empathy failure: "I was upset by your suggestion that I may be performing for you. I don't think I am doing that." I commented that he had seemed to feel a sense of disapproval in my remark, to which he had reacted quite strongly. He finally confirmed that idea by relating to further memories of his mother's attacks: "I wrote my first novel at age 10—she tore it up in a rage. Then I turned to painting. Now my mother wants to give me her portrait, which I can put in the living room and so never get away from her. I liked painting. I gave my first painting to my mother, who used it to show off to her friends. Then I dropped painting and took up the violin for four years, and finally gave that up. When Mother found that I was using my allowance for foods that were forbidden on the diet, instead of giving me my allowance, she put it in the bank. Then my father gave me money on the side. I learned to go along on the surface and to hide the rage, and, it's funny, as a child I didn't realize I was unhappy."

This led to a dramatic event reported in the next session: "Last week, my partner, my secretary, and my wife were all angry at me at the same time for frustrating their agendas. I felt absolutely furious, as though my head were going to explode. I remembered that this was how I felt just before my heart attack, **but this time I asserted myself. I told them off and said I was going to follow my own agenda,** which then led to a weekend of criticism."

I asked why he seemed, without being aware of it, to feel the need for these critical people. He responded: "Why did I need bad mirrors? I was never fed as a child. I thought I was a happy child. I thought my parents were caring and warm. I didn't feel deprived, but when I was very young, I was a rebel. By grammar school, I went into hiding, became invisible, and Mother was on center stage; Father disappeared."

He now again abruptly dismissed the past, and came back to the present to say that he would have to change his behavior. I reinterpreted that because it was so painful to remember these memories, the way he soothed the pain was to cut off the feeling and the memories and focus on the here and now. He responded: "It's humiliating to think about it. When I talk that way, I feel as I did as a child, a pitiful, whining brat. The only thing that mattered as a child was performance." I pointed out perhaps that was why he changed the subject from his painful memories of the past to performance in the present.

This led him into further memories: "My mother had a whim of iron and my father was more absent. I recall how bad I felt when my father didn't come home. I was left to the war with Mother, desolate, alone, no ally. She criticized him for his lack of perfection. We were both in the doghouse. Until age nine I went to bed at eight o'clock. On Halloween, I could stay up until eight thirty. I loved it, but all the treasures I brought home in my bag, mostly sweets, were thrown into the garbage. I got two apples, and my mother would put any money I got in the bank, telling me that she was saving me from self-indulgence. I got very angry and cried. Mother said, 'Don't you understand I am doing it for your own good?"

He added, "I'm a connoisseur of humiliation." I suggested that one of his ways of dealing with the pain of humiliation was to give up the self and focus on the object. The patient responded, "I'm feeling so depressed, I wish I could go back to the way I was when I came here." I replied that it appeared that the work in the sessions was so painful and humiliating that he yearned to go back to the state he was in when he started, even though that state may well have resulted in his heart attack. He said: "I feel diminished. It reminds me of the phrase, 'I planned a vase but it dwindled to a pot.'"

He reported memories from grammar school of being so sensitive to humiliation that he would fight at the drop of a hat. His external image was that of a fighter, but inside he felt a coward, scared to death. His father built a boxing ring in the backyard to help him. "Once humiliated, I fought. In third grade, I sat in the corner with a dunce cap on, so humiliated." Then he shifted: "I don't mind these memories. As I get depressed, I feel worse about self. If I forget, then I can function." I interpreted that getting access to these feelings was expressed as a repetition of the humiliation he felt as a child, but that actually they helped him to gain access to his sense of self. He questioned, "How far will this go? How deep?" I answered, "We'll have to see."

Comment

As the patient moved along the triad from self-activation to abandonment depression and impaired self to defense, I interpreted the defenses to bring him back to the depression—such defenses as focusing on the idealized object, shifting to the present to avoid the past, and transference acting out with me by compliance. He integrated the various interpretations and moved deeper into the abandonment depression, getting access to feelings of rage and humiliation, and then, following the triad, he returned to defense.

Ninth Month

Working Through Continuing—Memories of Humiliation, Being Attacked, and Rage and Rebellion

In a surge of self-activation, the patient reported that he had come to realize that he could do what he wanted to do. **"I can be I, but I have to focus on myself. I've decided to leave my partner, set up my own business. The wonderful part is that I feel self-esteem, not guilt, and this opens creative vistas."**

He then reported memories of his mother's demanding that he read and attacking him and humiliating him when he was unable to, and the harder he tried, the worse he got, the more humiliated he felt. This led to some positive memories, up to the age of 10, with his paternal grandfather, whom he described as being warm and caring. He used to sit on his grandfather's lap, and his grandfather taught him how to tell time and how to use money. His mother became jealous of his relationship with the grandfather and attacked him for it. When he was seven, his mother demeaned the grandfather in his eyes. "I can recall feeling guilty about the relationship with him, but I could identify with him. He was kind and full of stories."

The working through continued. He recalled being hospitalized with pneumonia at the age of six. "They didn't tell me where I was going. I was terrified. They said that we were going for a ride. I had a feeling I was going to die, but I didn't know what it meant, like being put in a box in the ground. I was in a rage about being lied to and in an absolute terror about dying. In the hospital, I sat up all night watching the shadows—terror at being left alone. My parents were gone. I was alone in the room."

He then recalled walking with his grandfather in the park six months later, seeing the flowers and the greenery and the birds and the trees. "I was happy. I recall thinking, 'This is happiness;

am I glad I didn't die.' Grandfather made the world different just by being there. He was a storyteller and involved me in his stories."

In the next session, he focused on self-activation, saying that he had read my book *The Search for the Real Self* after his coronary occlusion, but at that time he could not handle it. Now, he said, he understands why psychotherapy is necessary. He said: "I didn't numb out until my grandfather died when I was 10. I'm beginning to feel simple things I was numb to. I want to stop this focusing on others. Why do I do it? Evidently, if I assert myself, I have to be attacked. It must be related to memories of childhood." Then I questioned why he did not have more access to these feelings in his memory of childhood, because he reported them here.

He replied: "It's too painful knowing them. From three to six, I didn't passively-aggressively evoke Mother, but was overtly hostile and violent. I threw chairs and broke antiques. By the age of seven, I literally switched to being compliant and hating her, and then I began acting out in school with fighting and truancy. In the second grade, I was sent home for talking in class. I would not do the homework. I saw nothing wrong with this. I was afraid to fight, but when humiliated, I fought. I spent most of my school life in detention, and this humiliated my mother. I was a loser at home but could get even at school. I humiliated everyone—teachers, parents—I was a troublemaker. I thought I was doing my thing. I didn't feel I deserved the punishment."

The working through continued in the next session as he remembered a dream that brought to mind a humiliating incident in school when he had been beaten up by the class bully, felt humiliated, and was taken to the principal, who made him sit in the corner with a dunce cap on his head. He sat there fearing that he would be sent to the state penitentiary. He continued: "After that, I had recurring nightmares. Knew that if I did it again, the punishment would happen again, but I felt guilty for the first time, realizing I had done something wrong."

I interpreted that he had to put up with the humiliation at home, but he did not have to put up with it at school. He replied: "I haven't remembered this incident for 45 years." He then reported that when he heard from his wife that she had to discipline her daughter, he flew into a rage internally about his mother's statement, "Children are to be seen and not heard." He then returned to the theme: "Although I was a rebel and punished, I never felt that I was doing anything wrong. I didn't believe in the punitive god I was taught about. I remember, at age six, part of me wanting to run away and the other part feeling I couldn't make it. I didn't realize how controlling my mother was until I was in my 30s."

Tenth Month

Begins to Link Attacking Mother with Giving Up Self and Better Relationships with Women

The patient took a two-week vacation and returned reporting that he was trying to focus more on himself in his relationships and in his work. He continued to feel a greater sense of choice and freedom, but more depression and guilt (the triad). "I remember now that I only felt I was me when I was a little kid and rebelling. It lasted until I was six, and then I became a model child. For 20 years, I followed my wife's definition of what a good husband is. I have to nourish this focus on myself, but at least now I realize I have options."

In the next session, the theme continued: "I've surrounded myself with negative people because I have a negative image of myself. With my first wife, I had great difficulty focusing on myself. She used to put me down and had no respect for me, and I used to attack myself for not wanting to leave the children and for not doing what I believed in. I regret not leaving sooner, but now I understand why."

He then returned to the rebellion before age five. "I was broken at age five. If I objected with my mother, she would put me out of the house on the front stoop or put me to bed without dinner. Then I would steal food and hide it. If I didn't accept her structure, I was blown away. I became a cog in the great machine and underground, beneath this, became the counterpuncher. What do I want? Harmonious integration of all my parts."

The next session brought back memories of his being sick and insecure. He was put to bed, left by himself, and missed his mother, but when she did come, she would intrude and attack him. "I needed her, but she was the head torturer and inquisitor. I used to panic at the thought of getting sick. I was hospitalized at age six for pneumonia, but liked the hospital better than being with my mother. Later in childhood, I hid symptoms from my parents since I didn't want to let them know. I still tend to ignore and to ride out symptoms because illness means total vulnerability."

I pointed out that as he recalled the story, he told it with laughter, not anger, and he replied that the laughter was anger. "I have a lot of respect for the feelings of sick people as a result. It's a sublimation of how totally vulnerable I felt when I was sick."

He began the next session returning to the present, reporting how successful he was in his work because he perceived the reality of the circumstances and so was able to do well. Why did he suspend this capacity to perceive reality in his relationships with women? This led him back to the past: "My mother's threats cowed me as a child, and later, as an adult, I felt guilty. My first wife ordered me around all over the place, told me that every husband followed instructions this way. What did I know? When it came to divorce, I couldn't handle leaving and held on for five years and became a workaholic."

I interpreted that it seemed that without being aware of it, since he felt he had freed himself from his mother, he ended up repeating the same relationship with his first wife. He continued: "I have empathy with everyone but myself. My only identity is in doing, and I can't feel empathy with myself."

In the next session, he reported: "I don't remember being acknowledged as a child. I didn't know I had an unhappy childhood. My mother told me that the other mothers who weren't doing what she did didn't care. I have great difficulty remembering my mother as the witch she was. Actually, she told me she was the Madonna."

I interpreted that this must have something to do with his denial of reality and his reluctance to take on the denial because of the guilt and fear that it evoked. He replied: "I was forced to believe that being beaten was love. Why do I keep pushing other people to dump on me?"

I interpreted that perhaps he did this in order not to remember and really understand what had gone on with his mother, and that he was repeating it and reenacting it in his life to reinforce the denial. He replied: "I didn't realize that my first wife was like my mother. She and my mother fought like cats and dogs. They would put me in the middle, I couldn't win. The psychiatrist told me to be sure to have treatment before I remarried. I thought he was right, but denied it and did not follow through. After my divorce, I worked 16 hours a day. I remembered that my uncle had been ostracized for being divorced. I thought that when I married my second wife I was avoiding all those characteristics of my first wife. I can't acknowledge or accept that I was not acknowledged and that my performance ethic is based on sand."

Comment

Following the vicissitudes of the disorder-of-the-self triad, the patient controlled defense—moved deeper into the abandonment depression and impaired self with memories laden with affect. He then defended again and my interpretations of defense led him back again. Similarly, in the therapeutic relationship, he vacillated back and forth between transference acting out of compliance and therapeutic alliance and transference with working through of painful affect.

Eleventh Month

Positive Memories of Mourning the Death of the Uncle and of More Self-Activation and Wife's Attacks

The patient reported: "I have an avalanche of memories—things I never thought before. [These were brought forth by overcoming the defenses.] For example, I remember Father saying that the mark of the man is that he doesn't cry in his beer. I'm feeling more empty and lonely. A 50-year façade is cracking. I had learned not to cry. There has been a change. I no longer only become aware of my problems afterwards in retrospect. I see them as they are happening. **I feel more in command and less a victim. There is a tremendous sense of continuity, and I am focusing more on myself and not on others as before, and I am taking care of myself. I'm handling my feelings and I can cry.** I spoke to my mother on the phone and realized how self-centered she is and that I never mattered but went along out of guilt. My total function was as a puppet on a string to create an image."

In the next session, he reported that his maternal uncle had died, which brought back memories of this man who had been a positive model. "He was a father surrogate. He gave me my first bike at six. He called me champ. He confronted my mother. He's the first memory of a person who was very positive and supportive with me—I admired him. He made me feel I could do what I wanted. I spent three weeks in the summer with him and my grandfather and then I was able to be me. My mother had been neutralized. It was a shelter of creativity. An alternative to Mother's world. I gloried in it and was excited by it, and my bond with my uncle grew. The fact that my grandfather and uncle dealt with my mother made them powerful and awesome to me. They had identity and integrity, and every time we left at the end of the three weeks, I cried and cried."

The patient forgot the next session even though he had written the date down. I asked whether it might have been too painful for him to face the feelings of loss in the prior session, but he corrected me, saying that he had been planning to talk again about his memories of happiness and sense of identity with his uncle. **"A time when I was me, which was maybe why I forgot" (to avoid supporting his self). He went on then to recall in great detail his relationship with the uncle.** The uncle was a baseball player who gave him his own mitt, and this mitt made the patient feel invincible; he could excel with the mitt—he had total confidence in it. He felt that he was not worthless when he had the Excalibur of a mitt. He loved playing baseball, but in prep school, he had no free time between study and commuting. He had to give baseball up, and his spontaneity and identity went with it.

After an interaction with his mother, he reported her coldness, her attitude: "It's my way or the highway." It infuriated him. His self-esteem was wrecked, and then later he surrounded himself with mothers. I asked why. He said, "I am too empathetic with women in order to please my mother, but I am beginning to shift to pleasing myself, to having a new sense of entitlement. It's inches, but it has a momentum. Now when I am criticized by my wife, it makes me feel I am right."

In the next session, he returned to the years in graduate school. The rules angered him, but he did not know how to rebel. It was a dehumanizing system. This system called for performance, which fit his knee-jerk style. He said, "I had achieved and was very successful, but I was unable to get back to how I was in college." **He reported that he no longer was complying with his wife's and secretary's efforts to control his scheduling, insisting that he could control it himself,** and how, as a result, he was attacked by both his wife and his secretary.

In the next session, he reported that his wife, when in the office, literally flouted his directions, while in the home, she was too permissive and indulgent with her daughter, and yet he put up with both attitudes. I asked him why he did so. This theme of compliance with his wife continued in the next session. "I react as if my wife's entitlements are the Eleventh Commandment. Why am I so dependent on her? In practice, I focus on doing the best job I can, but with her, I focus on her approval, not on doing what is best. If I support myself with her, the marriage will break up."

I raised the question of what kind of marriage it could be for him without room for self-support.

Twelfth Month

Dealing with Wife's Attacks, Nostalgia for Lost College Self, Increase in Depression, Drinking, and Denial of Father's Lack of Support

His wife again began attacking him about having an affair and he again attempted to reason with her, which I then questioned him about. He said: "I feel humiliated by her charges, but there is no logic. My mother used to humiliate me publicly for disagreeing with her. I'm intimidated by the possibility of future public humiliation. What does her attacking me do for me?" (I suspected that both he and his wife served each other as external objects upon which to project and get rid of their inner negative objects.)

In the next session, he recalled how as an adolescent his fear of rejection by girls paralyzed him: "Throughout high school, I was very girl-shy. I couldn't take no for an answer, so I couldn't ask girls out. Plus my mother pushed my career and not dating girls. In college, I reversed and became the opposite to rescue my self-image. I had many dates. This created havoc at home. When I brought women home, my mother put them down. I went from being a wimp in high school to being macho in college. Both were acting out against my mother."

His compliance with his wife came up again in the next session when he reported her drinking bouts in the home, and I asked why he went along with it. He said: "I surrounded myself with these people. Where is the escape? What is normal? Why do I have this tolerance?"

In the next session, he repeated stories of his wife's attacks with such gusto that I raised the point that he was so enthusiastic that it seemed as though these attacks must do something for him. I asked, "Is it possible that your focus on her negative attacks allows you to avoid focusing on yourself?" He replied: "Like Sartre, I focus on the mirror, not on myself. My identity as a child came from my mirroring mother." (The mention of Sartre again raised the possibility of his transference acting out through compliance. I included a section on Sartre in one of my books.)

I told him that I wondered why he did not get over this obstacle, pointing out that he had great difficulty supporting himself, and it seemed to me that these negative attacks made it even harder. He replied: "I remarried my mother. How do I work on that?" I wondered why he felt so helpless about it.

In the next session, he said that he had been to his physician, who confronted him with the news that he was still 25 pounds overweight, which he was continuing to deny. He said, "I start to lose weight but don't have the will, and then I put it back on."

He began the next session with comments on his wife's attacks, but now reported: "I decided I don't need it. I tried to remember my childhood but couldn't. Why did I perpetuate the abuse? Maybe punishment equals love. Why do I put up with it? Nothing in my life to give me support. My first wife was very hostile, but I thought the second one was kind and thoughtful." (I suspected here that he was talking about acting out the impaired self in which the harsh, aggressive unit is projected outward and his impaired self is constantly attacked by others. This is the opposite of the narcissist, who projects the impaired self on others and plays out the role of the attacking object himself or herself.)

In the next session, he reported on a trip he had taken to his college town, where he recaptured the positive feelings he had about himself when he was 19 years old. "I was walking around the city. I began to remember what I felt like, the sense of optimism, of being my own person, of an unlimited future, successful. That was 31 years ago, but I've turned my back on those feelings. I wasn't looking for adulation from others then. I wanted to do what I wanted to do. I felt like a ghost. If I had seen at 19 what it would be like at 50, I would have choked. A cascade of depression descended on me. Life looked like the carnage of a train wreck. The ruin of a marriage, two bad wives, a bad partner, a controlling mother.

"Every place I looked, I was the person who did it. Overweight, high blood pressure, no one to blame but me. I had done it. Now I know why I focus outward. I can't stand the pain of focusing on myself. This is my first day in therapy. My past was in that town and I connected with it. I am trying to find a path back to the optimism of the 19-year-old when I still did things because I believed in them and wanted to do them. Too bad we couldn't see ourselves 31 years later then. I see my self-abandonment, what I did myself."

As the patient talked, he became more and more depressed. He then activated himself more with his wife. **"I told my wife that either the drinking had to go or I had to go, and I decided I would take charge of the office, and if she doesn't like it, she should quit. I stepped back into myself.** This contrast of memories between then and now broke the dam and taught me that I was the one who lost it. I feel a bitter loneliness. Where and why did I abandon self?"

In the next session, he attacked himself for expressing his feelings in the session. I asked: "Why such a harsh attack? It seems to me that you were making progress."

He continued: "It was the fear of failure and loneliness that kept me from fulfilling that 20-year-old promise. My father, who was my supporter, died when I was 21 and in graduate school. Mother had to work as a dental assistant. I felt guilty about her having to work. I was crushed by my father's death. He was my best friend and supported me. My mother was the opposite. She wanted me to be successful for her, not for me. She reinforced the guilt by emphasizing her sacrifice for me. I made a contract to pay her back every cent, and I did. I married right after graduate school. My wife objected to the payments to my mother. My wife and mother fought over me and I was in the middle. After my father's death, I allowed the flow of work to take over my life. I didn't consider any other options." (He had shifted the focus completely from self to object.)

I interpreted that the father's death, which brought a loss of support for him, left him alone. He did as he had at the age of three: he turned himself over to the maternal object, but rationalized it not as Mother, but as graduate school. The death of his father led to emptiness and loneliness, and self-activation was associated with these feelings. To defend against the feelings of loneliness and emptiness, he shifted to the object. He replied: "Two years after my father died, believe it or not, I went to the phone to call him, and only at the last minute did I realize that he was dead. I lost self-confidence after that. I did it." The patient reported: "I was overcoming more denial—I felt so depressed that I couldn't function. It's like looking at the picture of Dorian Gray. I was almost catatonic and disorganized and ready to give up. It's excruciating mental pain."

This led him to memories of his 10 years of alcoholism, when he drank excessively in his free time, although it never interfered with his work. He said: "Alcohol allowed me to blame everyone else. I had a bad wife. My first wife divorced me for being an alcoholic, and my drinking increased with my second wife because she was also an alcoholic. But she was so bad that her drunkenness caused me to decrease my drinking because someone had to be in control.

When I became aware of this since the last session, I decided to give up the occasional glass and ban all alcohol from my house. That's it for me, but it's very scary. I feel very shaky today about managing myself. I thought about taking Prozac, but that's just another drug."

I interpreted that perhaps he was more shaky about managing his depression on his own without the use of a drug rather than about only managing his depression.

His preoccupation with alcoholism continued as he began to recall childhood memories during grade school when he had not realized that his parents fought so much about his father's drinking. His mother constantly put his father down, which angered the patient. He said: "It seemed to me that it was Mother's problem. I only saw him have a couple of glasses of wine before dinner. I felt caught between him and my mother. However, when I was in high school, my father had to stop because of liver damage. My mother kept emphasizing that I was the son of an alcoholic. I resented her trying to alienate us. In the last three years of his life, he became depressed and drank too much, and I saw that she was right. My mother harangued him about the drinking, just as my wife harangues me about the affair.

"When I got to college, I wondered how my father could stand her. I started drinking around that time, and only this week have I realized fully that I was an alcoholic with a pattern very much like that of my father, but I have not been intoxicated for the past five years [a reevaluation of his first statement of not drinking for 15 years]. I feel full of rage, but I am not going to blame others, including my mother. Am I condemned to spending my life seeking out other mothers?"

I answered that he was condemned either to seeking out other mothers or to exploring the investigation of his rage in the sessions. I pointed out that he was not responsible for the hand he had been dealt, but since it was his hand, he was responsible for playing it, and that if he did not get to the bottom of these feelings in the sessions, he was going to be tempted to repeat them.

He continued: "I had to conform to my mother, and my father went along. However, when I was a very early preschooler, I rebelled overtly, and then it went underground. I was constantly in trouble in school. I would fight at the drop of a hat, but at home my rebellion was more passive. I would procrastinate in doing my many duties—cutting the lawn, washing the dishes, and so forth. One time, while on a ladder putting up the screens with my father, I, out of nowhere, hit him on the head with a hammer with all my might, and I didn't know why—I still don't know why."

I suggested that perhaps because of his need to idealize his father to support himself, he was unable to see him as he was, and also was unable to be aware of the rage he expressed at his father when he hit him on the head.

Thirteenth Month

Depression About Loss of Self, Memories of Father, Father's Drinking, Conflict with Mother

The patient had taken a vacation in the Caribbean, where he saw how close French mothers were to their children—how they respected their independence. The children seemed fulfilled and happy, and it brought to his attention how different his childhood had been, and he felt empty, hollow, and depressed.

He then reported the following dream: "My grandfather and I are on the subway together. It was the first time I thought about what I wanted to do. I was seven or eight and I wanted to be a conductor like my grandfather." *Free association*: "I could tell him all the things I couldn't tell Mother. That's what it was that made me cry when I left my grandparents. I could be me there. I had an identity. I didn't have to shape it. I could, after this dream, remember those feelings of identity for the first time."

The patient pursued it further in the next session, questioning: "How can I be real only two hours a month, when I am lecturing? What about the rest of the time?"

He continued: "The bond I had with my grandfather was real so I could be myself with him. I didn't have to be a part of my mother's agenda. I have to recapture those feelings of being independent and dynamic. I feel that my sense of self is starting to grow. **I'm**

starting to write. I'm putting two parts together and I have reorganized my office. However, I am beginning to sense the depth of my emptiness and the lack of warmth in my relationship with my mother [self triad] and the rigid rules. I dreamed about a memory I had of being in the crib and hugging a toy elephant to deal with my loneliness. The elephant was my only friend."

In the next session, the patient got further in touch with his denial of his father's drinking. "My father and mother used to have violent fights on holidays, and I remember feeling depressed and helpless and wanting to hide when I was about four years old. Until I became aware of this, I would have said that the holidays were wonderful, but emotionally I felt hurt and angry."

In the next session, the patient reported that the pain of self-discovery was mitigated by **an increase in energy and creativity.** "I have to change myself; no one rescues me. I'm reenacting the childhood pain to continue to try and prove myself, but I am realizing that pleasing others doesn't please myself. Why do I have such tolerance for the inappropriate behavior of my wife? I feel guilty if I leave."

I pointed out that he did not seem to see any options other than putting up with the abuse or leaving. He replied: "I did it with my first wife. Why do I let the other come first? Why do I cave in? It's my problem, not my mother's."

In the next session, he elaborated on how he had performed in college. He followed the rules literally with no allowance for his sense of self. He then reported that his wife again had attacked him for the supposed affair, and he had attempted to find a more respectful response. "I am so guilty about leaving her. Afraid that she may harm herself."

I asked him why he felt that his wife's welfare was solely his responsibility. He replied that although he had such anger about being constantly programmed, he felt responsible for his partner's welfare, as well as that of his wife.

He reported how successful his lectures had become now that he was more spontaneous. He had been too defensive in his lecturing and had put people to sleep, and he connected the change to treatment.

I pointed out the change was due to his being himself with his audience. He then returned to the conflict with his wife: "Why don't I see this tragedy for what it is? My need to be a good guy causes enormous denial."

I reinforced this view, saying that with both of his wives and with his partner, his focus seemed to be exclusively on the other and not on himself. He replied: "It's a false image of a good guy. It's inflexible and frozen. I can't allow myself to look bad in the eyes of the other."

Before the next session, I received a letter from his wife accusing him of having affairs. I gave it to him to read, and he immediately launched into an elaborate defense. I asked him why he felt such a need to defend. He replied: "I defend just because I'm attacked—it's a knee-jerk response whether the attack is true or not. I'm beginning to realize that what I'm defending myself against with my wife is delusion."

He went home and confronted her about the letter, and returned in the next session saying he now had a perspective on himself; he did not collude with her rage, but just removed himself and went to bed. He also reported taking back responsibilities for the finances—deciding to sell the house in order to pay his debts.

He continued: "I realize I'm super vulnerable to what people think, and I have to defend against any attack automatically. However, now I feel my life is turned around. I feel real, and I am taking things like they are, and telling it like it is. For example, when I went out to give my latest lecture, I tested out whether I was going because the people's response made me feel so good about myself or because I enjoyed the teaching, and I decided it was the latter. After I confronted my wife when she attacked this time, I didn't feel so defensive."

In the last session, he reported: "When at home, Father was usually drunk and Mother was attacking him. I didn't perceive it at the time; my memories of my childhood are very unreal, and I would have said until recently that it was happy. I notice that when I relax and reflect on my childhood, I can summon up these positive memories about my grandfather, and this allows me to deny and ignore the rest of it."

I interpreted that his way of dealing with the pain of his childhood was to deny its reality and substitute this fantasy based on the relationship with his grandfather.

Fourteenth Month

The Impaired Self and Memories of Mother and Focus on the Object

The patient continued to work on his need to focus on the object to defend against self-activation, seeing the price he had paid for it, and he began to activate himself more and to have more memories of the relationship with his mother.

He began the first session stressing how he asserted himself, unlike how he had acted previously, to deal with his wife's drinking, and how depressing it was to realize how negative his mother was: "I'm finally recognizing her hidden agenda, and this time I didn't participate. I felt angry at my having gone along with all their agendas." These two events—supporting himself with his wife and remembering his mother—are related. As he stopped the reenactment with his wife, he started to remember.

This led to a memory in the next interview of his impaired real self expressed at the age of 20 in a short story, as follows: "There was a young man in a garret, who was upset and depressed about not having achieved success as a writer, although he did copy-writing. He looked at the Christmas stores and was depressed about not being fulfilled. He saw the Christmas lights as promise unfulfilled. He became numb and cold. He couldn't participate in the joy of the people.

"A woman invited him to sit down with her in a cafeteria. They talked about their lives. He began to warm up and feel an identity [I think he meant to say connection]. She was an unsuccessful actress. She said she had to leave to work. He asked her what work she did, and she answered, 'I'm a prostitute.' He was shocked, hurt, upset, but he felt thankful because he had lost his numbness. He returned to his room and the numbness returned. He said that reality is real and fantasy is the escape of not learning to cope with the real."

The patient continued: "This Christmas season brought back memories of that story. I at one time did focus on reality. Then I turned it into fantasy. I had a literary reputation. I was depressed and numb, but refused to admit it. I only learned now what I said then. I didn't know then. I wasn't into melancholy or soul searching then. And the story was actually out of context for me. My other writings focused on being witty and humorous. This piece, however, wrote itself while usually I had to struggle through it."

In reporting the story, the patient had meant to say "connection" when he said "identity." I used this misuse to interpret that the way he found a sense of identity was through focusing on the object rather than on himself. He responded: "It's emotional parasitism. The host provides an essential nutrient that the parasite can't metabolize himself. That's why I surrounded myself with hosts."

I also pointed out that the hosts ignored his verbalizations because they picked up his need to focus on them.

He carried it further in the next session: "I've a better understanding of how parasitism gave me a sense of direction, but I'm beginning to realize that I can function with or without my wife, and I had a wonderful sharing moment with my grandson watching TV that recalled memories of my grandfather and my father. When I was four, my grandfather had a dog that I loved. I felt total glory with it, but my mother disapproved. My grandson taught me how to focus on myself. I always needed approval and still do. Why was I afraid to be me? I must support myself."

This led in the next session to further memories about his need to focus on the object. "When I was a child, my mother would hold up successful men that she had dated to whip my father into a frenzy. It made me angry and upset that I was used as a confidant for her anger at my father. The message was that success is everything. Years later, I saw that my father also had a lot of respect for success. My parents had money trouble and the depression reinforced my mother's pressure on me to succeed. I worried about my parents' going broke as early as age five. And my mother constantly talked about survival. And at five, I started a plan for surviving. In high school, my anxiety was not about failing but about being a success. And after high school, my father and mother wanted me to study business, but I was interested in the arts, which to my mother was synonymous with failure. In my second year of college, I decided I wanted to work in business. It was my job to fulfill Mother's dream, but I didn't become a pillar of the community."

In the next session, the patient reported: "I'm doing what I believe in across the board, but when they question me, I wonder whether they might be right." I asked why others' views shook his own view of himself. He replied: "I surrounded myself with critics to keep from expressing myself and then getting depressed." The patient then reported another interaction with his wife in which he had regressed from setting limits to falling into her projections. There followed a memory of his mother's control when he was 19, and how he turned his anger on himself. "Why do I tolerate my wife's attacks now? I feel a total anger at Mother's programming and I'm beginning to see the illogic in my wife."

I asked again: "Why did you pick a wife like your mother? What function does it provide for you?" He replied: "As long as I did what I was told, I had no problems. I was housebroken, like a dog."

I then reinterpreted that he needed the object to defend against focusing on himself. He continued, "I was taught by my mother that there was nobody in there." He next reported that his wife had stopped her therapy, which made him feel guilty. I pointed out that he was probably denying that she felt more support from him in the reality of the marriage, so that she did not need it so much from a therapist.

Fifteenth Month

Feelings of Inadequacy, Failure as a Father

The patient reported becoming more aware of his own fear of inadequacy for the first time, and that his workaholism and focus on the object were defenses against it.

This led to memories in the next session: "At age eight, I remember loving to listen to "The Lone Ranger" program. I was alone, totally protected by my parents, who were always right. It was a fantasy to deal with my fear of inadequacy. I thought that this was what I would be someday. I loved the mask. I could be all things to all people. On Halloween, I wore a mask, a Lone Ranger costume. I was always uneasy with men with mustaches and beards. They were masks. I lost myself in fantasy, and later I loved adventure stories."

The patient recited a long story about trying to combat his wife's drinking after he had colluded with her. He said: "I started to see our relationship as it is, grotesque, inappropriate. I have allowed others to think for me and to direct me as if I were invisible. I felt desolated, like I was on a moonscape in a vacuum and they fill it, and I allow it. Why? I think I'm beginning to turn the corner."

An interaction with his mother brought out further awareness: "Mother is not interested in my welfare. She wants what she wants." This led to memories: "At age four, I remember tackling her, sending her down the stairs. I can remember wanting to kill her. I felt murderous rage. At five, she'd get angry at me for not understanding words, when I was learning reading. I remember feeling that she was ridiculous. She had a whim of iron, no deviation from the party line."

After he reported his wife's drinking, I was able to point out the depth of the denial of his wife's alcoholism, and that although he verbally protested, he did not follow through. He responded: "I couldn't face my failure as a husband with my wife. If they had problems, it was my failure. Don't be a bad son, husband, or father. I had to focus on Mother, not myself. I was trained like a dog not to be bad in her eyes. I have a ring in my nose and I will follow."

I pointed out again how important it was for him to focus on others in this fashion as a way to avoid focusing on himself. He then further analyzed the cost of his denial: "I have two children who don't talk to me, a wife who's an alcoholic, and I've had a heart attack. My failure as a father makes me so depressed and I'm forced to face my own inadequacy. I was trained to perform for adulation." He then reported a dream: "I was a four-year-old and I was on this porcelain table and was about to die." *Free association*: "That's when I died." He then reviewed his first marriage to a woman who was more negative and attacking than his current wife and who turned his children against him, which reinforced his feelings of inadequacy as a father.

Sixteenth Month

Working Through Memories of Impaired Self with Mother and Father

Overcoming this denial and depression led to further memories: "I was a good citizen because I was terrified, not because I believed it. My so-called principles were my parents' principles, not mine, and were inculcated by fear. Why didn't they help me? There was no room for experimentation, creativity. Whatever the rule was, it was more important than yourself. I didn't realize that I had the right to find rules for myself, but went through life like a highly trained dog. I have to start challenging it. In my business, I am working now for my own glory. Now I've recast that role so I'm able to enjoy it more. My wife's drinking makes me see how monumental my denial was. My job is not to control her. I'm learning to not feel guilty. My job is to grow and live my life. I had to be a success at work, a good husband, a good father, et cetera, to deal with the fear and the guilt. I'm beginning to do what I believe in. I don't have to worry that the other will leave me and my world will fall apart."

This again led to further memories: "Why did I comply with my mother? My father complied also. And he backed her. One place I rebelled was in my diet, when I hid food, and I was in terror of saying no. For years, I felt guilty that I wasn't man enough to oppose tyranny even when I saw it in the movies."

I pointed out that if he did not comply, it was death. He continued: "I felt I was a coward, obsessed with a movie. I had great anger at my father for going along. Only when I got into my 20s did I realize his problems. He could barely manage himself and had to bury his feelings. He did well in the army by functioning as I did as a child, following the structure. But the marriage was bad and he drank a great deal.

"I figured that my way out was to divorce my first wife, who was much more like my mother, and get rid of the external mother, but I didn't get rid of the internal, so the denial kept on."

I pointed out that this was a result of his focus on the object, which was to deal with his fear of death if he focused on himself.

He replied that at about ages seven to nine: "I felt like a coward for not fighting and for killing myself. I was angry at myself. I was always in fights at school, had to prove that I wasn't a coward, but I got no support from my father. I couldn't understand why I felt abused when I was loved. How come the other children who were not loved as I was are happy? The Eleventh Commandment was, 'Thou shalt not speak evil of parents.' There was a primitive sense of something wrong, and what was wrong was me. So I surround myself with others and reinforce the fact that I'm wrong."

After another battle with his wife over her drinking and her attacks, the patient said: "I felt the old guilt trip and started to give in, and then some voice in my head said, 'Why are you taking this abuse?' And so I quit the argument and went to bed. The next day, I was flooded with guilt."

I interpreted that supporting himself leads to feelings of guilt. He then told me that his cardiologist had warned him about his weight, and that in not taking care of his weight, he seemed to be ignoring his own welfare. "Mother held me accountable for everything. Nothing was because I wanted it. I had to be a good person, a polished mirror. My childhood was a poisonous bush that has to be uprooted. I'm frustrated by my denials."

In reviewing again his memories of his rage as a toddler at his mother and how he was dependent on her whims, he gave examples of how, at age eight or nine, he would earn money, which was put in the bank. The other kids were able to use their money for candy, but he couldn't touch his. He had been interested in music, but his mother co-opted this interest. She wanted him to perform when it would reflect on her. So it no longer was his. He loved baseball, and since his mother did not like the game, baseball gave him his only feeling of achievement.

"I preserved an inner core. Now in my office, rather than comply with others, I support myself and then fume inwardly. I'm realizing that I treated my secretary just like I did my mother. The attitude probably caused my cardiovascular problem and my heart attack, so angry, but I'm feeling free. I no longer have to be what I was."

Seventeenth Month

Rage at Mother Leads to Separation Anxiety and Awareness That Self-Activation Equals Death

At a lecture to a codependent group: "I opened myself up to them. I saw their pain and became more aware of my own. It validated my emptiness. I and they, nothing special, nothing entitled. I felt very depressed after. We shared vulnerability. I've been a fraud for 15 years. After the talk, I had a memory right out of the blue of a scene at age three or four of me screaming at my mother. I wished she would die. I told her, 'I hate you.' Mother slapped me so hard that I lost bladder control, but I was able to step out of myself as if I wasn't there."

I pointed out that in order to survive, he had to split himself between the experiencing child and the observer. (Here he had described a dissociative experience.) He continued, "Frightening, I felt crushed. With the rage, I felt like I had an elephant on a six-inch rope."

He continued at the next session: "The rage is ancient. As a child, I was helpless, not allowed to show feelings. I had eight years of Jesuit teaching, 'Use your mind, not feelings.' And I was excellent at it. However, underneath what I felt was loneliness, fear, inadequacy, and shame."

I pointed out that he did not seem to consider the possibility of working through those feelings in the session. This led to further exploration of the rage in the next session: "I had another battle with my wife, but this one brought back memories of my mother. I denied because I hadn't realized I was being abused. I felt sorry for other kids whose parents were not as positive. Yet, I was depressed. I rebelled by not studying, by fighting, by being angry and guilty, not aware of why I did it, hating my mother, telling her I wanted her dead. My father had two personalities. When he was drinking, he was angry and aloof. I remember fighting my mother's prohibition against smoking at 15. And also when I had my heart attack. I had great difficulty giving up smoking. In prep school, I did extremely well. I really was performing for others to feel good about myself—president of the dramatic society and the French club, at the top of my class—I had to prove myself and deny the emptiness. Proving my mother wrong became my identity."

I interpreted that rebellion is not the same as self-activation. This led to further memories: "My father was close to his mother. He told me that one's mother is the most important person in a person's life, the one person who will stick by you. And that started the guilt. I was disloyal to both my mother and my father.

"At age five, I was on my tricycle several blocks away from the house. It paralyzed me and I had a panic. I thought I was going crazy. Then the mailman said hello. I realized I was okay and I pedaled off. The episode haunted me for years. I feared it would happen again. I'd be paralyzed, incapable of moving, being dead but alive."

I interpreted it as separation anxiety related to his rage. Being himself brought on the rage at his mother and father, which betrayed them and evoked the feeling that if he were to separate, he would die. He replied: "I had self-loathing for all ideas, drinking, overeating." I asked him why he had so little compassion for himself. He said: "I feel I want to be left alone. I have the energy to protect myself. Once I supported myself with my wife, I could do it with anyone. I still have the elephant on a six-inch leash."

I interpreted that he closed the door on himself by focusing on the object, but that by being more receptive and recapturing his sense of self, it opened the door to further development and expression.

In the next interview, he reported that, after another battle with his wife, he had had an anxiety attack while he was at work. He said that it must be related to the last interview.

I interpreted that the anxiety attacks seem to come as a repetition of the rage and the memory he had in the last interview. As he set limits to his wife, he could no longer idealize and cling to her and was on his own, as when he was on the bike. And he had a separation panic, a feeling that he would die. His mother's theme was,

"Comply or die." I interpreted that he seemed to need an attacking woman to deal with the fear of being on his own and dying.

He responded: "The memory of Mother punishing me physically with a switch. I was four and a half and I cried and that's when I gave up myself. I lost myself. It was the turning point. I still recall the table I was leaning on, the tears splashing on it." (Thus he began to experience consciously and with affect and memory what was presented in the dream earlier in the month.)

This led to further memories of how he also switched from focusing on the object mother to focusing on the father: "I used to bask in Father's charm and wit. At 13, I imitated him to fill the emptiness rather than develop a sense of myself. The more I could be like Father, the freer I'd be from Mother. And Mother attacked me for it. 'You're gong to be just like your father.' My writing came from my father, who was a raconteur and a short story writer. I was aware that I couldn't do it on my own since there was nothing there."

I interpreted that he idealized his mother to deal with his panic that he would die if he focused on himself. He then switched to idealizing his father to cover the emptiness, and since his father focused on the object, it reinforced his idealizing of his mother.

He said: "I had idealized my father, but while I was in graduate school, I went to a play with him, *A Touch of the Poet*, and I realized with a shock that it was the story of my father's life. I was thunderstruck; a story of a man who lived in past glories. I had immense sadness when he died a year and a half later, the story of dissipated talent living an illusion. Was I the same? I would much rather let others tell me how wonderful I am."

I interpreted this as reinforcing his fear of defeat because his idealization of his father rested on sand and threw him back on his empty inner self. This led to performance to please the object in order to fill the emptiness.

Eighteenth Month

In the next session, he reported a memory that preceded that of the bike episode. That was the last time he had communication with himself. "I thought about what I wanted to be when I was four. I wanted to be a chauffeur and drive a Rolls, like the one owned by a rich family in the neighborhood. And I felt I could do it because my mother would be dead. I would be happy only when free of my mother. Not long after this memory, my mother beat me with a switch for not standing in a corner for 30 minutes as punishment. That's when I gave up myself. That's when I started focusing outright on others. At three, I went to nursery school and liked it, but I was fearful that I wouldn't be picked up after school. I disliked it at night when the day was over and I had to go home. In college, I became a night owl. Under the pressure at home, I always found some escape angles, my grandfather, family, friends, and after age four, I had no feelings. Everything was performance and rebellion, an addiction to performance. I regulated myself by focusing on others. I was forbidden to climb trees, so I envied those who did, even though one fell and broke his arm. His broken arm confirmed to me that to do forbidden things brought punishment. What is the purpose of discipline anyway?"

I interpreted that the purpose of discipline is to strengthen self, not get rid of it. He said: "As of the last interview, I'm using feelings as my guide. I was shamed for feeling. As a child, I numbed feelings, but was always in trouble even though I got good marks. I had to unfocus rage and still have it."

I pointed out that although he felt it, the fact that he did so was not apparent here. He said: "It wasn't permitted by Mother. I could vent it with Father, but then he did nothing about it."

Nineteenth Month

Working Through More Anger, Guilt Leads to Feeling of Rebirth

He reported: "My good memories of Mother's Days of the past have changed. I'm beginning to see how bad Mother is, critical, stingy, tense, also maybe an alcoholic. And I felt sorry for her for the first time, but got angry at myself for allowing myself to be manipulated."

He continued with memories: "At age eight, I idealized my cousin who had been in World War II, and also my father. I cling to these idealized figures of the past and avoid the painful reality of the present. As these people age and get ill, I still focus on the past and deny the present. At eight, I admired my cousin but felt inadequate. But after graduating from school, I felt I was in the tradition of family greatness. I used to go endlessly to meetings to be 'ahead' of my peers. I thought it was for updating, but now I'm no longer doing it. I've got a monkey off my back."

I pointed out that since he was comfortable with himself, he did not feel that he had to be great. He again returned to memories of his mother: "It started at around age three. It was a fierce love–hate relationship. I spat at her, but was terrified of not being with her. The more I performed, the more I justified myself. It was a treadmill. As a child, rules were inflexibly written. Reward was being a good boy. I was afraid I would be the family flop. Mother crammed vegetables down me, so now I can't stand them. To be angry was to be disloyal. Who was I to think like that? It was egomaniacal to challenge. I was chronically angry and depressed, and finding out that that is who my real self is. Then the guilt comes."

I interpreted that it seemed that he felt that focusing on himself was not self-support, but was being arrogant. And then he felt guilty about it.

The patient returned from a week at an out-of-town meeting, announcing that the time away from treatment had allowed him to consolidate and see the enormous changes that had occurred. For example, at the meeting, he focused mainly on what he needed to know rather than on what he could learn to impress others. And, he said, it was totally, uniquely different.

"I reflected on myself and put a persona together, this time in realistic terms of just who I am. However, this led to rage at other people's agendas, my mother's, my wife's, et cetera. I was swimming in the pool and I ended up doing laps, exhausting myself to deal with this rage. My head was bursting with it, at the way these agendas had robbed my sense of self.

"The next day, I felt a genuine rebirth. It probably was the best I ever felt about myself in my life. And I immediately began picking up on my wife's manipulations rather than going along with them. I made some very important decisions for myself—to sell the big house I have and move into a more appropriate one, to set a regular vacation for myself—and as I see options and flexibility, I realize the rigidity that I have had in caving into other people's agendas. For the first time, I felt a congruence between the inner hurt self and the outer image. And I'm not going to focus on impressing others anymore."

SUMMARY

In 20 months of psychotherapy, mostly twice a week, the patient demonstrated clearly the disorder-of-the-self triad: real-self–activation leads to pathologic affect, which leads to defense. The defense of idealization of the object presented a tenacious resistance as it was reinforced by the identification with the aggressor dynamic. The patient had internalized the attacking maternal object to such a degree that he needed to find additional attacking objects later in life to reinforce this internal object representation. These later attacking objects (i.e., women) in turn reinforced the idealizing defense against self-activation.

In psychotherapy, the patient, through interpretation, got better access to real-self–activation, and he would be attacked and then would regress under this influence. At the outset, there was little awareness of this sequence, but further interpretation, with some confrontation, enabled the patient to use real-self–activation to set limits on these incursions and thereby achieve better continuity of access to his real self. This led to better consistency and continuity of affect and memory for the working-through process.

Since performance and achieving in the eyes of the other (object) were the keystones of the patient's defensive system, there was, and remains, a continuing question of how much the content of interviews was based on transference acting out of this dynamic (i.e., he was doing it to please his fantasy about me) and how much was due to genuine working through (i.e., self-activation). The intensity of affect and the nature of the content itself, together with the changes in self-activation, would argue for the latter, but it is always necessary to keep a weather eye out for the former.

PART THREE
Countertransference and Projective Identification

9

Countertransference and Projective Identification I

Overview

Countertransference can be defined in the strict sense as those emotions in the therapist that derive from his or her unresolved earlier relationships with his or her parents that are projected onto the patient. It is used here in a broader sense, not only as meeting that definition, but also as encompassing all those emotions in the therapist that interfere with the ability to provide a therapeutically neutral frame.

Why is the neutral frame so important? In Chapter 4, I pointed out the importance of therapeutic neutrality in that it provides the essential frame within which the patient's transference acted-out projections can be identified, measured, and worked through. Very often in treatment, poor management of these frame factors produces loopholes or leaks in the structure of the therapeutic frame, which then promote hidden and regressive transference acting out and resistance. This transference acting out becomes institutionalized into the regular recurring frame and produces a powerful resistance. Once the therapist has altered his or her therapeutic objective stance to resonate with the resistance, the therapist's most powerful tool has been lost.

Often the patient's persistent, dedicated, artful, and insidious efforts are pressed with such fervor and such a flavor of reality that the therapist can feel caught between humane consideration for the patient and therapeutic objectivity. The therapist who starts to think in this way already is caught in countertransference.

I cannot emphasize enough that the maintenance of this therapeutically neutral frame is a life preserver that sustains the integrity of the treatment under pressures that come from both sides of the desk: the patient's transference acting-out projections and the therapist's countertransference.

Let us now take a look at why countertransference becomes such a major issue in the treatment of the closet narcissistic personality disorder of the self.

THE PATIENT'S TRANSFERENCE ACTING OUT OF PROJECTIONS

The patient begins treatment by relating initially through the projection and acting out of the fused self- and object representations. Patients often report, when well into the treatment, that their childhood had been like living in a concentration camp where their parents were the guards. The way they learned to survive was to figure out the emotional Achilles' heels of the guards so that when the patients were in need, they would be able to evoke the proper response. Therefore, they had become professionals at this process. Thus from the outset of treatment, they are monitoring the therapist to discover his or her emotional Achilles' heel. And they may not necessarily reveal that fact, nor will they evoke it immediately; instead, they store it away to be used when emotional crises arise in the treatment.

In addition to the intensity of the acting out of the projections, there is the brittle and fragile therapeutic alliance, which makes it doubly difficult to keep these projections within the limits of reality. These forces cause countertransference to be a greater problem in the treatment of narcissistic patients than, for example, of neurotic patients, as illustrated by the following example. A patient with a neurosis reports his symptoms and the therapist makes a comment. At the next session, the patient reports that he had been thinking about the comment, and in doing so realized that he became more anxious . He says that, as a matter of fact, he had a dream, and then he describes the associations to the dream.

A closet narcissistic patient reports symptoms and the therapist makes an observation, "There are 100 things that can happen, and none of them will be what I just described. The patient with a neurosis may not hear the therapist, may distort what was heard, or may instantly deny, avoid, or otherwise defend against what was said. The patient may not return at all, may return late, may return without remembering what was said, or may return having distorted what was said.

How can we understand these differences in behavior? The patient with a neurosis begins therapy with a firm therapeutic alliance. Thus, from the outset, the therapist and patient are allied and are working jointly on the problem, which automatically seems external to the therapeutic alliance.

With the closet narcissistic patient, since there is so little therapeutic alliance at the outset, the therapist is the problem. The patient at the beginning of treatment relates to the therapist on the basis of his or her projections. The patient comes to treatment not to get better, but to get the therapist to resonate with these projections. If the therapist resonates with the idealizing projection, the patient perceives that his or her defensive self-representation is being responded to. The result is that the patient feels good, and treatment stops.

If the therapist resonates with the harsh aggressive unit, the patient dumps on the therapist all the rage that he or she was unable to express to the parents, and treatment momentum stops.

When they reach the middle of the working-through phase, and not before, many patients will confide that they do not come to treatment to get better, but to get what they were deprived of in childhood.

THERAPIST COUNTERTRANSFERENCE

There are, of course, two sides to this issue—the patient's projections and the therapist's response. I have described the characteristics of the patient's pressure to induce the therapist into countertransference. Let us now consider why therapists seem so vulnerable to countertransference.

Therapists undertake their work for a variety of reasons, but one important element in their motivation, it seems to me, is what I call a rescue fantasy. To the degree that their self-development was deprived in childhood, they project this self-representation on their patients, and then do for their patients what they always wanted to have been done for themselves. If the therapist had healthy parents and a relatively healthy development, and thus mature self- and object representation, this fact will be the basis of some of his or her satisfaction in treatment, since the therapist does help the patient to remake his or her personality, recapture a sense of self, and overcome childhood deprivation.

On the other hand, if the therapist's parents were not that healthy and the therapist had severe difficulties with the development of a sense of self and so does not have good self- and object representations or a good differentiation of self from object, the therapist eventually will project that deprived self on the patient and do for the patient what he or she always wished his or her parents had done for him or her. In other words, the therapist will end up treating himself or herself, and the patient will love it, because then the patient does not have to participate in treatment.

PROJECTIVE IDENTIFICATION

There has been much debate about whether projective identification is purely intrapsychic or is also interpersonal, and as to how much the patient's actual behavior evokes it. The term will be used here in the sense of the patient's projecting upon the therapist usually negative affects associated with either the self- or the object representation, and then behaving in such a manner as to coerce the therapist into actually accepting and feeling this projection. This behavior can be quite subtle and indirect, consisting of such things as facial expression, tone of voice, and body posture, as well as more overt behavior.

Why does the patient operate in this fashion? In early development, the closet narcissist was the recipient of a projective identification on the part of a parent. The parent projected onto the child some unwanted negative aspect of the parent's sense of self. I recall a patient on whom both the mother and father projected their negative, inadequate, helpless, hopeless senses of self. The patient was required to behave in a helpless and hopeless fashion without any self-activation, or else she would be attacked by both parents. In this manner, she managed to contain and process these negative affects for both parents.

The child learns that the way to deal with painful affect is to project it onto others and coerce them into containing and processing it. These children develop an exquisite radar to search out therapists' negative self-images that they can then evoke to take on their own negative self- and object images. For such patients, this mechanism operates in all other relationships, as well as in psychotherapy. The degree to which it will evoke a countertransferential response depends, first, on the therapist's acceptance of the projection, and, second, on whether this projection also happens to fit one of the therapist's unresolved negative self-images. If it is the latter, the countertransference induced can become quite intense and difficult to resolve. In other words, the fate of the projected identification will depend on whether the therapist is reacting purely to the hear-and-now behavior of the patient or whether this content of the projection fits an unresolved problem of the therapist from the past.

As a prototype, let us return to the woman whose parents projected their negative sense of self-helplessness, hopelessness, and so on, on the patient's self-representation. Whenever the patient attempted to activate herself, she was severely attacked by both parents. This resulted in an intrapsychic structure of an underlying harsh attacking aggressive unit—a self-representation of being bad, inadequate, hopeless, and helpless. This was defended against by a grandiose-self–object representation of an idealized object that provided support and admiration for compliance in giving up the self.

In psychotherapy, the patient could project either of these representations, or she could alternate between them. She could project the attacking object representation on the therapist; experience the helpless, hopeless, inadequate sense of self; and feel that the therapist dislikes her and is devaluing her and attacking her. The patient might actually conduct herself in treatment in such a fashion as to provoke this reaction; for example, by not paying the bill, being late, attacking the therapist, and defeating all the therapist's efforts at intervention.

On the other hand, she might project a self-representation of being inadequate, helpless, and hopeless onto the therapist and experience herself in the role of the attacking object, in which case she would devalue and attack the therapist and try to obstruct all therapeutic endeavors. In this latter operation, of course, the patient is defending by turning passive responses into active responses and identifying with the aggressor.

The therapist's job is not to react to projections, but to reflect and interpret. In so doing, the therapist enables the patient to become aware of the projection, to contain it, and to make it available for working through in the psychotherapeutic session. At the same time, the therapist's accepting the projection and giving it back to the patient without reacting to it begins the process of defusing the intensity of the affect and bringing the projection within the boundaries of reality. The projection is thus "metabolized" along with its powerful negative affects.

Following are some examples of therapists caught up in a countertransference based on projective identification, which is one of the most common dynamics of countertransference in work with closet narcissistic patients.

A therapist reports seeing an attractive woman patient who had a closet narcissistic disorder. She presented with severe constant somatic complaints and verbalized her frustration at her husband's lack of response to her wish to be taken care of by him. The therapist said that he also felt helpless and frustrated by her persistent complaints, but that he was somewhat attracted to her and felt a real need to take care of her. I was able to interpret to him on the basis of his report that the way the patient was dealing with the frustration and helplessness evoked by the denial of her wish to be cared for, was to focus on her somatic symptoms and her attractiveness as a way of getting attention. And when that did not work, it left her feeling even more frustrated. The therapist immediately recognized what was happening; he lost his sense of frustration and helplessness and was encouraged to return with confidence to interpret the projective identification to the patient.

In another case, a young woman patient, upon entering the office of her therapist, made a comment about the therapist's dress and shoes, and then reflected on her own difficulty in choosing clothes. She said she wondered if she and the therapist might be the same size, and whether she could wear what the therapist was wearing. Later in the session, the patient talked about her difficulty in activating and supporting herself, and then turned to the therapist and asked, "How do you support yourself?" Rather than reflect and interpret this behavior, the therapist responded by trying to give the patient direction and advice on supporting herself. This patient's psychodynamic background was that she had to be the caretaker of her mother and to give up herself in the process. Thus, in the therapeutic relationship, she was placing this impaired self on the therapist and experiencing the role of the object representation, expecting the therapist to function for her as she had for her own mother.

Another therapist reported seeing a patient who had been in a local prestigious training group, but had to drop out of the group and out of treatment. Unable to face her feelings of humiliation and embarrassment at the implied inadequacy in herself, the patient started treatment with a new therapist, whose ability she questioned. Did the therapist, the patient asked, have the ability to help her, the patient? The therapist identified with this projection, becoming very anxious as to whether in fact she did have the capacity to treat this person. In this way, she identified with the patient's feelings of inadequacy, humiliation, and embarrassment, rather than reflecting the question back and interpreting it to the patient as follows: "Perhaps you were so concerned about my capacity because it was so painful to face up to the feelings of humiliation and embarrassment you had, and your way of soothing them was to place them in me."

One of my patients, a closet narcissist, had had an extremely devaluing and attacking mother and was married to an even more devaluing and attacking husband. Her sessions were marked by complaints about her husband's behavior toward her and his devaluation, as well as her difficulty in supporting herself. However, as she began to activate herself in her life and with her husband, and he no longer fulfilled this function for her, she was required to project it upon me. She felt that I was bored, uninterested, and devaluing, just as her husband had been. The proof of this projection was that when her husband returned to his abusing behavior, the projection on me disappeared. It seemed that it was so painful for her to face in her psyche her mother's devaluation of her that she had to find an external object upon which to project it, and then coerce it into feeling and processing this projection. This may have had a lot to do with her choice of a husband, since the husband had taken on the projection and carried it out. However, when he ceased doing so, as a result of her self-support, she had to place it on me and the treatment.

A schizoid-appearing therapist presented a case of a closet narcissistic woman who began treatment with flagrant acting-out idealizing of the therapist. She wanted advice, she wanted to sit next to the therapist, and she wanted the therapist to do various things for her. The more the patient acted out this idealizing, and the more the therapist experienced it as a reinforcement of the commanding object's wish for her to be a slave, the more anxious, angry and distant the therapist became and the more she withdrew and withheld from the patient. The more she withheld, the more the patient felt abandoned and escalated her acting out. It was necessary to bring the therapist's countertransferential withdrawal to her attention so that she could regain therapeutic neutrality and be able to set the necessary limits for the patient.

Projective identification, of course, is not the only mechanism for the evoking of countertransference, but it is a common and powerful one that most often goes on unconsciously.

MANAGEMENT OF COUNTERTRANSFERENCE

The first step in managing countertransference is to identify it. When this is clear, it is appropriate for the therapist to focus as much on the countertransference as on the patient, since the countertransference is now the obstacle to further therapeutic process. And the first thing to do is to do nothing until the countertransference is understood. In two words, "Shut up." One cannot get in trouble for what one does not say, and unless the patient is in an emergency state, he or she will get along until the therapeutic neutrality is restored.

Once the countertransference has been understood, the therapist has a variety of options. The therapist can review the patient's behavior and see what the patient has done to evoke the countertransference. This should be done even if the countertransference stems from an unresolved, infantile conflict of the therapist that was evoked by the patient. If, however, on further observation, it becomes clear that the patient is not doing anything to evoke the countertransference, then it becomes strictly a problem of the therapist from his or her past, that he or she must manage by getting a consultation, further treatment, or whatever else is indicated. But if the countertransference is evoked mostly by the behavior of the patient, the therapist has some further options: First of all, if the countertransference has resulted in overt behavior with the patient, it is necessary to acknowledge this and apologize to the patient. With narcissistic patients in particular, where failure of empathy is a constant issue, whether the countertransference is real or is based on fantasy is very important. Patients will forgive mistakes as long as the therapist eventually gets on the right track. They will not forgive dishonesty.

If the countertransference has not resulted in overt behavior, the therapist can use it as a litmus test or signal to indicate what the current issue is for the patient, and then interpret it to the patient. For example, I had a patient, a professional, who was extremely obsessive, compulsive, and intellectualizing, and I had great difficulty deciding when the patient was intellectualizing and when he was expressing feeling. I finally realized that if I became bored and started to go to sleep, the chances were that the patient was not expressing feeling. At these times, I would not tell the patient that I was about to fall asleep, but I would ask him if he were expressing feelings at that moment—and he would invariably say that he was not. If the treatment is far enough along and there is an adequate therapeutic alliance, the therapist can report such a feeling and link it to the patient's behavior, which then makes it available for working through. For example, I was seeing a patient with a closet narcissistic disorder and anorexia nervosa who was referred to me after her therapist had to stop treatment with her. In the course of her sessions with me, there as a good deal of devaluation of me and the treatment, but there was no element of anorexia, which surprised me until I realized why. She did not require the anorexia because those affects were being discharged on me in session. What was happening was that she had had to play the role of her mother's caretaker despite her mother's constant vilification and devaluation. She was externalizing and acting out her rage at the loss of her therapist by projecting that devalued self-image on me and playing out the role of the devaluing and attacking object, thereby externalizing rage and depression. Interpretation of this then made it available for working through.

The key to identifying the projective identification is found in the details of the therapist's feeling about the patient. This is illustrated by the clinical examples presented in Chapters 10 and 11.

10

Countertransference and Projective Identification II

Clinical Example: Defensive Fusion Evokes Directiveness

EXAMPLE 1

Projective Identification

Patient's Impaired Self Evokes Fusion* Defense (i.e., Directiveness with Patient)

The patient, a 42-year-old married homemaker with three adolescent children, had a closet narcissistic personality disorder. In the past year, she had obtained a full-time job that she loved, but the long hours required much time away from home. Her husband objected strongly to her working, and when he began to consider a job change that required relocation, she threatened to leave him rather than move. The couple came in for a marital consultation. The therapist decided to see the woman once a week in individual psychotherapy and referred the couple to another therapist for joint marital therapy.

**Fusion:* The therapist reacts to the patient's affects by providing the wished-for response—joining or fusing with the patient. The patient expresses wishes to be directed, reassured, and cared for, and the therapist tries to do this rather than reflect and interpret it.

The Therapist's Report

Therapist: I had some trouble with this client right off the bat. I was having a lot of anxiety problems myself through her sessions—especially when she was being defensive and trying to put me on guard. There was one session where I had a clipboard in my hand and was starting to take notes, but she started to get on me and say she was very uncomfortable talking to me, very uncomfortable having me sitting there writing notes. I tried to get into some mirroring interpretations, and I literally stopped writing. I took hardly any notes that session. I was aware that I was trying to focus all my attention on the patient and basically trying not to screw up, but I was anxious.

J.M.: She is a closet narcissist. When she complains about your notes, what is the basis of the complaint?

Therapist: I'm not paying enough attention to her.

J.M.: That, or you're focusing too much on her.

Therapist: That could be. I have to get better at this. I'm not as fast as I should be. There are times when I'm taking notes where I'm just scribbling things down.

J.M.: Unless you consider your behavior inappropriate, you don't want to alter it because of what a patient says.

Therapist: I haven't. I've stuck with my clipboard, and I'm taking better notes.

J.M.: You're going to take process notes, I assume.

Therapist: That's what I'm doing. Actually, since I've referred her for marital therapy, that also has dropped away; I sit there writing all I want, and she doesn't mind.

J.M.: One of the big problems with that is that she is backing off and lying low. Why do you think she is?

Therapist: I don't know. I'm a little surprised to hear you say that, to tell you the truth. I've gotten more affect in recent sessions. She's talked a lot about her guilt, about wanting to leave her husband. Maybe I'm missing the point.

J.M.: The husband's agreeing to see the marital therapist has taken both of them off the hot seat. They came to you as an alternative to separating. Now, what we have is an arrangement that, for the foreseeable future, puts separation way, way in the background. They're not going to separate; they're going to work on their problems.

Therapist: Yes. The only thing I should add is that near the end of my assessment period, the wife did come right out and say that she was not going to give up her career, and that she would rather leave her husband than do that. If he had to move again, she wouldn't go with him.

J.M.: I understand that, but do you see how the immediacy of that has been removed by the arrangement? So that fades into the background. The pressure of that. So she can relax more. There are some good aspects to that, right? Because you want her to act in an integrated way after reviewing it. But I think it's important to keep in mind. Maybe there's more to it.

Therapist: I had some more difficulties in dealing with her in our last session. I need some help figuring out what was going on. She really got me on the defensive in a way that hasn't happened before. I think part of it has to do with your comments about the pressure being off, the marital separation being pushed away in the background. Let me read my process notes.

She comes in, sits down, looks at me, and asks, "Where should we start?" I thought, "Uh-oh." If I had a borderline, I would confront that, but I wasn't sure what to do with it. I was not happy with my response. All I said was, "Where would you like to start?" And wondered if I should have interpreted instead.

J.M.: Why not?

Therapist: Why not, yes. I was off balance, to tell you the truth. I guess I could have said something like, "What makes you look to me to start the session today?"

J.M.: That's a confrontation. Sometimes you do have to confront, but not now with this patient.

Therapist: She said it in a kind of flip way. I wasn't sure if she was kidding or what.

J.M.: Also, when in doubt, you can say nothing. She what she does with it.

Therapist: That would have been better than what I did, I think.

J.M.: We're back to the problem. What is she doing? She's offering you an opportunity to fuse with her. And you have trouble with that.

Therapist: Yes, I do.

J.M.: And since you've got to report to me, you get uncomfortable about it.

Therapist: Yes.

J.M.: And this blocks your freedom to evaluate and respond. So I think that what you tend to do when you're in a corner is generally to reach for a directive response. So here you're saying, "Don't push it on me. Take it yourself." See what I mean?

Therapist: I think that's true.

J.M.: So I think you have to become aware of that.

Therapist: And I must say that I think I would have responded that way even if you weren't going to be going over this case with me. I can be put off balance like that.

J.M.: It's important to understand your countertransference. What puts you off is the invitation, because it stirs up your own impulse. And that makes you anxious because you have learned that's not the road to take, so you're stuck. You can't do what you want to do, and you're blocked then on thinking through what you ought to do in reality.

Therapist: Exactly. I'm stuck for a better alternative.

J.M.: This being stuck has to do not with your intellectual process; it has to do with your emotional process. To begin to think about what is appropriate for you to do is to frustrate this wish, if you follow me. As soon as you start to think about how you should handle this overture, what you're doing is frustrating your own wish to fuse with her. And so you're blocked at doing that. Not that you couldn't figure it out, but the countertransference emotion blocks you.

Therapist: Well, things went on from there. I think what I did, taking that directive stance, got things off on the wrong foot here. She responded by saying: "The marital sessions have been going well with the other therapist. She has pointed out some things to us that I guess, if we were aware of them, we had put in the backs of our minds. Something that has been missing all these years is feelings. My husband's feelings, his inability to express them, that has been very hard for me, and that has made me try to be stronger, like him. And that has made him not aware of feelings and trying to fix things. That's the part I'm the most aware of, the feelings. That's the part he always leaves out. And that's the part I care the most about. And in these marital sessions, that has left me with a much better feeling; we're able to talk about it more." There were a few other things in there I didn't get, but basically she was saying that she was quite pleased with the marital therapist's work with them, and felt as though they were really doing well, making progress.

She caught me . . . I realized I was doing this. I was concentrating very hard. I think I was still cogitating over the initial misstep I had made. I also felt . . . I could hear in "the therapist is doing very well" her putting more pressure on me, like, "What are you going to do?" So I was frowning. She looked up at me and said, "You're frowning," and smiled a little bit at me. Once again, I didn't know how to respond to that well, and I got defensive. I just said, "I'm listening." That's all I said. And she chuckled.

The patient knew that the therapist was vulnerable to fusing with her because of his response to the initial "Where do we start?" overture. She now increased the pressure by devaluing the therapist, evoking his impaired self, which he then would defend against by fusing with her through directive responses. I did not convey all this to the therapist, but instead I said the following:

J.M.: When she looks at you and says "you're frowning," what is she doing? What's going on?

Therapist: On one level, she's trying to put me on the spot, and she's doing a good job of it. Because I feel on the spot. I felt kind of devalued. I really did. And it goes on. I began to feel like I was no good, or really second-rate. I felt compared with another therapist, and felt like I was coming out second best. It was stirring up all kinds of stuff in me. She was really putting me on the spot. And I was not handling it well at all. I think she picked up on that because the next thing she said spoke directly to that. She started to compare me directly with another therapist, saying that she liked what that therapist was doing, that she didn't think I was doing.

J.M.: Like what?

Therapist: She said: "Maybe this is dumb, but I talk at you, you don't respond. The other therapist interprets our feelings to us. Sometimes people need that." Well, at this point, I was really starting to get angry. And I got confrontational, I think. Well, I did. I said, "You don't think you're getting that in here?"

J.M.: That's not so bad, because that is what she is saying.

Therapist: But I think I was getting angry, too. Because I was feeling like I was getting knocked. Having this patient come in and me feeling not very good with narcissistic patients in general, getting this kind of evaluation of my performance was really . . . it hit me where it hurts, is one way to put it. She chuckled when I said that, and she said, "Well, I'm in here for a different reason." Then (I didn't get all this down because she was talking fast and I was flustered) basically she started talking about her resentment about being placed in the "sick" role, that her husband still sees her as having a problem and her coming in to see me reinforces that idea, that she's the one with the problem, and she doesn't like that. I think at this point I began to recover a little bit.

J.M.: Because she has taken back the projection of her inadequate self in you and started now to do the work. This has gotten her off your back.

Therapist: In spite of what I did, I think, more than because of it. Because if she had kept after me, I was going to be in big trouble. But I did manage to recover somewhat here. I said something like (using stock things), "It's so painful for you to focus on yourself that you protect yourself from the pain by focusing on the marital conflicts instead." She responded to that by saying, "I'm in here to work on myself." She seemed flustered, she started to flush a little bit. She seemed uncomfortable, even a little irritated with me. She then started to talk about how she's very hypersensitive to criticism. Talked about how she had been criticized at her job recently and how that's very hard for her to handle. Again, I began to think, She feels like I'm criticizing her now.

J.M.: No, I don't think so.

Therapist: Okay.

J.M.: She's starting to do the work. She's elaborating on what you said to her.

Therapist: I guess I was still tangled up in my own countertransference, being very defensive. I kept my mouth shut for the most part.

J.M.: That was smart.

Therapist: She went on and on about the criticism. Then I said something that was not quite a mirroring interpretation, but she paused. I said, "It's difficult for you to accept the criticism because it makes you feel pain about yourself." She agreed with that, and then started talking about how she reacts at those times, that she gets in a very bad and irritable mood, starts dumping on people, being snappy and short, getting mad at things that really are of no consequence.

J.M.: I'd hold that there right now. She's a closet narcissist, right?

Therapist: Yes.

J.M.: What do closet narcissists do? How do they defend?

Therapist: They try to find that idealized object and bask in that glow so they can feel special and have their grandiosity . . .

J.M.: All right. So they operate off the other person.

Therapist: Right.

J.M.: Now this woman comes in from a marital session. What can she do, easily, in a marital session?

Therapist: She can keep the focus off herself.

J.M.: How?

Therapist: By focusing on the marital relationship, and especially her husband.

J.M.: All right. So, when she transfers from that to seeing you individually, what happens to this operation?

Therapist: Well, it takes it away.

J.M.: Right. So that's what she was reacting to, because individual therapy, for her, takes away the reinforcement of her idealizing defenses. Let's go back to the beginning of the session.

Therapist: Right. She wants to focus on me.

J.M.: How does she handle that? She says what?

Therapist: Where should we start?

J.M.: Right. What is she doing?

Therapist: She's trying to put the focus on me, in order to have me take the lead.

J.M.: Right.

Therapist: Is that an effort to idealize me?

J.M.: Yes, so that she doesn't have to focus on herself. And so the dynamic that you're struggling with is a combination of what her internal intrapsychic dynamics are and the difference between a joint and an individual session, and how it reinforces or frustrates that dynamic. So you see that it has nothing to do with you. You're seeing a clear example of transference acting out. But somehow you missed grabbing the difference between the joint and the individual. You're going to have to use your knowledge to try to limit this countertransference too, right? So when she walks in, the beginning of the session is a moment of self-activation, is it not? Therefore, it mobilizes all of our patient's defenses. So when you get that first shot out of the gun, you know what it's going to be about. Right? When she comes in and it's her moment to reflect and so forth, what happens? Rather than do that, she turns it over to you.

Therapist: Right.

J.M.: Now let's go back to the beginning. What might you have said then, at that point, if you were in command?

Therapist: Taking a cue from the things you have just suggested, in terms of her first statement, maybe I could have said . . . would it have been too much to have said, "It's painful for you to come in here and start focusing on yourself right away, so you try to deal with the pain by trying to toss it over to me and have me take the lead?"

J.M.: That's fine.

Therapist: Okay.

J.M.: And then when she goes on to talk about the marital session, you can say, "It was evidently much easier for you to operate there than here." You notice that she goes on and says that herself, even though you don't say it.

Therapist: Yes, that's true.

J.M.: Then why does she turn to you and say that you're frowning?

Therapist: Once again, she's taking herself off the hot seat.

J.M.: Right. She's focusing on you rather than herself. And when she says to you that you're frowning, you say . . . the initial response should always be, "I wonder why you shifted from yourself to me." Or if you have enough grasp of the situation, and you think she has enough awareness as well, you can run an interpretation. "It's so hard for you to focus on what you were thinking about, that you shifted over to me as a way of soothing it."

Therapist: Okay. Again, in spite of me, she started to go in that direction anyway, interestingly enough. I see what you're saying. I even came into this session feeling defensive.

J.M.: Why do you think you're so vulnerable to this?

Therapist: A couple of things, I think. I feel I'm not very good with narcissists in general. I've had very little work with them. I have difficulty with this woman. I'm very worried that I'm going to mishandle it early on and lose the case. So these kinds of things are weighing on me.

J.M.: I wonder why you feel so vulnerable to feeling the patient is attacking you and your competence. Why does it evoke feelings of inadequacy about yourself?

Therapist: I guess I have some doubts about my own competence, and they're hitting that bull's-eye. For whatever reason they may attack it, they hit me in my Achilles' heel if they do that.

J.M.: My guess is that either your mother or you father, or both, attacked you in this fashion. Is that right?

Therapist: Yes. More my father. More overtly.

J.M.: The work with the narcissistic disorder stirs up something in you that has more to do with you than with your patient.

Therapist: Yes. I think my father is almost certainly a narcissistic personality, and he is very attacking and devaluing whenever he gets crossed. And there were some times growing up where he made it clear if I didn't do what he thought I should do, I was totally devalued. I was thrown out of the house. I was denigrated and called names, all kinds of stuff.

J.M.: So you developed this inner image of yourself as being no good and valueless and worthless. Unless . . .

Therapist: Unless I do what the narcissist wants me to do.

J.M.: Right. You see, this fits hand in glove particularly with closet narcissists and transference acting out. If you're not perfect for them, you're no good. I think what happened is that you become anxious and ill at ease in advance.

Therapist: Yes.

J.M.: You're anticipating. I think by the way, that you're right here; this is where your level of experience comes in. Since you don't feel experienced and you're going to make mistakes, this places you in the position where you were with your father. You're not going to be doing it right. And then you get the narcissist who comes on with that and you've got a combination. So the anxiety itself tends to block freedom of thought and exploration, and experimentation, in your head. Now, I think you have to find a way to get a hold on this, so that you put some barrier between your feeling these things and your getting them into therapeutic action. You'll have to think this through. In general, if you put a stop . . . if you're feeling uncomfortable, like you're being attacked, the best thing to do at that point is probably to say nothing or just reflect it back to the patient, until you get a better hold on it. And try to force yourself to think, What is this patient doing, why is she doing it, and what's going on right now? As we talked about it, you did pick up what was going on.

Therapist: Yes, eventually.

J.M.: The key was the switch from joint to individual therapy, and her difficulty managing it. Do you follow me? If you're feeling yourself defensive, the best thing is to say nothing. The second is to reflect it back. As with this one, or routinely almost, you can say, "I wonder why you shifted this focus from yourself to me," or, "Did you notice what happened just now?" Generally, they're talking about something that is painful to look at, so instead of looking at that, they turn it over to you. You had better be equally alert, not just to the criticism, but also to the invitations to be idealized and to fuse. It sounds like she's giving you a chance here; it sounds as if it did not go too badly, considering.

Therapist: Quite frankly, I think I got lucky. She did just sort of take the reins and start working. But, as you said, I think more and more of how this works with me. Early in my life, I was more idealized, but when I went off to college, there was a definite break in the other direction.

J.M.: Probably that's what saved your life. What about in your treatment? How much did you touch on all this?

Therapist: A fair bit. I had two years of once-a-week treatment. And I think, for short periods, I had twice-a-week therapy. The therapist I had was highly nondirective. I think he was more analytic. He didn't say much.

J.M.: Not analytic enough, evidently!

Therapist: Really. And the other thing was—this is important, it's something that has always bothered me—I never got emotional at all in those two years. It was all intellectualized.

J.M.: Yes, that's bad. That's probably what he was most comfortable with, too.

Therapist: There was only one or two times I even felt emotion stirring deep in the pit of my stomach, but I shoved it right back down. I never shed a tear during the whole two years. So I don't think I touched any of this stuff on an emotional level.

At the next session she was calmer, even when she came in the door. Which was striking. I expected her to come in angry. But she didn't. She was pretty calm and matter-of-fact, said okay when we talked about the insurance, and really didn't have anything much to say one way or the other. [The patient had been expecting the therapist to handle the insurance rather than checking it herself.]

J.M.: What you should have said to her, in my view, was, "I'm struck by the fact that you really didn't check out your policy when you undertook this responsibility."

Therapist: That's true. But I didn't say that. Well, the insurance thing came to an end and I just lapsed into silence. She looked at me and smiled, then asked, "We're ready to start talking?" (as a theoretical sort of question) and then sort of chuckled. Then she said, "There are some things I wanted to talk with you about from last time." (We didn't get to the end of the session last week.) At the last session, she had started to discuss the situation at her office, where a male colleague who seemed attracted to her was coming by more and more, wanting to spend more time with her, joke around, eat lunch with her. She's beginning to pick up that this fellow's interest seems to be growing into something more than just friendship. She asserted last time that she had absolutely no romantic interest in him whatsoever. She likes him as a friend, and is wrestling with the problem of how to handle this because she doesn't want to hurt his feelings.

She started to bring this up again and basically reviewed the situation. She said, "I don't want to hurt his feelings. I still am the kind of person who doesn't want to hurt anybody's feelings, and I guess I always will be." I asked at that point, "Do you think that will never change for you?" She said, "No, I want to treat others the way I like people to treat me." I said, "For you, it's one step further; you can't allow yourself to hurt someone else's feelings for any reason."

She said, "Right," and then started to discuss how she wished not to hurt other people's feelings because it made her feel bad—rehashing the same sort of stuff—didn't want to do anything like that. I said, "Hurting anybody's feelings makes you feel pain about yourself, and in order to protect yourself from the pain, you've discounted your own feelings and pleased the other person in the past." She said "Yes," and then started to get into more specific detail about the situation with this man's joking around with her, coming around her so much; he had made no passes so far, but she gets the feeling that is coming. I said, "It's painful for you to assert your own needs and feelings when you don't want to do something." She said that that would be extremely embarrassing for her, that she hated that, and she would rather do anything than feel embarrassed like that.

J.M.: So at this point, you're on the main line, aren't you? Her impaired self? That's what you want her to do. As long as you've got her on the main line, let her do it.

Therapist: Okay. Well, I'll just tell you what I did say. I hear what you're saying. I said, "You're exquisitely sensitive to being embarrassed or humiliated or made fun of." She had started to bring up times in the past when she had been teased, even as a child, and how incredibly painful that had been for her. "But you're stuck because, in this situation, in order to protect yourself from this, you have to give up your own feelings and please the other person." She said: "Yes, that's because I know how I would feel. I don't like that at all. It's the worst feeling I can ever have. There's something wrong with someone who wants to hurt other people's feelings. What makes people different? Why aren't we born with the same amount of feelings?" I said, "That question takes us away from looking at what makes you feel so sensitive." And she chuckled, saying, "That's the bottom line. I don't like to have my feelings hurt. I'm very sensitive to that. Look, I'm 42, I've always been this way, and I'll probably be this way for the next 40 years, but I need to find a way to deal with this." Then she paused, and I just said, "Agreed." She started talking about how she was an unusually high achiever because she cared about hurting other people's feelings. She said that people always tell her their problems, that she's the kind of person everybody always comes to "because they know I'm a caring person." But she avoids telling other people her feelings because "I don't want people to know I have any problems. I even have a comeback. I'll always throw it back at them. It's not real mean, but I'll throw something out to take the attention away from me."

J.M.: That is a beautiful description of the closet narcissistic defense, isn't it? And that's what she is going to be doing with you over and over again. That's what you have to be alert to and interpret, rather than react to. This is better, but you're still a little too active. Your job, you know, as with this patient . . . either the patient is talking about the main line, which has to do with the sensitivity and/or her need to defend against it by idealizing. When she's on that track, you just let her go. And particularly important, let her go when she hits a silence. When she is doing it, in other words when she is spontaneously talking about the impaired self or the defense, she is activating herself. Which will lead to what?

Therapist: Well, that will lead to some feelings, some depression, I would guess.

J.M.: Right. And then she is going to defend against it by what?

Therapist: Taking the attention back off of herself again.

J.M.: Turning to you. So that's what you want . . . once she's on the main track, you sit back and let her do it. And wait. What is going to happen is that she is going to become silent, and if you don't interject in the silence, inevitably she is going to come around to you. And then you interpret. And you relate that it's so painful for her to look at all this that her way of soothing that pain is to focus on you rather than her.

Therapist: Okay. She started to talk more about this particular person in her office.

J.M.: By the way, what is overlooked here, and what probably in general is denied in the service of this defense . . . if she's not interested in this man, she views telling him that she wants to be a friend, as "hurting his feelings." Whereas the reality is that she's doing him a service. And why is she doing him a service?

Therapist: Because she's not leading him on.

J.M.: Right. There are two options at that point: to lead him on by activating her idealizing defense, or to tell him, as nicely as she can, that she wants a friend and she's not interested romantically. And this whole latter part is denial. She sees that her only options are to idealize him and ignore her needs, or support her needs and "hurt" him. She's overlooking that she is also doing him a favor by keeping him from getting in too deep.

Therapist: Yes. And I was just thinking that in spite of what she is saying, she is certainly enjoying all the narcissistic supplies of having this man pandering to her.

J.M.: Sure. Particularly in this situation.

Therapist: She was getting back to this situation more, with this man in the office, and she was talking about how . . . well, giving more examples of how she would throw it back on him, that she's not going to share any of her feelings with him at all. He had asked her a few things about her family, her kids, and stuff like that. She never stayed focused on that very long. She always gets back to him. I did say something again. I think I may still be hooked by that thing that happened last session; I wonder if that is operating on me. Her complaint.

J.M.: What?

Therapist: Oh, she said something to the effect that I never say anything, that I just sit there and listen.

J.M.: She's resenting having to activate herself and the frustration of her need to idealize.

Therapist: I wonder if that is tugging on me still. I am saying things here when I should be keeping my mouth shut. I said: "It's very painful for you to take the risk of even beginning to show your feelings or have the focus on you. And the way you protect yourself is to throw it back on the other person." Which, as I read it, is really pretty redundant, something I've already said. She said, "Yes, but it's not something mean. I don't want people to know what I'm like inside." She started to talk about how, in the past, she had found she could overcome problems and things that pained her by learning about things, by studying them. She talked about times earlier in her marriage when she would be confronted by some sort of challenge (sometimes just some sort of volunteer thing), and she wouldn't know how to go about it, but she would go to the library and get the information, learn, and then do it. She said: "But I don't want anything negative to come back on me. Where that came from, I don't know. I think some of that came from my husband. I think some of the things I didn't have I tried to learn from him. I wasn't the confident person. I think I learned that from him." I said, "What made you not . . .?"

J.M.: You just can't do that. You're not letting her do it. And she's trying.

Therapist: I see what you mean. The session continued like this. I jumped in periodically.

J.M.: She's really doing pretty well. You see, you're making the right interpretation, and she's responding. But then you won't let her do it.

Therapist: I need to get out of her way.

J.M.: Right.

Therapist: I asked her, "What made you lack confidence before you got married?" She said, "Nothing was ever expected of me, I always had somebody to tell me what to do and when to do it." She made an interesting slip here, but I didn't say anything about it. In talking about her family, she said "the five of us," and then she caught herself, saying, "Wait a minute, there were six of us, four kids and two parents." I thought, She is so focused on everybody else in the family, she can't even count herself. Then she went on: "We never had any goals to reach. Then in the marriage, we did have goals. If we want this, we have to do this and this and this. And if you want something, you learn it, you get information from books, and I found I did do that for myself. I just had to give myself a little time to learn about it. But I don't like to be made fun of. I don't like to be teased. I always throw it back on the other person." I said something again.

J.M.: You see, every time she gets to the point where she might investigate her narcissistic vulnerability, that's where you move in. As if you don't want to hear it. Do you follow me?

Therapist: Yes. And when I'm doing it, I'm thinking I'm trying to nudge her, but I'm trying to do it for her.

J.M.: You're thinking what?

Therapist: I'm trying to nudge her in that direction.

J.M.: But it's not your job to nudge her. Your only job is to reflect and interpret, and that's all the nudging she needs. I think that inside yourself you don't have confidence in your operating on your own. And so I think you have trouble seeing that it's possible for patients. At that point, when they have to do the work,

I think you're responding to your own anxiety. And that's why you move in, to relieve it. So I think what you're going to have to do with this woman (let's start with her; you've made some movement so it's not all that bad a session) for the next session is, in your process notes, first of all to err on the side of *not* intervening rather than intervening. Second, when you want to intervene, figure out in your own mind why you're doing it and what you expect from it. And, I want you to particularly note where she starts to try to investigate her impaired self that you are impelled to move in. And don't move in. Make a note where you wanted to move in, but don't do it. Then you and I can discuss it and what there is about it.

Therapist: So it's conceivable, especially since she's working as well as she is, that I might say nothing for practically the entire session.

J.M.: Absolutely. That could be the best thing you can do for her. Your job as the therapist is to create conditions that allow patients to activate themselves and do the work. You can't do it for them. For example, with this patient, if your interpretations are appropriate and effective, you have created the conditions. And then she will start to do the work. But then you know what's going to happen. She'll start to do it, her anxiety and depression will mount, and she'll try to come back and draw you back in. So you first have to do your job, which is the interpretation, and then you sit back and monitor. You're like the anesthesiologist at the operation, checking the blood pressure, pulse, and temperature, but she's got to do the operation. But then you must be prepared. You know she's going to run into trouble, and when she does, she is going to do the same number. And then you have to decide, "Am I going to interpret this at this moment?" You can either reflect it back, "Why do you turn to me?" or, "Looking at yourself has been so painful that you're doing here what you do elsewhere, which is to change the focus to deal with the pain." As far as I can see, that's about the only thing you have a right to say to this woman. And I don't think she needs that much, she already has it. She started taking the bait from you, which is a confirmatory sign as far as diagnosis is concerned. But because you came from this overactive position, she probably doesn't believe your correct interpretations in the first half of this interview, so she is going to come back and test you again to make sure you meant them. And you have to be prepared not to do it, but to reflect it back or to interpret it.

Therapist: Okay. I can go on.

J.M.: Go on, Let's hear the rest of it.

Therapist: I think I read this to you. I said; "But for you, it's more than just not liking it. You can't feel good about yourself if that's going on." She kept saying she didn't like it. That got a reaction out of her. She said, "Is that like when somebody is beating on you? Should I let them do that?" That drew me into responding to her, so I think I really derailed things completely here.

J.M.: What did you say?

Therapist: Well, I got back to the example of the man in the office—her fear that he would not react well to her confronting him and her not being able to feel okay about herself in that situation. I just pointed out, "You're taking care of yourself there, but you can't feel okay about yourself when you assert your own needs."

J.M.: Okay, she's already started what I thought she would start. She's starting to test you. She threw out a little teaser to see if you would pick it up.

Therapist: She reacted strongly here. She started talking fast and got a little flushed. She started talking about how she avoids conflict by pleasing others. She said, "I don't like conflict!" She said that it worked well for her until she got out in the working world recently, and now it's harder to operate that way. "It all comes from the same feelings, same sources, but I work to cover it up. Cover up the flaws. The insecure feelings, the selfishness, I hide it real well." Then she started discussing this example of the kind of woman who comes in looking frumpy, with mussed hair, and you know she's had a bad day. She said, "But if you keep yourself up well [meaning cosmetically], then they'll never know when you're feeling bad." I spoke up again.

I said, "So you perform and keep up this front and convince everybody else that you're fine." She chuckled and agreed, saying that she does fool people 99.5 percent of the time. "I never want them to have any idea that something is wrong. I came into this world alone, and I'll leave it alone." Then she started talking about how the only time she lets down and can be herself, let herself be in touch with her feelings, is when nobody else is in the house. "Then," she said, "I can let down the way I want to and feel the way I want to feel." But she was careful to specify that meant that her husband was gone, the kids were gone, she was by herself, and she knew she would be alone for hours. And I said something again. "That's the only time you feel safe to be yourself and not perform."

J.M.: That statement is mirroring. That reinforces defense. Can you see how you're working at cross-purposes with yourself? She is ready to work, and if you back off and stick to your therapeutic neutrality and reflect and interpret, I think she is going to be a very good patient.

Therapist: I think so, I see potential. But I've got to get my act together. Obviously. I still am anxious going in.

J.M.: Next week . . . if you intervene, I want to hear what you thought before you intervened. I don't want to hear about your shooting from the hip. All right?

Therapist: All right.

The following week

Therapist: I guess that the place I should start is to talk about my reaction to our discussion last Monday, because it does bear more on this countertransference issue. In all honesty, after that discussion, I was feeling pretty terrible, more than I have felt in quite a long time over just about anything else I can remember. And I realized that that was a lot of my own countertransference reaction. I was dazed for a couple of hours, and then one of the most illuminating things I did was to take the tape that I had made of our discussion and listen to it again. And it was striking for me to notice that when I listened to it on the tape, it sounded maybe a tenth as bad as I had experienced it when I was going through it. I think it's something you have already touched on. You've spoken about how you see my anxiety about being reproached or criticized and wondered if it had something to do with my parents. I think this certainly is tapping into . . . the first thing that comes to mind is my father.

J.M.: You mean that part of your reaction was that you thought I was your father giving you hell?

Therapist: Yes.

J.M.: You're doing a bad job.

Therapist: Yes. And I felt awful about myself.

J.M.: You must have also felt angry.

Therapist: That's another strange thing. That was, at most, a peripheral feeling. I mostly felt terrible and extremely anxious.

J.M.: I think this may provide a clue to the problem with your patients. Which is, I suspect, that you feel . . . you're describing how bad you felt about yourself.

Therapist: Exactly.

J.M.: Now, you felt that in consequence of what I said to you. So, if we turn that around, I think what it suggests is that you are looking for the kind of mirroring from me in—order to maintain yourself—that you feel the patients are looking to you for. Do you follow me?

Therapist: Yes.

J.M.: Because when it is interrupted, you feel so bad about yourself.

Therapist: Yes.

J.M.: What you're doing with your patients then is projecting this wish upon them, a wish that is really yours. And this comes, I'm sure, from your father and the disappointments that were involved in all that.

Therapist: Yes, I think so.

J.M.: The two things you've told me so far, which are the best, are, first, that you did listen to the tape again. It would have been very easy to avoid that. That was setting limits to your own projections.

Therapist: Yes. I felt compelled to do that, I had to do that.

J.M.: And the second is that you did learn, when you set the limits, that this is an intrapsychic issue.

Therapist: Yes.

J.M.: Which is very important.

Therapist: Yes. I literally felt myself cringing as I listened to that tape and that section came up. I was amazed when I listened to it that it truly didn't sound that bad at all. But I felt as if I had been blown to smithereens or something. I felt awful.

J.M.: So you can see now . . . when you were feeling that awful, I become the ogre who made you feel that way. So you can see, with your patients, when they start to attack you for being so awful, that they are going through that same experience. And you have to be able to maintain your own neutrality, and ask, "Why are you feeling this way?" as opposed to stepping in and making them feel better to make yourself feel better.

Therapist: Well, I'm looking on it all as a painful growth experience. Part of me is pleased, or valuing this, although it feels awful. I see what you're talking about. What happened, as the week progressed and I brought this up with all my patients, was even more illuminating. Attendant to what you were just saying, I had all these fears about patients' getting angry with me and quitting, marching off—if I told them they would have to be responsible for their insurance—that I wouldn't have any more patients and I would go broke. But, of course, it went much deeper than that. One thing that struck me very hard was that most of the patients had absolutely no problem with it [the question of insurance]; they nod and say it's fine, and don't even care to discuss it [i.e., turning responsibility for the insurance back to the patient]. At the next session, she again began with, "Where should we start today?"

J.M.: Were you ready for that?

Therapist: Well, I had a couple of lines we had talked about. I decided just to say, "Why are you turning to me?"

J.M.: That's fine. Great.

Therapist: She said: "I get tired of talking about me. It's good that I talk, I know that. But what am I accomplishing? What goal am I trying to reach? I guess that I haven't decided how this is going to be good for me." So I thought, Okay, she's testing me again.

J.M.: Right. She's throwing it out for you to move in.

Therapist: Yes. So I had my stock lines ready. I confess to you that I had them written at the top of my pad so I would have them in case I needed to refer to them. And I did. I said, "It's painful for you to focus on yourself, so you're doing here what you do elsewhere—you want to give the lead to me in order to make yourself feel better."

J.M.: That's terrific. That's right on the money. What did you get back?

Therapist: She said: "But I'm not trying to change that, am I? I don't like to focus on me. I don't mind hearing what other people have to say. I guess I just have another purpose for it. Does that answer your question? I know I'm trying to get over being so sensitive, but am I trying to talk to other people more?" And I just said, "It's painful for you to focus on yourself so you soothe yourself by focusing on somebody else." She said: "I guess so. But I don't know if you have to go with this. I need some input, I need some help from you." And then she just stopped and stared at me.

J.M.: Now you have the whole issue right there on the desk in front of you?

Therapist: Yes. I just came back with a similar sort of thing. I said, "It's painful for you to focus on yourself so you're trying to change the focus to me and have me take the lead so that you can deal with your pain." She said: "How am I supposed to focus on this? I'm trying to deal with too many things at one time. It just confuses me. I don't want people to know what is inside of me. I don't know if I ever will. That's not going to make me a better person. I don't think it's going to make me get along better with my spouse. I get along with people okay. I get along with people okay if I go along with what they want, and if I don't want to, I just back off. I don't know if that's bad." She paused for a long time after that. I didn't feel any pressure, I just sat there and looked at her. And then she said: "I'm better about telling people that I don't like something. I guess I haven't decided at this point if that makes me feel better or not. If everything is in harmony, you don't have to complain. I guess I get my feelings ruffled easily lately. People say the hair is still standing up on the back of my neck when I have conflict with them. I guess if you're irritable, it sends people a message. It's like winning or losing. I don't care if I win or lose, especially if it's at the expense of someone else. If someone else needs to win, that's fine. I'm not competitive at all." She started to flush, and looked away from me more. I just sat there silently. "I'm just thinking out loud. It doesn't fix anything." I had an urge there to say something, but I resisted.

J.M.: Good. You've got her centered right now, exactly where she ought to be.

Therapist: Right. I knew she was trying to get me to take the lead again, so I just decided to sit there. She looked down and away more, and continued to flush. She finally said, "I guess I need you to tell me what we're trying to do." I said (once again), "When you start to focus on yourself, it's painful for you, and here as elsewhere you try to deal with the pain by looking to me." She said, "Well, okay, but I'm not sure what we're trying to fix."

J.M.: You've got to be careful here. I think the writing down at the beginning of the change, to contain yourself and get the job done, is okay. But you've got to be careful about it. Because what's going to happen is that rather than doing it yourself, you're going to start mimicking me. And it will come out after a while a little bit programmed and not attuned to the vicissitudes of each situation. Keep that in mind. This is an example right here. She has moved, as a result of your input, from focusing on others to focusing on herself. But what she is saying is, "I don't know what I want out of this treatment." Do you see? You should reflect that back now, not just that it's painful. Do you see? She is in doubt and confused about what she wants out of treatment, and she wants you to tell her what to get out of treatment. At that point, instead of asking, "What's so painful?" you could add . . . what would you say at this point to be more precise about where she is at?

Therapist: The next thing I did say was, "You look to me to tell you what kind of person you're trying to become." I felt that's what she was wanting me to do, to tell her how she should be—as though that should come from me instead of from her. That was my stab at saying it. I wasn't responding well to it, I guess, but I thought that if she wants me to tell her how to be, we'll just be right back in defense again. If I tell her, she'll do it. So I need to make her do it.

J.M.: What she's saying is, "I don't know what I want out of treatment." Is that what she is saying? You now can say, "When you do focus on yourself, you seem to feel helpless about what you want." Do you follow?

Therapist: The self-activation problem.

J.M.: Right. What happened in the rest of the session?

Therapist: She kind of thrashed around with it more. She started to go with it, talking. When I said, "You look to me to tell you what kind of person to become," as a question, she chuckled. She said, "I know that you're not going to do that. I want to be middle-of-the-road. I want to be my own person, but I'm still struggling not to be the person my husband wants me to be." Then she started to contrast what has been expected from her and how she always tried to do it, with who she wanted to be herself. She went on to say how she was beginning to stand up for herself more with her husband, and it was less of a problem for her. I should tell you how the session ended, though. She just started rolling after that, and I don't think I said much.

J.M.: Because she has described the problem that arises with trying to operate as a closet narcissist. She gives up herself and idealizes the other person. In the process, she loses her sense of self—who she is and where she wants to go. So she has recaptured some of that and has begun to assert it with her husband, which puts her in conflict with him because he liked her the way she was. Now that you have been able to control your countertransference, she starts to do the work.

Summary: Example 1

The patient projects her impaired self on the therapist and coerces him to identify with it by devaluing him. The therapist massively identifies with the projection because it hits the center of the target of his own unresolved feelings of inadequacy about himself. In order to relieve his feelings about himself, he countertransferentially becomes directive and caretaking with the patient, which evokes further resistance. When he identifies the intrapsychic source of his countertransference, he is better able to control it, stop the directiveness, and make appropriate mirroring interpretations of narcissistic vulnerability. The patient responds by taking back the projection and by beginning to reflect on her impaired self.

11.

Countertransference and Projective Identification III

Clinical Examples: Too Much Activity and Direction; Distancing

EXAMPLE 2

Projective Identification Evokes Anger and Fusion Defense

A 40-year-old woman, a patient with a closet narcissistic personality disorder who had been in psychotherapy three times a week for several years, decided to cut down to twice-a-week therapy to avoid the criticism she anticipated from a brother who was coming to her home for a prolonged visit. She felt guilty about this decision to avoid self-activation and expected to be attacked for it.

The therapist resonated with the patient's projection of the criticizing affect. He took in the projection, felt the criticism, and then defended against it by projecting the idealized object on the patient and becoming too active, confrontational, directive, and mirroring rather than interpreting.

The Therapist's Report

Therapist: I told the patient, "There's no doubt but that this is one of the more difficult dilemmas you are caught up in—the desire to be yourself and to support yourself versus the thought of being criticized by your brother. And it seems that you're dealing with the dilemma by avoiding this, rather than trying to find a constructive way to manage and understand your fears."

J.M.: I think she's certainly going to take that as criticism since it is a confrontation. Contrast that with the following: "Your brother's visit, since he can be critical, poses an acute dilemma between your need to support yourself and your fear of criticism. Your effort to soothe and deal with this dilemma is more on the side of avoiding criticism than of supporting yourself. What may be most important is not the fact that you're coming one less time a week, but the reason why you're coming one less time a week, cutting down on your work here. Have you thought of that?"

Therapist: You're right. She took it as a criticism, which is kind of interesting because I found myself with the feeling of trying to be firm.

J.M.: More confrontational. This is a countertransference response to her projective identification. She feels guilty about the decision and expects to be criticized. She projects this criticizing object on you, and you resonate with it.

Therapist: Right, right. She did take it as a criticism. And she said: "As far as I'm concerned, I've done a courageous thing in agreeing to see you twice a week. I was thinking of taking one or two months off and then coming back after Christmas when my brother would be gone. And, I just don't think I can or will stand up to my brother. He is gentle, but not that gentle. It's hard for me to feel as though I have permission to be, without getting permission slips from people to add to my portfolio, giving me permission just to exist."

I said: "This is what you have been working hard toward in the last several years—the ability to support yourself in the midst of criticism and to tolerate the painful vulnerability without yielding to pressure, because, as you do yield, it reinforces these feelings of needing permission to exist, to just be and to have your own need."

J.M.: That's better. Did she take that in?

Therapist: No [laughs]. She said: "I just think it's the way for me to go, not only for him, but for me, and I'll risk your being angry with me for making this decision. It makes me nervous to do it, but I'm nervous about a lot of things." That was the end of the session, which was on the day before her brother was to arrive.

She is petrified with pure fear, and she is all set to do battle with me if that means the price of being safe, to avoid it with her brother. At that point, it became very clear to me that she was drawing her line, that she felt she needed just to get through this trauma.

J.M.: You are avoiding dealing with her projection of criticism, you have to say that this has nothing to do with you or your anger. You're not angry, and the issue's not you, it's her and what this portends for her.

Therapist: At the next session, she reported that her treatment had come up with the brother, and to her surprise, her brother responded positively. She said that she was feeling proud of herself for approaching the subject and not running from it. She felt good for not doing that—having approached the scary thing and have it turn out to be friendly or even loving.

I said, "I'm curious how your tremendous relief of being understood by your brother influences your decision to cut down on your sessions, which was based on your fears of not knowing how he would react to you." She contemplated that and said, "I hadn't really thought about it, that if it's okay to see a shrink, then the number of times may not be a big deal. People won't think that I'm a closet alcoholic or a person who's having these deep problems."

She then discussed with her brother her feelings about people being mad at her even when she just walks into a room. She turned to me and said: "Do you have any ideas or thoughts about this?" I replied, "Do you have a desire to talk to him about these things?"

J.M.: She's turning to focus on you again.

Therapist: Would you have interpreted that?

J.M.: I don't see why not. She explores a little bit, and then she turns to you in defense and asks you for your contribution.

Therapist: Right.

J.M.: Which is a form of defense—focusing on the object.

Therapist: Okay!

J.M.: That's what I thought.

Therapist: She had said, "I'm going to cut down, and if you're angry with me, then so be it." I was feeling kind of gun shy about that and still trying to feel out where solid ground was in myself. The second part was that it felt to me that in comparison with the first session, to which she came in staunch denial, in this session she was beginning to thaw out and warm up a bit. I suspect I was feeling gun shy and not wanting to rock the boat, because the acting out of cutting down on the sessions seemed to be somewhat acknowledged and contained in the session. And I think I probably was feeling [laughs], "Let's not rock the boat here."

J.M.: But I think it's more your countertransference. To protect yourself against her projection on you of the attacking object, you are identifying with the projection of the idealized caretaking object. In either case, the projections, rather than being interpreted, are acted on. You react rather than reflect.

Therapist: I think you are right, actually.

J.M.: I think you have some anxiety about the criticism projection, and that somehow you think you will be able to avoid dealing directly with it by interpretation. That's not going to happen.

Therapist: I think I would be in favor of dealing with her projections onto me, as they come up, as we talked about before.

J.M.: Okay, but try to be sure that you're making a clinical judgment and not a countertransferential judgment.

Therapist: Right. What was going on here was a lot more of my own countertransference.

J.M.: Yes.

Therapist: Because the predominant feeling that I had in the room with her was one of still trying to recover from the session before—to get myself back on solid ground with her.

J.M.: But that's an illusion, right? [Laughs]

Therapist: [laughs] Yes, yes.

J.M.: That's your countertransference projection.

Therapist: That's right. [Laughs]

J.M.: When she doesn't feel criticized and she's in fusion with you, then you're back on solid ground.

Therapist: In the next session, she described her husband's making some comments to help her, but she felt it was criticism. Then there was a pause. She began to cry. She said, "I suppose I want people to understand and to care, but as soon as they tell me how to solve it, even if it's out of good intentions, then I feel I'm doing it wrong.

J.M.: Here is a golden opportunity for you to interpret her need to project.

Therapist: Really?

J.M.: She gives her husband some credit for his motivation. She perceives the reality of his motivation. However, she's saying that despite that fact, she still experiences it as criticism. But the therapist caught in his countertransference is unable to respond.

Therapist: Let me go on to salvage some of my lack of response, because I didn't say a word. In fact, it didn't even cross my mind. She continued: "I wasn't thinking about how I was perceiving his advice yesterday, but I didn't realize I was this bothered by it. I guess it made me feel small and inadequate again. I guess what I need to do is to tell him how I feel, like your lecturing me right now! Is that right or am I just overreacting? I don't want to be so on edge that I'm ready to pounce on anything that comes up."

J.M.: But she is.

Therapist: She is, right.

J.M.: And she is with you particularly.

Therapist: Would you still intervene at some point?

J.M.: Yes, because I think now she's giving you the material. This is the first material I've heard that she has any awareness that this feeling of criticism could come from something other than the external object. She is certainly bordering on saying that it hurts so much that she can't tolerate the hurt, and her way of soothing that is to feel that it's the other person who is criticizing her.

Therapist: I missed that completely.

J.M.: I think that you had better think about that, because we've been talking about it for three weeks.

Therapist: I think I need to be able to understand that my job is not only to deal with the projections that she has with me, but also to reinforce her reality testing as it applies to others.

J.M.: This kills two birds with one stone. It gives you access to what you have not been able to get access to in her relationship with you, which all revolves around her feeling of being criticized. And it links the two to the same source. Whether it's her husband or whether it's you, when any comment focuses on how bad she feels about herself, it feels so bad that she can't tolerate the idea that this is inside her, and she has to soothe it by feeling that the other person is criticizing her, not that she hurts.

Therapist: I got it. I have it locked into my memory bank. Whether or not I get access to it when I need it depends on my countertransference. I hope it does, but at least I now think I have it clearly in my head.

Therapist: [reporting patient's interview] She said, "I don't want to tell you that I didn't tell my brother where I was going, that I was coming here." I asked, "How come?" She replied, "I don't want to hear another lecture." Then she moved on. "I went to choir. I was late and the director said something about my being late in a laughing manner, and that was okay, but the choir then laughed, too, and that wasn't okay anymore. I told the director that I wasn't really glad to be there that night. The director came back later and dramatically apologized. Then another choir member came up and said, 'Just laugh it off.' I said, 'I can't, as it hurts my feelings.' Another friend came up and said, 'That was pretty hard, wasn't it? They both didn't let you feel or have your own feelings.' She seemed to understand. I told her something that was risky. I said I automatically expect people to be mad at me, and when things like this happen, it reinforces it. What he said wasn't all that terrible. It was the laughing from the group. I didn't like that." I then asked, "How did you experience that?"

J.M.: Your comments mirror her or fuse with her, and only create more resistance—to say nothing of the fact that the necessary interpretations are not made. I think, particularly at that point, that you are fusing with her to express your own countertransference. I don't think she needs it.

Therapist: So at that point, just . . .

J.M.: Just don't say anything. Every intervention in this session has been in that direction. It suggests that maybe her cutting down and her reacting to your confrontation as criticism have put you in a bind. You are very anxious about either remaining silent and being seen as withholding or interpreting and being seen as criticizing. What you end up doing is intervening in a way that mirrors and fuses with her, trying to direct her, so to speak. But she doesn't need it, and it creates more resistance.

Therapist: I think that's right on, because I know how anxious I felt in the previous session, just feeling kind of gun shy. [The therapist then continued with the patient's response to his intervention.] She said: "It hurts so much. That's one of the more painful things in my life I want to hide." She cried deeply at this point. "It's not a casual thing for me. That's an understatement. I suppose somebody has seen into me somehow and is threatening to know how inadequate I am. I don't think it's the people, it's just the pain at being laughed at by a group of people."

[The patient now, on her own, began to investigate the pain associated with criticism.] "I guess I experienced that a few times in school while growing up. Knowing the answers at times proved to be dangerous. I don't remember who said it later on, but someone said I keep hiding my life under a bushel. I wonder if that was a leftover from being laughed at and humiliated in a group of people. Once I stand out, I then can be laughed at. So I learn how to please the crowd to avoid the shame and ridicule. And I know I was laughed at at home. I was laughed at when I did anything that was contrary to how my mom thought or what she expected of me."

At this crucial juncture, when the patient was doing quite well despite her therapist's countertransference, the therapist intruded again, directing the patient.

Therapist: I asked, "Do any examples come to mind, either at home or at school, of when you were laughed at?"

J.M.: Your countertransference took over again and caused that intervention. On the surface, that material sounds like she's working through, but I don't think she really is. I think she's kind of intellectually plugging into the present experience what she thinks about the past. And then when you intervene in this way, you take over the process for her and create more resistance. Then you both are using fusion with the object to defend against your anger and her feelings of being hurt and criticized.

Therapist: I had another thought that her taking such a strong stand with me left her feeling pretty vulnerable, so maybe she is trying to get back into being a good patient.

J.M.: So you're both doing the same thing, skirting around the same issue. So you'll feel better and she'll feel better and the psychotherapy will just drag along.

Therapist: That is what she is saying, that she's learned to be compliant toward the object, on either a group basis or an individual basis. And she's acting it out in front of my eyes by being compliant with me so that she doesn't have to deal with the vulnerability of having stood up to me in the previous session [The therapist continued the patient's report.] She went on: "There is something I do remember and it's important because I keep thinking about it. When I was young, one morning I was still in bed and my parents found me asleep. I still feel the shame of this. Instead of Mom just talking to me directly, she turned to Dad and said, 'Look at that lazy, irresponsible bum.' And she would add, 'I can't understand that, I can't understand her.' The translation is, I'm wrong. Because Mom can't understand that, it means that somehow I'm bad or I'm wrong."

J.M.: Again it sounds like historical working-through material, but I don't think it is.

Therapist: I think you're right.

J.M.: It does give you an idea of where the fear of criticism comes from. If her mother isn't approving, then she's wrong.

Therapist: Right.

J.M.: So in her relationship with you, if she doesn't feel she's pleasing you, by definition she's wrong and you are criticizing her.

Therapist: Right, right.

J.M.: And it's so painful that she can't contain it and she has to act it out. To deal with your countertransference in the next two sessions, unless you can clearly establish to yourself a theoretical reason why you want to intervene, don't do it. Make a note on the material where you wanted to intervene and we'll discuss it. I think you're afraid that if you don't say something, she's going to attack you for not saying anything. [Laughs] And if you do say something, she'll attack you for criticizing her.

Therapist: Actually, I think I'm more scared of you than of her.

J.M.: You may be reenacting with me what she does with you—acting in a compliant manner to protect yourself against the fear of being criticized, and so your therapeutic reflexes become immobilized.

This therapist in previous supervision had shown a principal countertransference problem of anxiety about being the target of a patient's aggression that he defended himself against by being directive, caretaking, and mirroring. This, of course, was the mirror image of the patient's problem, and through projective identification, he accepted her criticizing affect, which reinforced his need also to resonate with her omnipotent object defense and be soothing, reassuring, and so on. This paralyzed the capacity of his real self to act in a free, self-activated, spontaneous manner, and to interpret the problem rather than identify with it.

Summary: Example 2

The patient defends against the attacking object by projecting it on the therapist. The therapist first resonates with the projection and angrily confronts. Then the therapist defends against the anger by moving into directive, caretaking interventions that fuse with the patient and evoke more resistance.

EXAMPLE 3

Projective Identification Evokes Distancing* Defense Against Fears of Engulfment

Therapist: One of the things that I've been noticing with the supervision of all my patients, but especially this one, is that the core issue for me is keeping myself at a distance, or in some ways it's not being a fully human interaction or a fully live interaction; I'm keeping patients at a theoretical distance. I've been thinking about that. There's some way in which my patients are relating to me that I am not responding to. I'm trying to keep them at a distance.

J.M.: With this closet narcissistic patient, treatment has been stalling. I think he is expressing and exposing himself more in the world . . . I think some of it is pathologic and some of it is healthy. Some of it is the real self and some of it is the grandiose self. He's stepping into the spotlight more at work by making a job change. He's been more and more sexually involved with his wife. He's started to develop some friendships outside of work and has gone to some functions.

Therapist: I think he is wanting to be more spontaneous or wanting to not be so perfect with me or wanting to use his own words rather than to follow whatever words I use. He's somehow looking to see whether it's possible to be himself with me without being attacked.

I think I get uncomfortable being cast in that light, either as the person who's going to attack him or as the person from whom he wants something. He wants to be mirrored by me or is waiting to see if it's okay for him to step out into the spotlight and shine. I think I've been missing that he's worried about my

---

**Distancing:* The evolving therapeutic alliance stirs up anxiety about intimacy in the therapist, who defends by putting distance between himself or herself and the patient by blocking the perception of the patient's therapeutic need for an interpretation, which is necessary to further the therapeutic alliance and deepen the treatment. When offered, the interpretations are inadequate.

attacking him. I think I've been so concerned about doing the therapy right or pure or in a classical way that I think I've been subtly signaling him that he had better not step out of line; he had better do this exactly right. For example, there's a certain way to talk, and don't you dare talk any other way.

I'm not 100 percent sure, but that's what I've been thinking about. The last time you and I talked about him, some six weeks ago, he was doing pretty well. Then he began to feel very insecure. He had a panic attack when he decided that he might have AIDS, somatic complaints, a fear of dying. A week after that, he continued to be very depressed, had problems with sleeping, was very worried about what others were thinking. A lot of this seemed to be related to his decision to leave the firm that he was in and go out on his own. In addition to feeling that he was going to die or be a failure, he did talk about some history: how he wouldn't apply himself in college, how he took easy courses rather than hard ones, and how he really limited what he could do in the world because he was so afraid of failing. The week after that, the fourth week, is when things started to seem to stall out. He started getting worried that I was tired of him, that I was tired of listening to him moan on.

J.M.: Do you see how he's just shifting there to defense?

Therapist: He was shifting from himself on to me.

J.M.: Right.

Therapist: And onto the situation.

J.M.: Right.

Therapist: And this is where things really started to bog down.

J.M.: What did you do? Did you interpret this?

Therapist: Eventually I did interpret it. I interpreted it along the lines that he was doing with me what he does outside. I interpreted that as he had been focusing more on himself and feeling more of the pain in himself and identifying more clearly for himself all of the ways in which he felt bad and how this limited him, it really exposed him more. I said that he was dealing with me in the way he dealt with the outside world, that he was imagining that I was viewing him in a boring, moaning light, and that he was going to pull back as a way of protecting himself. He talked about wanting to leave the office, wanting to run out of the office. I don't think it went so well, because the following week, he showed up late for an appointment. And the week after that, he showed up 35 minutes late for an appointment. This was about two and a half weeks ago. In the session for which he showed up 35 minutes late, he was in a rage. He was pissed off at the world. He was pissed off at me. He was pissed off because of the fact that it was so hard for him. He was buying some computer software for the computer that he's going to be using on his own, and he just decided to blow me off and said he wasn't going to rush back to see me. It really seemed like attempts to act out.

I again came back with an interpretation pretty much along the lines that, as he had moved into this job and as he had moved into looking at himself more closely in the sessions, this had made him more intensely aware of how bad he felt about himself. I pointed out that he was then imagining that this bad feeling about himself was going to cause him really to fail, that it was actually going to spread to this new job and he felt that he wasn't going to be able to succeed, and that he was angry at me for not relieving this bad feeling and ensuring that he would be successful. It's hard to say whether that was on the money or whether or not it worked—he's since been coming to appointments early on a regular basis. Actually, for both of these two sessions that I have to read today, he showed up a half hour early, but I guess my dilemma is that, in some ways, he's seesawing—he seems to me to be seesawing back and forth.

He's made progress. He's moving out into the world. He's putting himself more on the line. He's trying to exercise his ability, and this is also stimulating him. You know, there is increased awareness of the impaired self, but then also I think it stimulates his old ways of coping with it, that he wants to merge with a grandiose, omnipotent object and somehow be made whole. I think he's sort of going back and forth, and I think that's what's happening in the sessions with me.

I'll read these two sessions to get a sense of where he stands. These two sessions are better than those in the middle two or three weeks.

Patient: "I got here early. I got here at four-thirty. I'm feeling as though I'm going to die. I went to see my physician, and I told him about my concerns, and I told him about my side. I'm now worried that I have liver cancer. The doctor examined me and told me I had nothing to worry about. I know that this is psychological, but I really had to get a reality check. It really is so bad, I had to see the doctor. It's weird. Saturday I was really in bad shape. It got really bad just before the Christmas party.

"I had this feeling that I was going to die. I went to the Christmas party, and I really had a bad time. I had a dream also. I had this dream about my wife. I was at an amusement park with her and I lost her, and it was this crying image that I had of her that she was frightened, and I was frantic. And when I woke up, I had this terrified feeling of being lost.

"I remembered feeling that as a kid. I would wake up fatigued; you know, I guess in my dream I was sobbing. When I woke up, I had that sobbinglike feeling. It really, really threatens me to think about those feelings. It really made me just now jump from that feeling. I really feel a pain in my stomach. I want to really get away from it.

"You know, I just realized that, as I was talking to you, I thought that you were going to criticize me, and I actually heard you. It was as though you were like my father. He would have controlled me. He would have tried to control me."

Therapist: This is what I think is going on with me. I think that in some ways I have been controlling, signaling to him that he can't be as spontaneous with me.

Patient: "I was nervous about the party. I felt really uncomfortable. I was very aware that a girlfriend was there. I talked to her briefly, but I didn't really flirt with her. I was worried about talking to her, and I was talking to her boyfriend. I didn't want her boyfriend to think that there was something weird going on. I felt very awkward saying hello to them. I gave her sort of a social kiss on the cheek, but I really had these bad feeling. I was trying not to let anybody see how bad I felt. On Thursday when I was here, I also had those feelings, and I really wanted to run away from them. I don't really want to feel that—I guess I felt terror in the dream, as though it was a feeling like I had lost my other or I had lost some of my bearings. I was panic stricken in the dream. I guess in real life, I feel like that, too. I guess in some ways I had lost my girlfriend—I was looking to her like my mother. I don't know if talking about this brings the feelings on more or not. It seems like it makes them more intense. I'm feeling it right now. The feeling is welling up in me. I really wish I didn't have these feelings. Today I saw my girlfriend, and I said hello to her. I didn't want to talk to her, but I had this feeling, I was wondering how I looked to her at the party. I really feel hurt. I have been hurt for a long time."

Therapist: Let me tell you how I'm listening to this. This is better than a lot of the weeks, and I hear him focusing on himself, exploring himself, exposing some of the impaired self. But I also hear the attacking object or the controlling object coming in and also the desire to please the object.

J.M.: These are all linked together, it seems to me.

Therapist: There is just a hint in this session that's been more pronounced in other sessions, wanting these feelings to go away, wanting, you know, wanting them to be relieved.

J.M.: Yes, sure.

Therapist: He doesn't say it right out, but he wants me, I think, to make these feelings go away.

J.M.: I think you can interpret the whole defensive arrangement to him, including his wish for you to soothe it, to take it away.

Therapist: Okay, okay.

The therapist returns to the patient's report.

"In the dream, there was this feeling that I wanted to find my wife. When I talk to you, I feel sort of guilty. I feel it's wrong to talk about these things, that it's wrong to feel these things, it's wrong to feel the way I feel. I guess in the dream I lost her. I had this panic feeling that I wanted to get her back. It was kind of dramatic. It really made me panic. When we were away on vacation, she did get lost, in a department store, and I panicked; I was running through the store yelling her name, running around. And my cousin said it was no big deal. I was so happy to see her, I felt like I was going to cry. It really scared me.

"It would kill me if something happened to her. I guess that real-life situation came out in the dream. In the dream, what upset me most though was I—her eyes, there was terror in her eyes. I saw this look of terror in her eyes, that she couldn't find me, and I realized the feeling that what I was seeing in her, the terror, was really my own feeling, that I really feel lost and alone and in danger.

"It's hard for me to say that for myself. I guess it's easier for me to do it through her. I don't feel as bad when I see it in her. I'm nervous that she is such a focus of my feeling, that that's unhealthy, that it'll hurt her. I don't know if it's normal to feel as much as I do for her. I'm afraid. I'm afraid of what's going to happen to her. I really am upset about this, and I really realize how important she is to me."

Therapist: I'll condense the material up until when I make a comment. My patient went on worrying about screwing his daughter up and that his feelings for her are going to screw her up. And then he also described this fear, a terror of being engulfed, that he will just be sort of eaten up, that his parents sort of did that to him, and also that his father really wasn't there for him. His father was very controlling, and he said how he really doesn't get involved and that he had to do everything for himself in school. Neither his mother nor his father was much of a help to him. He then talked a little bit more about his mother and the feelings that he had with her and how vulnerable he felt with her, and how some of this comes out in his relationship with his wife.

He was feeling good toward his wife just before the party. He was feeling very sexual, has been much more sexual. He's been more spontaneously sexual with her, which is a big change, at least since when he first started seeing me. He went on talking about this feeling of loneliness and how hard it is for him to feel really connected and really involved with people. And then he started shifting.

Patient: "I'm really feeling bad, and it's really hard for me to stay on top of what the reality of all this is. I . . . I . . . I don't really think it, but I do think it. I think that you're judging me, that you think that I'm defective, and you think I'm stupid."

J.M.: So he just shifted, didn't he?

Therapist: Yes.

J.M.: At this very point, as he was talking about his mother and father, he then shifted from transference, therapeutic alliance, and beginning working through to transference acting out.

Therapist: Yes.

J.M.: And he's already given you the clue to how to get at this with him when he says, "It's so painful for me to feel this terror inside myself. I guess I put it into my wife." So when he's beginning to explore his impaired self with his parents, it feels so painful, and so on.

Therapist: He puts it "into me."

J.M.: When he feels the attacks, he puts it into you.

Therapist: Yes, I missed that. I'm in the ballpark, but I don't get it exactly. He continued for a little bit more about my viewing him in a bad light. I came in and made a comment: "I think there are several places in which you are putting yourself more on the spot—at work, with friends, and here—and I think that as you focus more on yourself and hear and express these painful feelings about yourself, it really makes you feel even more sensitive and more vulnerable to being hurt, and that's so difficult for you to imagine. You then imagine that I am going to attack you and you check yourself." I think that is sort of in the ballpark, but I think the way that you put it, putting the pain into me as opposed to experiencing it himself, is really the issue.

J.M.: But also, the other part you left out was its link with his parents, which is a very important link, because that is going to be the pathway out of projecting it on you. And probably we could hypothesize that as he got into it at that level, I mean linking it with his parents, probably the next level has to do with feelings of being attacked by them. You see what I mean?

Therapist: Yes.

J.M.: Because that's where he stops, and then he starts to defend. So we could guess that that's what is coming next.

Therapist: My question is that I'm feeling that we're teeter-tottering back and forth, and I'm having trouble seeing exactly what the next level below is in terms of what he is defending against.

J.M.: All you have to do is deal with the defenses that he is presenting.

Therapist: Yes, then that will just emerge.

J.M.: I mean that you can only guess at the moment.

Therapist: I was feeling that there's this teeter-tottering back and forth, and I've sort of been at this place with him for six weeks. And we'll work on it for a while, and then he'll pull back, and I'm feeling like I'm stuck on a plateau. I'm not sure if it's him or both of us.

J.M.: When you made your interpretation, what came back?

Therapist: He said I was really sensitive.

Patient: "You know, when you coughed—you just made a cough a little while ago—I imagined that I was going to end up getting hurt by you; I mean really hurt. I am really afraid of being hurt by you—I can feel it. I'm ashamed of how sensitive I am, and I'm also ashamed of myself. At the office party, I really felt ashamed of myself. I've always had this secret wish to play a guitar, and I've fantasized about playing guitar and having people admire me. I really felt awkward at the party, and I felt I really screwed up.

"Some of the people that I've been hanging out with and playing music with were at the party, and they got the band to let us play. I felt my heart pounding. I felt that I really was going to be embarrassed. I felt so ashamed about how I felt, I really felt very awkward. I couldn't be spontaneous. I couldn't express myself. I went blank on the song that we were going to play. I was hoping people would say good things about me, but, of course . . . I guess it's a good example of how incredibly ill at ease I am. It scares me to death. I mean, I was really terrified, I could barely play. I wish I weren't that way. When I see people, I think that they're just going to see through me. What I would really like to do is just let myself be myself. I feel as though I want to be a show-off, but I feel all of these painful, panicky feelings. There was no way that I could express myself. I was so afraid and fearful of making a mistake that I was out of touch with myself. I guess that could be a good metaphor for life, that you have to be in touch with yourself to express yourself. It's the same in other, areas as well."

Therapist: What I got back from the intervention was an elaboration of how painful it is for him to be in the spotlight and how sensitive he feels about making mistakes and being attacked.

J.M.: It sounds pretty good. He's staying with it.

Therapist: At the end of the hour, he elaborated a little bit more about being more spontaneous and being himself and how hampered and controlled he felt. He elaborated on feeling jealous of other people's abilities to operate smoothly. He then ended the hour saying he felt so uncomfortable at times that he felt as though he were going to die. He's more focused on himself and is exploring his impaired self, and I think he is trying to explore how it comes into the picture and how it hampers his self-expression.

At the next session:

Patient: "I feel like I have nothing to talk about. I feel kind of unsettled. I had a fight with my wife yesterday. I had just come from a meeting, which I did well at, and I made a point that I felt good about, and I was really right about it. But I'm feeling somewhat unsettled.

"I did work on a project today, and I solved this problem, coming up with a theoretical model that no one has presented before. And I really felt good about how I worked, and it worked really well. But I just get afraid; I don't want people to be looking at me as though I'm goofy. I think that I should be hanging out with my colleague more. He's pretty good at this stuff."

Therapist: At this point, I think he's more in defense. He's fighting with his wife; he wants to hook up with this colleague. I do hear him actually applying himself in a real way to the mathematical models and acknowledging himself and feeling good about it. I hear some positive side. But this seems like a pulling back from the session before.

J.M.: It is.

Therapist: This is where it's sort of teeter-tottering back and forth. The first session was fairly intense, and I was tracking him; he seemed to be getting more into it. Then he came back and he was at a different place; and he was not where he was the session before. I wondered, Where do I come in? And what happens if I don't come in for a while?

J.M.: I don't think you have to wait, unless you're either unsure of the pattern or unsure of your own countertransference. In both instances, you are justified in waiting until you are certain of these. Otherwise, I don't think you have to wait. The first was a good working session right to the end, so I see him in defense in the second session. I would immediately start thinking about the time between when he left and today. Has something happened that's changed things? I might take it up with him right at the outset by saying: "You seem to be in quite a different state today than you were when you left here. I wonder what happened to that state." Do you think he just detaches, or that he might shift to his wife? Or what?

Therapist: I think that what happens is that it's just unbearable for him. I think when he gets up to that level of pain, he can maintain the focus on himself with the support of therapy; but when he gets outside of the hour, it just becomes too much. And then I assume he starts to act out rather than feel upset. He gets upset with his wife and turns to others for mirroring and for encouragement. He gives up the struggle. That's what I'm thinking is happening outside of the hour. Therapeutic support is not continuing outside of the hour.

J.M.: You're probably right, and I think you should interpret that to him.

Therapist: I never even thought of doing that.

J.M.: I think this is the point where you're having trouble.

Therapist: Yes.

J.M.: Why don't you think of doing it? Is it because when you do interpret, you are moving a step closer to him, and that creates anxiety?

Therapist: Yes, absolutely. As long as he has his fix outside of the hour and continues to do that, he's not going to rely on me more.

J.M.: Right.

Therapist: And it's really . . . it's . . .

J.M.: Safe.

Therapist: To make a comment like that—it is drawing him more into the treatment, more reliant on me.

J.M.: Right. Even within therapeutic neutrality, the idea of interpretation—moving you closer to him and him to you—is pretty accurate, because, emotionally, that is what happens. The patient begins to depend almost completely on the sessions and on you to deal with this material.

Therapist: He's indicated that these are killer feelings.

J.M.: And he needs a sign from you that you can handle them in order for him to be able to go deeper himself. I think he's more than ready to go deeper.

Therapist: Yes. I think things are cooking also, because he made a job change that puts him more on his own.

J.M.: Psychologically, the job move has the same emotional effect as a move to being on his own, to being on center stage, to focusing on himself.

Therapist: And he really is on his own, standing on his own feet. So I think that, in reality, he's taking steps in that direction, both with work and with his wife, and I think with me as well. There are a number of levels on which he's moving in the same direction. At the beginning of the session, I didn't make a comment, but his wife responded with critical comments. And it really enraged him, and he felt really criticized and put down by her.

J.M.: I don't think you can go in on that alone, because I don't think that's what's on center stage here. I think that center stage is his exploring the pain of focusing on his impaired self, followed in the next session by the need to defend.

Within that context, I would interpret that it also appears that the kinds of feelings that he was talking about in the session, about your attacking him, have become reenacted in his life, which may take him further and further away from focusing on himself. I think that's where the intervention belongs—because if you intervene only about the wife, and even if you are successful, you aren't going to get very far.

Therapist: No, its a confrontation of a specific defense without the center stage.

J.M.: Right. It misses the boat of the central defense.

Therapist: Halfway into the next session, I made a comment: "It seems to me that you have been really trying to stay focused on yourself more and investing yourself more in exploring the painful feelings that you have about yourself, and that this also matches up with your other endeavors outside of treatment, where you are applying yourself more at work and with friends. This increased investment makes you feel even more vulnerable to feeling hurt and feeling criticized and attacked by me, and what you do in response is to feel a need to control yourself and to protect yourself from the anticipated attack that I might make." He replied that he felt with his wife that he was sensitive to attack, and he was also feeling tremendous anxiety in treatment, and that he was very concerned that I might tell him that he's fucked up, and he's fucking his life up, that he is sick and disgusting.

And at the end of the hour he said: "I guess there's only two minutes to go, so it's safe to say I feel very embarrassed about what I really want you to say to me. I want you to tell me that I'm okay. I want you to make me feel that I'm okay."

J.M.: [laughs] This is the other side of the transference acting out, isn't it? What could you have said to him at that point?

Therapist: I could have said: "As you are becoming more invested here and really digging into looking at some of these painful feelings you have about yourself, it is deathly frightening to you. I think you stay with that for a certain amount of time, and then it is so painful that you put it out into the world, you put it out into your life. And I think that you sometimes put it out into me. I think what you are describing now is really a desire to have me wash it all away, to make it all go away so that you don't have to focus on these painful feelings."

J.M.: I think that it would be good to contrast it with his transference acting out. First, when he focuses on himself, he feels ashamed and bad and painful, and he's afraid that he's going to be attacked, and he puts that fear of being attacked on you as a way of dealing with it, as if you were going to attack him. The other side of that coin is the wish that you would give him the acknowledgment that he has so much trouble giving himself, and thereby wash away the pain. I think he's ready for that kind of interpretation. The reason I raise this with you is that whenever a patient who is afraid of being attacked says he wishes you would acknowledge him, he expresses a positive. It's important to say something, on the spot, and not to leave it open.

Therapist: That's a narcissistic injury.

J.M.: Yes, leaving the expressed wish waving in the wind—at least acknowledge it, you see, acknowledge the wish even though it's defensive in nature. So I would look for that in the beginning of the next session and for an opportunity to respond. You could always bring it up again. But I think you may have trouble doing this, by the way.

Therapist: If the past is any predictor of the future, I will.

J.M.: Right, so keep an eye on that. I do think it becomes clearer and clearer that the issue here is your distancing countertransference and not the patient's resistance, but you can't test his resistance until you resolve your countertransference. My guess is that if you do, he will come right along.

Therapist: I've been thinking that the same countertransference comes into play with another patient, a woman with a borderline personality disorder, that occurs with this narcissistic patient. I think it arises when the patient is afraid to move from the testing phase into the working-through phase. I recognized that this woman sealed off her real self by detachment and really hasn't hoped or wished or trusted in another person since being betrayed by her parents. I think it's at this point in treatment that the patient feels a renewal of hope that he or she can find an environment or relationship in which to develop and be himself or herself and not have to protect the real self that I react to by distancing emotionally.

I think I saw that the issue for her was whether she could really trust that another person—me—was not going to repeat what her parents did. I think now it's the same thing with the patient with the closet narcissistic personality disorder. He seems to be in a similar place in his treatment; to go into some of these painful memories and to recall them time and time again, he projects onto me that I'm going to repeat with him what was done to him as a child. I think I respond by distancing to that effort to deepen the relationship.

J.M.: You have the reciprocal anxiety.

Therapist: Exactly. I think that's a real primary defense of my own: to keep a distance and to protect myself from objects. When my patients by their progress start dismantling that defense, it stimulates a lot of anxiety in me because it's something that is deeply wired in; that's not something that you start fooling around with.

J.M.: But you must have an anxiety similar to that of your patient. If you allow the patient to depend on you, your self will be engulfed by the patient's needs.

Therapist: I think it has to do with being engulfed, being co-opted, or being intruded on or losing what is real or unique or individualistic about myself. My mother was very strong; she had clear ideas about how she wished me to be, and many of them didn't match up with who I was. I erected many defenses to seal off and protect what was uniquely my own from being co-opted and being mixed up with her stuff.

I'm thinking that this is what's going on with the closet narcissistic personality disorder patient. He is beginning to trust me and to have a therapeutic alliance with me, and it is touching on my own defenses against that developing. I think probably there's a parallel process going on in this supervision with you as well.

J.M.: Sure, it has to be. Did this issue get on the table in your analysis?

Therapist: This is an issue that's been on center stage in my treatment forever. I have had a lot of treatment, and I've had several courses of treatment. Once I was seeing an analyst who ended up dying—

J.M.: After how long?

Therapist: I saw him, I guess, for eight years.

J.M.: That must have been a real blow!

Therapist: In the middle of the analysis, he had a major coronary. Then the treatment was interrupted. His health was declining and I was probably one of the last patients that he stopped seeing, and about six months later, he died, which I think reinforced this distancing defense against addressing this basic trust issue. I then went on to see another analyst and got at least an intellectual understanding, and I also made some progress with it, as a defense. I don't think it has been really fully and thoroughly worked through.

J.M.: Here's another opportunity for you to work on it.

Therapist: Yes. I think it is another opportunity.

J.M.: By the way, talking about the reciprocal with me, it just occurred to me that the phone supervision fits right into the distancing defense, doesn't it?

Therapist: I think you're right about that. In fact, I was thinking about that because the phone does keep me at a distance.

J.M.: Do you have reactions to what I'm saying that you're aware of but that you haven't mentioned?

Therapist: No, although I do think I really tried to be perfectionistic. I'm concerned about doing it your way; it's a balance. I'm trying to learn from you, but also I'm not exactly like you. I'm different from you and my mother. Before I call you, even though I've talked to you a lot of times, I always get a little bit anxious, and it's curious to me, you know. I notice that after I'm talking for a while, I'm not anxious. But usually in the first few minutes, I do get anxious.

J.M.: But maybe that is tied to the projection, and the contact relieves the projection.

Therapist: My struggle with my patients is that this whole issue of basic trust and fear of intimacy and fears of being intruded on and co-opted and engulfed are what is preventing me from being more effective with patients who are further along in treatment. This is sort of the snag I'm hitting. I noticed it also with another patient. She's sort of at a similar place, and I've noticed that there have been some reactions that I have found startling. I anticipated that you would be stricter or more critical, and you haven't been. I think my image is always a kind of a caricature of who you are!

I think it is anticipating or worrying that I have to do what you want, and also sort of testing the waters that I could be myself. I'm not only viewing you through the lens of my mother. I'm also maybe viewing you in a parallel way to the way my patients view me as having the potential to be. I have a similar type of difficulty with this patient. She was avoiding really focusing on a feeling like that of a little, lost Brownie and feeling quite a bit of pain and being very clear that she was on the edge of something, looking over and being afraid of going into it and not wanting to go into it. And I would keep on missing that. She would go off on all these tangents in terms of everyday conflicts or everyday concerns and would do all sorts of things to avoid what was really center stage, which was this very painful sort of family that she grew up in, a lot of painful feelings that she had defenses against feeling and expressing. I was sort of unconsciously colluding with her.

J.M.: Well, at least now we have your countertransference on center stage.

Therapist: I'm really going to track it for myself and try to focus on working it through and not having it intrude into the work with my patients.

I'll read a little bit more of my report on the narcissistic patient. He really did seem to focus on himself and painful feelings in himself, and this led to painful memories organized around Christmas. And then it came into the transference. He projected onto me that I was going to see him as an inferior, as stupid, a bore, a pain in the neck, wasting my time. I interpreted the projection, and he got back to memories and elaborated on history.

At the next session, he seemed to be at a different level, much more on the surface, tracking himself and reporting being more on the surface. He ended the hour thinking that I was going to view him as stupid and as a whiner and complainer. And I interpreted that again.

J.M.: In this second session, you ought to have linked the interpretation of defense to the work of the prior session. In other words, when he moved into history rather than defensed. Starting to explore his past history was further self-activation, which stirred up more vulnerability. So then when he came in the next time, he was defending against the vulnerability that was stirred up in the prior session. It's important to link those two. This is how you get continuity. You see what I mean?

Therapist: Yes. Now I see it, but before I didn't.

J.M.: I think this is caused by your distancing defense. If you do see it and act on it, it evokes your fears of engulfment.

Therapist: And also conveys to him what is on center stage, which is all of these painful memories and the feelings that he has about himself. He's elaborating on them, and it really does draw him into a more intense relationship with me, and also the possibility of giving up the defenses erected against those painful traumatic experiences and having a new type of relationship.

J.M.: Well, but you don't want to introduce that yourself unless he does. What I am stressing here is more his internal process. You link for him that when he explores and works on a certain level of narcissistic vulnerability, it exposes his painful feeling, and then he defends by feeling you're attacking him, but when he's able to contain that, he's able to go back and explore further. However, the other transferential aspect I would use only as he gives you evidence for it.

Therapist: Yes. He hasn't introduced this as a theme at all. Although he has said that I'm the person he trusts most, if there's anyone.

J.M.: Well, but he still is vacillating between seeing you as a distant object and seeing you as an attacker, and it's not until he really contains the projection on you as an attacker that he's going to develop a solid therapeutic alliance.

Therapist: To return to the patient's report.

Patient: "I'm really enjoying my time off. This last week of not going to work has really been good. I've been spending a lot of time with my wife and with my daughter, and I'm thinking that this will be a great Christmas. It's been very easy spending time with my wife. In fact, I've been keeping the TV off and not sitting in front of the TV set and just really making time to play with her. It makes me very nervous. I don't know. I guess it, in some ways, has to do with coming here. I woke up the other night in the middle of the night. Yesterday, I went out to lunch with a fellow worker. I had some things I wanted to talk about with him. I guess in some ways it all has to do with the stuff about Christmas. I'm worried that my wife will get upset about Christmas. I remember something that happened about 10 years ago, when my wife and I first got together. I'd forgotten to get her a present, and I remember that she got really upset. In fact, that reminds me about my father. I had $12, and I had spent $8 on a present for my mother, and I'd spent money on my brothers and sisters, and all I had left was 29 cents. I had forgotten to buy a Christmas present for my father. I was so afraid that I had hurt him and of what he would do, that he would blow up at me.

"I had a lot of feelings about my father. I really feel sad for him now. I feel that he was really a lonely person, but at that age, all I thought of was that I was going to get blamed, that he would blow up at me. I guess I blamed myself for his not having been around when I was a kid. I remember one Christmas when I was eight that I got the family up early, and my father got angry at me and took the belt down and spanked us. It was awful. We were all crying and he was screaming.

"I guess it was right around that same time that I had that incident with the rod in my mouth. I guess I really felt bad the whole time back then. That's when all of this started. I remember walking around with that rod in my mouth and I tripped and I thought the rod could have gone to the back of my throat and killed me. It scared me that I thought I was going to die. I was afraid that I was going to die.

"The other night, in the middle of the night, I woke up with a dream. I don't remember the dream, but I had this horrible feeling; I felt as though I were going to die. I could feel it in the pit of my stomach. I could feel it in my chest. I just got this strong feeling, this real strong sense of insecurity. I had this feeling that this is all stupid and you're sitting there and I'm just wasting your time, that you feel that I'm just stupid.

J.M.: Hasn't he just shifted to the present from the history?

Therapist: Yes.

J.M.: So now, rather than pursuing the investigation of history, he's defending by attacking himself through you.

Therapist: At this point, I decided to come in. And I said: "As you're focusing on yourself and the painful feelings you have in yourself, and you're spontaneously recalling some of the experiences that are tied to feelings, you recall how you got attacked for being excited about Christmas. I think that here with me, also, you anticipate the same kind of hurtful action on my part for your expression of the painful memories—and the feelings that you have about yourself.

What I was trying to do here was link that the exploration of himself and his memories was stimulating so much pain in him that he was defending against it by projecting it on me.

J.M.: I don't think it comes across clearly and there's a little too much verbiage. It lacks clarity. It seems such a clear example of exploration of painful self, an inability to hold onto it due to the pain and a need to defend by projecting on you. You're taking a step closer to him in the treatment, and I think that what happens is just like with your patient, you get anxious about it—maybe without realizing it. And then the way you defend yourself is by taking a step back from a clear-cut, concrete focus to generalizing. It's a form of distancing.

So what did he say to your interpretation?

Therapist: He said: "As a child, I really did worry about getting too excited. I was really very worried about getting excited. It makes me sad to think about that. You know, I think about my daughter and how spontaneous and how excited she'd get, how much of a love of life she has. That was scared out of me. I didn't dare get excited. I was disciplined for getting excited. I'd be embarrassed, I'd be humiliated. It just made me feel awful. I learned not to get excited. I was always worried about being stupid with my father."

J.M.: Even though the interpretation wasn't as clear as we would like, he certainly got the message, and he went right back to work.

Therapist: Yes, he did.

J.M.: But now, at this point in the session, you should be on the alert for his going back into defense again.

Therapist: I think he's a really good patient. I think he really is trying to make use of treatment despite my problems.

J.M.: Yes, absolutely.

Therapist: He's taking a vague statement and extracting meaning from it—which, I think, reflects his motivation.

J.M.: It reminds me, you know, of Mahler's famous statement that it's astonishing to see what extraordinary lengths some children will go to to extract whatever supplies are available in the environment.

Therapist: [continuing his report] The patient said: "The whole family used to get scared. Every time that you would express yourself, you were afraid that you would get yelled at or slapped. It was a very scary place. My father would be the one who would hit you. I guess sometimes my mother would hit, too, but that was rarer. She would always wait for my father to get home, and then he would take the belt down. I remember sometimes I would fake tears in order to have him stop hitting me so it wouldn't be so bad. He'd lose his temper and he'd get physical and he'd beat us up. And she would always say that we were difficult."

He then paused and said: "It makes me uncomfortable. I don't know what really happened. I'm trying to piece all of this stuff together. I guess all of these things are perceptions of mine when I was a child. I don't really know how to deal with them."

At this point, I saw that he was pulling out a little into defense, but I was waiting to see whether he was going to return to work with it.

The patient continued: "I can still feel that sense of the rod in the back of my throat, that I could have died; it was killing me. I get the scary feeling in my stomach. I feel these butterflies. I just zoned out. I'm the hero of that book that they made into a movie, *The Accidental Tourist.* There was a sick quality to the way he lived, and he could never cry and he didn't have any tears. I just thought about him and I thought that in some ways I feel sort of like him.

"I wonder if I will ever be able to get to the part of me that feels alive, that I can allow myself to be in the present and to really express myself. I'm afraid that I won't make enough progress. I don't know if I'm going to succeed in this process here. I feel like I have all of these thoughts and it's difficult for me to be myself. I guess I was really afraid of people finding out that I felt this way. I get this real sense of sadness. I feel right now that I'm focused."

J.M.: He is beginning to express more of a mild sense of hopelessness.

Therapist: And then projecting onto me that I'm as stupid.

J.M.: Does he do that? He hasn't said that yet.

Therapist: He does, the next thing.

J.M.: I think at that point it would be a great time to track this whole situation for him. He focuses on himself then, and you could point out exactly how he started to drift away and then cut off feeling altogether, and then raised great questions about his ability to do this work when he's actually doing it.

Therapist: Yes, well, needless to say, I didn't do that. [Laughs] I waited a bit until his being afraid of how I was going to see him got more pronounced. I said: "As you're focusing on yourself, I think that you then feel quite a bit of pain about your life and your situation, which stimulates in you this feeling of being stupid, and as a way of coping, you put that feeling out onto me."

He told me that he does feel a lot of pain and feels very vulnerable, and that he is very worried about how I view him. He said that he wishes that he could really be himself, and that all of his life he has admired people who can be in the moment and can say spontaneously what's on their minds. He went on: "I wish that I could be myself. I kind of feel like a child now. It's very painful. I feel that I'm going to be criticized for speaking up and for saying what's on my mind. I worry about it with my wife and I worry about it here. Sometimes I feel that I get hurt if I say what's on my mind. My mother used to do that all the time, and I think my wife does that, too. I was so afraid of that happening all the time, that I could get hurt if I spoke up and said what was on my mind. I always felt as though I had to perform for my mother, that I always had to do what was right."

J.M.: He has taken in and elaborated on your interpretation. But you'll note that my comment again related to interpreting the entire tracking process. I think that's what you have to keep in mind."

Therapist: I have to say what I see and put it in a form that he can hear, but really, essentially just conveying to him my observations about what's going on informs him about how he is coping.

J.M.: But all you have been handling so far is the projection in the transference, rather than helping him track what he's doing, his defenses. I think the reason is the same distancing countertransference problem. When you talk about the projection, it's important to relate it to the painful self as a defense. When he starts to focus and to explore himself, it feels painful. He feels attacked, criticized, and put upon. It's so painful that he can't contain it inside his head, and the way he soothes it is by putting it out on you. It's important to introduce that idea of the relationship between containment and projection. You see what I mean?

Therapist: Yes, that he's unable to contain it.

J.M.: It's too painful to be able to hold onto and contain, and so the way he has found to soothe it is to put it out on another—in this case, to put it out on you.

Therapist: So essentially it's explaining to him the reason for his putting it out onto me.

J.M.: It's also providing a kind of role model, because what he must do for a time is contain it. He's going to have to contain it if the psychotherapy is going to work.

Therapist: I guess that saying it that way is, in some way, quietly giving him a vote of confidence, saying that he's capable of containing.

J.M.: Absolutely. The other thing is his raising these questions about whether he is going to be able to do it. These questions come up at a point when he actually is doing it, and rather than feel more confident with each bit that he does, it raises his anxiety about the opposite, that is, that he's not going to be able to do it. This is a paradox you could point out to him.

I think that for the next go-around you should concentrate on linking up the projection on you as a defense against the pain of exploring himself and his trouble containing it, and see if that doesn't help. It seems to me that he already is using the transference interpretation to help him stay on track. But I think you can do it more precisely. So how did he finish?

Therapist: He finished the hour by saying: "I think in terms of trying to take charge of my life, and I guess I don't know if I really can take charge of my life. In college, I used to be worried about being stupid, and so that would always take charge of me. I'd end up not taking courses that I was really interested in. I'm really worried that I'm going to do that with my life and that I'm not going to make anything out of my life. I really do want to make changes though. I really want to make real changes that count."

J.M.: That's a pretty good end! In general, it was not a bad session.

Therapist: Yes, but then he came back in the next session in his typical way, in more defense. On Tuesdays he seems to get into much more historical material, much more affect, much more pain, and is able to stay with it for longer periods. And on Thursdays, he comes in and reports feeling less in touch. He reports feeling blocked.

J.M.: Do you interpret that for him?

Therapist: I guess it's just recently that I've become aware that it's always on Tuesdays and Thursdays.

J.M.: Is he aware of it?

Therapist: No, I don't think so.

J.M.: But he is aware that he goes in and out.

Therapist: Yes, he's aware that he goes in and out.

J.M.: But does he then elaborate and try to explain or explore how he goes from being in to being out between sessions?

Therapist: Not between sessions. He is trying to understand why he is blocked in the session.

J.M.: I think we can hypothesize that what happens outside the office is exactly what happens in the office. He begins to explore and cuts off feeling and projects on you, which puts an absolute stopper on the contained affect. So you can assume that when he leaves the office, probably what happens is that he goes back to projecting and cutting off. I think you have to look again at your countertransference, too, because you'll note again what I am talking about. I'm talking about a tracking process, which is getting you in closer and closer. When you take it up with him, you want to be sure that you're ready to handle it. He could be testing you. At any rate, those two things certainly go together, and I don't see any reason why they couldn't be taken up.

Summary: Example 3

This patient is ready to move from the testing phase into the working-through phase. As he explores his impaired self, he defends against his vulnerability by projecting the attacking object on the therapist. The therapist reacts more strongly to the patient's progressive move toward a therapeutic alliance. This evokes the therapist's fears of engulfment, which he defends against by distancing—he has difficulty perceiving the need for and actually making the interpretation necessary to allow the patient to proceed deeper into the working-through phase.

Summary

The key psychodynamic theme of the closet narcissistic disorder is the disorder-of-the-self triad: self-activation leads to anxiety and abandonment depression, which lead to defense. The crucial defense against the six affects of the abandonment depression is the idealizing of the omnipotent object, which also regulates the grandiose self.

The crucial therapeutic intervention is mirroring interpretation of narcissistic vulnerability—that is, the patient soothes the potential pain of focusing on the self by focusing on the object. This intervention helps the patient to convert the transference acting out of this idealizing defense into a therapeutic alliance and transference. This move is signaled by the patient's facing and working on the impaired self and the emerging abandonment depression. At this point, the patient is feeling bad (i.e., depressed, anxious, angry, etc.), which is the sign that the impaired self is emerging and therapeutic progress has taken place.

The defensive part of the triadic theme then enters, and the therapist must interpret the defense again and again to bring the patient back to the abandonment depression. The triadic theme repeats and repeats until defense is overcome. Repetition, as reported in this book, is the essence of the therapeutic work. It is slow, difficult work for the patient and a trial of patience for the therapist. Efforts to hurry it or avoid it are bound to fail. The therapist's resolve to stay with it must be as strong as the patient's need to defend against it.

In every successful case there comes a poignant, vivid, unforgettable moment when the patient breaks through the defenses and gains access to and recaptures the central affects of the authentic impaired self. This is usually expressed in an idiosyncratic dramatic metaphor such as the disembodied heart of the prostitute. Paradoxically, this moment, which is sad and painful for the patient, opens the window to a shaft of hope and foreshadows the progress to come. The patient is on the way to recapturing an authentic real self. It makes all the effort worthwhile for both of the partners in this endeavor. After all these years of doing treatment, when I see yet another patient making this breakthrough, I still feel a sense of wonder at the extraordinary resilience of the human condition.

Patients' projective identification defense mechanisms evoke the most countertransference problems. The therapist must be alert to both the negative affects a patient projects and the efforts of that patient to coerce the therapist into accepting the projection of these affects.

When the projective identifications are reflected rather than reacted to, and when the triadic defense is consistently interpreted, an opportunity is created for the patient to work through the abandonment depression and overcome the closet narcissistic disorder of the self. The real self emerges and consolidates.

References

1. Masterson, J. F. *The narcissistic and borderline disorders: An integrated developmental approach*. New York: Brunner/Mazel, 1981.
2. Masterson, J. F. *The real self: A developmental self and object relations approach*. New York: Brunner/Mazel, 1985.
3. Masterson, J. F. *Psychotherapy of the disorders of the self: The Masterson approach* New York: Brunner/Mazel, 1988.
4. Fairbairn, W. R. A revised psychopathology of the psychoses and psychoneurosis. In *Psychoanalytic studies of the personality (an object relations theory of the personality)*. London: Tavistock, 1952; New York: Basic Books, 1954.
5. Federn, P. *Ego psychology and the psychoses*. New York: Basic Books, 1952.
6. Freud, S. Further recommendations in the technique of psychoanalysis: Recollection, repetition and working through. *Collected papers*, vol. II. London: Hogarth Press, 1953, pp. 366–376.
7. Guntrip, H. *Personality structure and human interaction*. London: Hogarth Press; New York: International Universities Press, 1964.
8. Gunderson, J. G., & Singer, M. T. Defining borderline patients: An overview. *American Journal of Psychiatry*, 132:1–9, 1975.
9. Jacobson, E. Denial and repression. *Journal of the American Psychiatric Association*, 5:61–92, 1957.
10. Jacobson, E. *The self and the object world*. New York: International Universities Press, 1964.
11. Kernberg, O. *Borderline conditions and pathological narcissism*. New York: Science House, 1975, 163–177.
12. Klein, M. Contributions to the psychogenesis of manic depressive states. In *Contributions to psychoanalysis (1921–1945)*. London: Hogarth Press, 1948.
13. Klein, M. Mourning and its relation to manic depressive states. In *Contributions to psychoanalysis (1921–1945)*. London: Hogarth Press, 1948.
14. Klein, M. Notes on some schizoid mechanisms. In J. Riviere (Ed.), *Developments in psychoanalysis*. London: Hogarth Press, 1946.
15. Klein, M. *The psychoanalysis of children*. London: Hogarth Press, 1932.
16. Stern, D. *The interpersonal world of the infant: A view from psychoanalysis and developmental psychology*. New York: Basic Books, 1985.

17. Mahler, M. *The psychological birth of the human infant.* New York: Basic Books, 1975.
18. Kohut, H. *The analysis of the self: A systematic approach to the psychoanalytic treatment of narcissistic personality disorders.* New York: International Universities Press, 1971.
19. Kohut, H. *The restoration of the self.* New York: International Universities Press, 1977.
20. Guntrip, H. *Schizoid phenomena, object relations, and the self.* New York: International Universities Press, 1969, pp. 41–44.
21. Winnicott, D. *Maturational process and the facilitating environment.* New York: International Universities Press, 1965.
22. Goldstein, W.M. Classification of projective identification. *American Journal of Psychiatry,* 148:2, 1991.
23. Masterson, J.F. *Comparing psychoanalytic psychotherapies.* New York: Brunner/Mazel, 1991.

Index

James F. Masterson is Director of the Masterson Institute and Adjunct Clinical Professor of Psychiatry, Cornell University Medical College. Dr. Masterson conducts workshops and seminars throughout the United States. He is the author of numerous journal articles and several widely acclaimed books, including *Comparing Psychoanalytic Psychotherapies*, *Psychotherapy of the Disorders of the Self*, and *The Search for the Real Self: Unmasking the Personality Disorders of our Age*.